Egypt Before the Written History

THE LOST KNOWLEDGE OF ANCIENT EGYPT

Mohamed Ibrahim Elbassiouny

Egypt Before the Written History

THE LOST KNOWLEDGE OF ANCIENT EGYPT

Copyright © 2023 by 4BIDDEN KNOWLEDGE. All rights reserved.

This book or any portion thereof may not be reproduced or used in any manner whatsoever without the express written permission from the publisher except for the use of brief quotations in critical articles, reviews, and pages where permission Is specifically granted by the publisher.

First Edition

ISBN: 979-8-9871224-4-0

LCCN# 2023947724

Although the author and publisher have made every effort to ensure that the information in this book is correct, the author and publisher do not assume and hereby disclaim any liability to any party for any loss, damage, or disruption caused by errors or omissions, whether such errors or omissions result from negligence, accident, or any other cause. Likewise, the author and publisher assume no responsibility for any false information. No liability is assumed for damages that may result from the reading or use of information contained within. Read at your own risk. The views of this publication do not necessarily reflect the views of 4biddenknowledge.

Books may be purchased by contacting the publisher and author at:

4biddenknowledge Inc
934 N University Dr #417
Coral Springs, FL 33071

4biddenknowledge.com

info@4biddenknowledge.com

To my beloved wife Noha, who supported me in my life and in my career, she is one of the main reasons that we have this book written.

Table of Contents

Foreword..1

Introduction..3

Names of Ancient Egypt..19

Religion of Ancient Egypt...35

Capitals of Ancient Egypt...47

Theories of creation in Ancient Egypt................................59

The Geology of Egypt..93

Pre-Dynastic Egypt..117

Dynastic Egypt...143

The Primitive Techniques and Tools of the Pre-Dynastic and the Archaic Periods..185

The Mystery of the Stone Vessels from the Pre-Dynastic Era......217

The Sequence of the Tomb Development from the Pre-Dynastic Egyptians to the End of the Dynasties.........251

The Lost Technologies and Advanced Knowledge............303

About the author..389

Foreword

by Billy Carson

In the shadow of Egypt's towering pyramids, amidst the shimmering sands of the Sahara, and along the serene banks of the Nile, a civilization of remarkable ingenuity and enduring mystery once thrived. The land of pharaohs, mummies, and hieroglyphs has long held humanity in its thrall, captivating our imaginations and sparking endless fascination. It is a realm where time seems to stand still, and where the echoes of ancient wisdom continue to resonate across the ages.

Egypt Before the Written History "The Lost Knowledge of Ancient Egypt" by Mohamed Ibrahim beckons you to embark on a captivating journey into the heart of this enigmatic civilization, where the sands of time cannot obscure the brilliance of its achievements. Within these pages, you will encounter the intellectual and spiritual legacy of a people who left an indelible mark on history, one that reaches far beyond the boundaries of their empire.

Egyptian civilization, with its pyramids, temples, and mummies, has long been a subject of study and admiration. Yet, beyond the iconic imagery lies a profound depth of knowledge and wisdom that has only begun to be fully appreciated in recent years. This book serves as a key to unlock the hidden chambers of that knowledge, shedding light on the mysteries of ancient Egyptian science, medicine, religion, and philosophy.

From the precise art of mummification to the precise measurements of the Great Pyramid, from the complex religious beliefs that guided daily life to the profound insights into the nature of existence, you will discover a civilization whose wisdom and innovations continue to astonish and inspire.

As we delve into the depths of Egypt's ancient wisdom, we must also grapple with the tantalizing notion of what might still remain undiscovered beneath the shifting sands of time. The allure of lost knowledge, waiting to be unearthed by future generations, adds an air of excitement and adventure to the study of Egypt's heritage.

"The Lost Knowledge of Ancient Egypt" is a testament to the enduring allure of this remarkable civilization. It is an invitation to explore the depths of a culture that, though long gone, still whispers its secrets to those who are willing to listen. As you embark on this journey, may you be captivated, enlightened, and inspired by the timeless wisdom of Egypt's ancient sages.

Prepare to uncover the treasures of the past, and may this book be your guide in unraveling the mysteries of "The Lost Knowledge of Ancient Egypt."

Billy Carson
4biddenknowledge Inc
http://4BK.TV

Introduction

How the pyramids were built? What is the function of the pyramids? Hundreds of millions of people, or maybe even billions, from all over the world with different levels of education and knowledge (commoners, students, engineers, artists, handicraftsmen, scientists and others) have all asked these questions at one point.

Also, in any talk about Ancient Egyptian Civilization, these questions are also asked:

- How were the pyramids built?
- Why were the pyramids built?

In this book, I will try to answer these two questions and explain some of the advanced techniques that may have been used to build the pyramids. Also, I'm going to add 2 more questions;

- When the pyramids were built?
- Who built the pyramids?

I can say that these questions are not from modern times. No, these questions were asked by the visitors of Egypt in the last 3000 years. Most of these visitors (if not all) unfortunately didn't have any chance for credible sources; that's why many of their stories about Ancient Egypt are false stories and fantasy.

The Greek traveler and historian **Herodotus** visited Egypt around 450 BC. Herodotus traveled all over Egypt, and he wrote extensively about Ancient Egypt, writing about the time he witnessed and the ancient history he didn't witness. To tell these stories, he depended on local stories and maybe even local guides during his journey through the ancient sites and structures.

Herodotus mentioned the Great Pyramid in his book (History), and he stated that it took 20 years to be built. He also tried to add more information about the Great Pyramid by giving some measurements of the width and height of the sides of the pyramid.

Yes, we know that some of the stories are not correct, especially the story about the daughter of the king who was sent to work as a prostitute in order to bring supplies and materials to the construction, but we must appreciate the passion of Herodotus to write about the Egyptian civilization.

No wonder Alexander the Great, after his battle with the Persian army in Syria, marched to Egypt.

Alexander the Great defeated the army of Darius III in the spring of 332 BC in the battle of Issus. Instead of following Darius, who retreated further east, Alexander went to Egypt.

In my opinion, he was following a call in his heart and his mind to go to Egypt. He didn't enter Egypt as a conqueror—no, but as a descendant of the Egyptian kings. He visited the Oracle Temple of Amun-Ra at Siwa Oases because he had some questions and he was looking for answers. After the death of Alexander, Egypt came under the power of Ptolemy I, who established the Ptolemaic Dynasty in Egypt.

The Egyptian priest **Manetho,** who served during the 3rd century BC, wrote one of the most important books about Ancient Egypt: Aegyptiaca. In this book, he wrote about the Ancient Egyptian dynasties from the very beginning to the very last rulers.

Diodorus Siculus is another Greek historian who visited Egypt around 60 BC. He didn't spend as much time traveling inside of Egypt as Herodotus, but he made some interesting notes about some ancient Egyptian structures and symbols. He mentioned that he saw the casing stone of the Great Pyramid during his visit to the area. He also stated that the bodies of Khufu (Chemmis) and Khafra (Cephren) were buried in secret places to avoid the revenge of the workers and their families. What he meant was that the workers hated the work of building the two pyramids and would this out on the former rulers given the chance.

However, it was not only the Greeks who wanted to travel to Egypt, but also the Romans, like the Roman geographer Strabo, who visited Egypt around 25 BC. **Strabo** visited the Great Pyramid, and it seems that he didn't like the idea that this pyramid was used as a tomb. He also mentioned that there was a movable block working as a door to the entrance of the Great Pyramid (Fig. 1).

Because of this information, Flinders Petrie went to Dahshur (south of Giza) and explored the Bent Pyramid and the Red Pyramid, and he stated that the door of the Bent Pyramid was the same technique because of some pivot holes on the entrance like the door of the Great Pyramid and he left behind some drawings for the entrance of each pyramid.

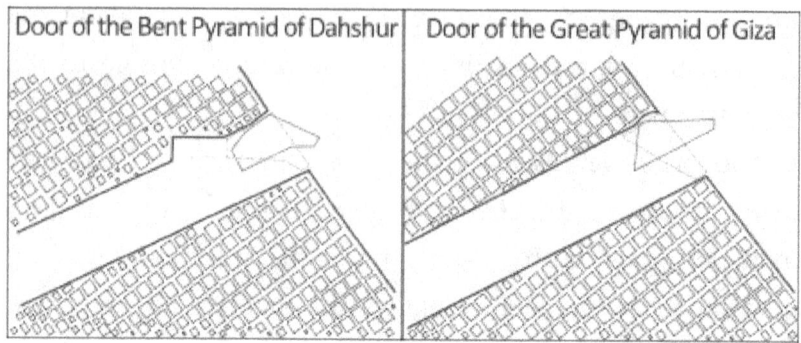

Fig. 1

Pliny the Elder was a Roman writer who visited Egypt in the first century AD. He agreed with Herodotus when he said that it took 20 years to build the Great Pyramid, but he said that this work required 360,000 workers. In his opinion, the king built the pyramid for economic reasons.

Ibn Zulaq (919 – 996 AD) was an Egyptian historian who wrote about Egyptian Islamic history.

He is quoted as saying that if you were to see the two pyramids in Egypt (the Great Pyramid and the 02nd Pyramid), then you would think that no human, no Genie could build the structure; the only one who could have built the structures was GOD.

Al Maqrizi (1364 – 1442 AD) is another Egyptian historian who wrote mainly about the Islamic history. He showed great interest in the Ancient Egyptian Civilization and the history of Egypt in general. He mentioned and described a pyramid in Dahshur (south of Dahshur). This pyramid is not well known even in modern days, but this pyramid was rediscovered in 1957 and is referred to as the Amen Qemau Pyramid.

In modern days, because of our technology and our good understanding of many other fields of science, we are able to explore even more questions about Ancient Egyptian civilization!

Another ruler from Europe who showed great interest in Egypt and the Ancient Egyptian Civilization was Napoleon Bonaparte. In 1798 AD, he led a huge expedition to Egypt, with around 40,000 soldiers and 10,000 sailors. A military campaign like this during the time of fights between England and France can be explained as a move by France to threaten England and to cut the connection between England and India, but it is very hard to explain why Napoleon took hundreds of artisans, painters, and scholars with him on this campaign.

In my opinion, this campaign was not to conquer Egypt; it was to study Egypt and the Ancient Egyptian Civilization. This is evidence because after this campaign, the French wrote a huge book about Egypt called Description de l'Égypte ("Thee Description of Egypt"), which covers almost all the sites of Egypt from north to south and from east to west.

There is a story about how Napoleon spent the night inside the Great Pyramid, and when he came out, he was shaken and was white like a ghost. There is another story about him meeting the Red Man inside the Great Pyramid. While there is no strong evidence to support these stories, we still believe that the purpose of the campaign was not for military purposes.

Because of the French expedition and their discovery of the Rosetta stone, we are able to read and understand the Ancient Egyptian Language.

I believe the story of Alexander the Great was repeated by Napoleon Bonaparte; both were following the call from Egypt.

In modern days, many scholars and experts have sought to understand the achievements of Ancient Egypt and find answers to these questions.

Luis Walter Alvarez (1911 – 1988) was an American physicist who won the Nobel Prize in Physics in 1968.

He wasn't impressed when he visited the pyramids of Mexico, but he said that the Pyramids at Giza were the most interesting ancient structures, and no one yet had managed to explain how they were built.

He led a project to X-ray the Great Pyramid, hoping to find secret chambers inside it, but the project didn't achieve its target.

Dr. Mustafa Mahmoud (1921 - 2009) was an Egyptian physician, philosopher, and author. He was well known in Egypt and in the Middle East because of his weekly TV program, Science and Faith.

Dr. Mustafa Mahmoud made an episode titled "The Pyramid The Miracle," in which he talked about the construction of the Great Pyramid and stated that building the Great Pyramid required high technologies and advanced techniques. He said that the only possible way to lift those huge blocks was anti-gravity technology.

Engineer Hassan F. Imam (Ph.D.) (1934) was a professor of rock mechanics and rock and building material engineering, rock tunneling engineering, and environmental geology at Cairo University.

He was the expert consultant for the restoration project of the Step Pyramid and the restoration project of the Serapeum.

I met him in 2012 at the re-opening of the Serapeum after it was closed for restoration and asked him about his thoughts on how the Serapeum was made? He told me that there were no clear answers to this question.

We must understand that these are not the only questions concerning Ancient Egyptian Civilization; there are actually many more questions about these great achievements of Ancient Egypt. The more advanced technologies we get, the more questions we have.

Some of these questions are:
- How did they cut these huge blocks of stones?
- How did they cut the obelisks?
- How did they transfer these huge blocks of stones, and how did they transfer the obelisks?
- How did they lift up these heavy blocks?

There are just a few of the hundreds of questions mankind has about Ancient Egypt, but there is no single opinion that can give a definitive answer to convince us.

These are the most famous questions about the Ancient Egyptian Civilization, but in this book, I'm going to ask more questions about the other unexplained megalithic structures in Egypt and present my ideas about them with the available evidence or at least with some logical conclusions.

In this book, we will talk about:
- The challenges of cutting huge blocks of stones weighing more than 50 tons from limestone, alabaster, and rose granite. The biggest blocks were cut from the rose granite quarry at Aswan, and many reached the weight of 1500 tons.
- The perfect precisions in angles, as well as how smooth, highly polished, and flat surfaces were achieved.
- The unique structure called obelisks and my own ideas about the functions of the obelisks

The information you will read in this book supports the fact that there was an advanced technology used to produce these objects, and this will lead us to talk about the existence of another civilization in Ancient Egypt, earlier in time and highly advanced.

In this book, I will explain all that I have learned in this field after almost 20 years of leading tours, exploring and visiting most of the sites all around Egypt from north to south, from east to west, studying the Egyptian people, many of whom still uphold Ancient Egyptian traditions; and most importantly, meeting and working with some professionals in their fields (engineers, sound engineers, geologists, geophysicists, astronauts, doctors, and mathematicians) who add to my knowledge about Ancient Egypt. But let me first tell you my story about how I became interested in this field.

So, I'm very convinced that many of the ancient sites were originally healing centers, and if the temple was huge, then it served as an academy (college) and hospital, so we can say that the priest was originally a healer and a scientist.

I was very lucky to start reading about new opinions and theories concerning some of the Ancient Egyptian sites. The first surprise for me was when I heard about Dr. Robert Schoch and his theory about the Sphinx. I was very interested because I had so many questions about these sites and their histories, but there were no answers.

Re-dating the Sphinx theory opened the gate for me to start searching for more evidence and logical opinions.

I toured with Christopher Dunn in 2013, 2018, and 2019, and during this time, I came to understand his opinions about so many Ancient Egyptian sites and sculptures as a master engineer. I then had the chance to tour with Dr. Robert Schoch in 2014, 2015, and 2019, where I was able to hear "new" stories from the experts. This was my first time understanding the great need for science in Egyptology. I'm not exaggerating when I say that we need all kinds of science in order to understand our ancient history; we need engineers, geologists, chemists, biologists, physicist, botanists, and even zoologists.

And as if destiny wanted me to be very sure that I was heading the right way, I met so many other people who were also experts in their fields, including geologists and engineers. Some of them knew Dr. Robert Schoch and Christopher Dunn, and some didn't, but they all agreed about the possible existence of an earlier Ancient Egyptian civilization and the existence of advanced technologies, either during the Ancient Egyptian times or during this earlier Ancient Egyptian civilization.

I understand that the ideas and opinions I present in this book are not aligned with mainstream stories and opinions about the tools and techniques of Ancient Egypt, and I don't want to underestimate the work of the Egyptologists, which was done through great efforts for centuries, and I can't deny that so much of what I have learned is based on Egyptology.

However, what I can say is that so much of the information and so many of the stories about Ancient Egypt are accurate. Most of what we know about the Ancient Egyptian rulers and royal families is accurate, but when we talk about Ancient Egyptian technologies, we can't say it is accurate!

Because Egyptologists collected this information and these stories from the writings on walls, statues, obelisks, and papyrus, we can say writings are an important source for our knowledge about Ancient Egypt; although it is not accurate 100%, it is still the main source for Egyptologists to date and relate to the objects they have found from Ancient Egypt.

Again, when we talk about Ancient Egyptian technologies, we will find that there are almost no writings about it. The Ancient Egyptians didn't describe how they built the pyramids or how they cut the obelisks; nothing was mentioned about these megalithic structures, so Egyptologists, in order to explain these methods and techniques, used their "imagination."

I can say that their claims about the primitive ways and primitive tools being used to build the pyramids and cut the obelisks are based on the level of technology that existed in the 19th century, when Egyptology became an official science.

We must understand that the Ancient Egyptians mentioned detailed information about so many professions, like in the tombs of the Old Kingdom at Sakkara, you will see that the artisans represented so many details of carpentry, butchery, land cultivation, harvesting, bird breeding, animal breeding, fishing, and animal hunting (fig. 2 and 3). But as I mentioned above, the ancient historians didn't bother to describe how they built the pyramids, the temples, or how they cut the stones from the quarries.

Fig. 2

Fig. 3

One of the best examples of these scenes of daily life activities is in the tomb of Ti at Sakkara (5th Dynasty, Old Kingdom). Again, we can see they represented so many things, even the process of making a sandal!! (Fig. 4)

Can we say that making a sandal is worth being represented on the walls of the tomb of Ti but not the process for building a pyramid!?

Fig. 4

Ti served during the time of the 5th Dynasty, so it means he witnessed the construction of a pyramid, at least one pyramid. How did they forget to represent this great project? Not only this, but they didn't show how they cut the blocks from the quarry, and they didn't show how they moved the obelisks out of the quarry or how they were loaded onto ships? We have a carving for King Unas from the causeway (5th Dynasty) showing 2 boats transferring 2 or 4 pillars from Elephantine Island to the temple attached to his pyramid at Sakkara, and there is a similar scene for Queen Hatshepsut where they transfer obelisks. I always wondered about these 2 scenes. Were they fake? Was it true that Unas and Hatshepsut did this job?? I don't think so, but if the answer is yes, maybe the size of the pillars and obelisks was smaller than what we believed (Figures 5, 6, 7).

Picture from the Causeway of Unas Pyramid, Sakkara
Fig. 5

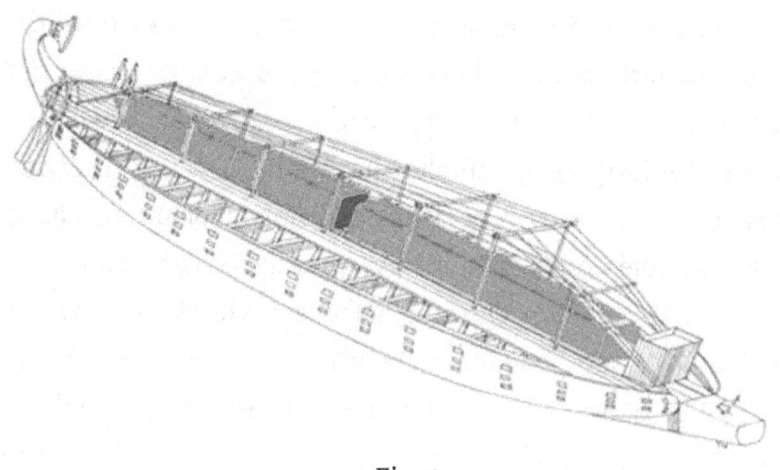

Fig. 6

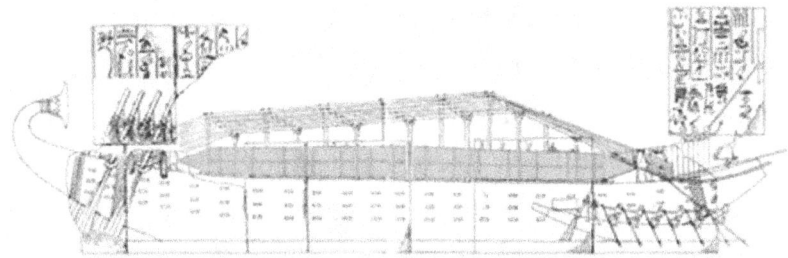

Picture from Hatshepsut Temple, West Bank, Luxor
Fig. 7

After seeing much evidence on the Ancient Egyptian sites, on the walls, and on many scattered blocks from different materials like granite, basalt, alabaster, and limestone, I became very confident about the ancient advanced technology, but the question was, did this high technology exist during what we know as Ancient Egyptian Civilization or did this high technology exist in a civilization preceding the dynasties civilization?

In my opinion, the answer is very clear when we do a good analysis of the era before the dynasties, an era we call the pre-dynastic.

What was found in the tombs of pre-dynastic cultures and groups of people is proof that there was an earlier advanced civilization that ended around 10,500 BC or, to be precise, the end of this Ancient Egyptian Advanced Civilization was between 10,500 BC and 9,700 BC, the end of the last Ice Age.

In this book, we will gain insight into Ancient Egypt, focusing not only on its history from thousands of years ago but also extending back millions of years. This exploration will allow us to understand how and why the land surface and formation of

Egypt took its shape and to learn when large mammals such as elephants, hippos, rhinos, giraffes, and other animals existed in the region. We will also investigate the oldest possible date for the prehistoric Ancient Egyptians who settled in the area, based on solid evidence found scattered across various locations in Egypt. Additionally, we will delve into the cultures of the pre-dynastic era, acquiring more knowledge about their industries and symbols.

You will find so many words in Hieroglyphic to make sure you know the Ancient Egyptian way of writing so many of the names and titles related to Ancient Egypt.

Names of Ancient Egypt

E gypt has always had a special effect on its visitors, and this effect can differ according to the culture and origin of the visitor. Not only do the visitors or travelers to Egypt feel this special effect, but also the locals. Because of my travels all around Egypt, I can tell you that each person in this country sees it in a unique way; each one perceives the energies and sees the beauty of Egypt differently.

Over the last 5,000 years, Egypt has had many names, including ancient names and modern ones. Many of the ancient names were not repeated in various sources, leading us to think that these names were more like titles or descriptions, representing certain meanings for Egypt. Other names were repeated in most of the sources, confirming that these were the official names for the country.

Egypt is the modern name used by Western people. The name "Egypt" comes from the Ancient Greek name "Aígyptos" (Αἴγυπτος), in Latin it was "Aegyptus," and in Middle French, it is "Egypte." But what is the origin of the name "Egypt"?

Some scholars believe that the origin of this name is Greek, theorizing that the Greeks called Egypt according to the Aegean Sea, the country south of the Aegean Sea. This opinion is not accepted, and it has been proven that the name "Egypt" is derived from an Ancient Egyptian word.

"Misr" is the modern name currently used by the natives and all the Middle Eastern people. جمهورية مصر العربية This is the complete formal name for the country; the short name is مصر

The formal Western name for Egypt is Arab Republic of Egypt; sometimes you see it written as A.R.E. as an abbreviation.

Again, many scholars think that the name "Misr" is derived from a Semitic origin, from the Hebrew word (Miráyim/Mitzráyim/Mizráim). I see that the name is an Ancient Egyptian name and was being used by the Hebrew; the name existed before the Hebrew language existed.

The name Misr was mentioned in other sources:

In some Akkadian texts, we can read in one of the Akkadian texts the word "mii ru"; this name is for Egypt (mi-i-ru).

In some texts from the Neo-Assyrian Empire, we can read the name "mi ru" or "mi irru" in some Assyrian texts; it is like the Akkadian name for Egypt.

Again, the name is an Ancient Egyptian name, and it was being used by the neighbors of Egypt.

So, let's learn more about the names of Ancient Egypt.

Kemet

Kemet is the official name for Egypt in Ancient Egypt; this name, Kemet, was found written almost everywhere: on documents, temple walls, tomb walls, stelas, and other surfaces.

Most people explain Kemet as the "black land," and some interpret it as the "land of black people." If we look carefully at the meaning of Kemet (according to the Ancient Egyptian language), we will find that it originally comes from the word "Km," which means "black" (color). However, Kemet also has other meanings that must be mentioned here to help us understand the term:

- Profit
- Total up
- Final account
- Large (granite) jar
- Holy herd
- Twinkling and mineral

In my opinion, Kemet means "fertility," because I think Kemet refers to the black layer of silt that covers the Nile Valley. Egypt used to receive a new layer of silt every year because of the Nile flood. This layer of silt includes many minerals like copper, zinc, manganese, iron, and gold; it also contains important elements like cobalt and iridium. Therefore, I believe that the suitable meaning of Kemet is fertility.

I believe that the name Kemet is the origin of "chemistry" and "alchemy." I imagine the early Greeks when they visited Egypt and found the locals practicing a very interesting science that dealt with liquids and substances. They named it "Kemy"

(Chemi) after the name of the country, and later it became "chemistry."

The Arabs did the same thing, naming it "Kemy" (Chemi), but they added the definitional letters (al), so the name became "Alchemy."

الكيمياء

In my own opinion, the name Kemet refers to ntr Osiris (Ausir), because Osiris represents the fertile layer of the Egyptian land, and maybe that's why they represented him in green color and sometimes in black color.

Deshert

There are other names for Ancient Egypt, like Deshert (desert), which means "Red Land" or, in another sense, the Egyptian desert. If you look at the map of Egypt, you will find that Egypt contains two huge deserts: the Eastern Desert and the Western Desert.

Some scholars think that the name Deshert is the opposite of Kemet, because they compare between the desert of Egypt (yellow sand and red sand) and the Nile Valley (black silt or mud). However, this is not correct because the name Kemet applies to all of Egypt, not just the Nile Valley. So, I can say that Deshert is part of the name Kemet. Also, I can say that the name Deshert refers to "ntr Seth" (Set); the nature of Set is like the nature of the desert, with tough conditions and not easy to deal with.

Deshert is the name of the crown of the North (north of Egypt); the red crown of Lower Egypt (north of Egypt) is called Deshert.

Ta-wy

Ta-wy is also one of the Ancient names for Egypt, meaning "the Two Lands." Some opinions suggest it refers to the East and the West sides of Egypt, as the East represents the power of the Sunrise, and the West represents the power of the Sunset. Alternatively, it may refer to the North and South of Egypt (Lower and Upper Egypt) because, according to Ancient records, the two parts of the country were politically separate in the early beginning. They were united by King Narmer (Meni) at the beginning of the dynasties. I think Ta-wy refers to two Egypts: the first Egypt is in our dimension in the first life, and the second Egypt is in another dimension in the afterlife or in the second life. This is because "Ta" doesn't mean a small piece of land or limited land; rather, it means all the land, or in another sense, it means Earth. "Ta" means land, and "wy" is the way to express duality.

Many of the Egyptian rulers had the title "Neb-Tawy," which means "the lord of the 2 lands." So, if we talk about the north and the south, it doesn't make sense because the title "Nsw-Bity," which means "King of Upper and Lower Egypt," covers this meaning.

Ta-Mry

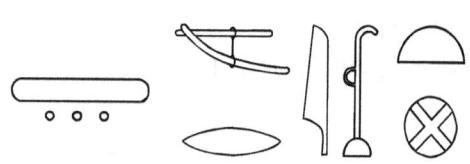

Ta-Mry is another name for Ancient Egypt; this name means "the beloved land" or "the land of love." There is an opinion that says the name "Mary" could come from the Ancient Egyptian word "mry," because sometimes the letter "T" joins the word to become "mryt," and the regular way to pronounce it is "Meret," but I pronounce it "Maria," the same as the Western name Maria.

This name could relate to the name Kemet if we understand that the main symbol in the word "Mry" is the hoe or the plow, which is very connected with cultivation. The word "Ta-Mry" is very close to the Arabic word "Tamar" (طمر), which means to put the seed under the ground (seeding). I believe it is a way to explain one of the natures of Egypt as the fertile ground for life, or we can say Egypt is the womb.

Medjer

Medjer is a name that may not be listed much in our books and research about the names of Ancient Egypt, but it is a very important name for Ancient Egypt. Medjer means "the fortress" or "the fortified land," which describes the condition of Egypt's land as a protected land. If you look at the map of Egypt, you will see that this country was protected by nature: from the North by the Mediterranean Sea, from the East by the Red Sea, and from the South and the West by the vast Sahara desert. I think the modern name for Egypt (Misr or Masr), which is used by the Egyptians and Arabs, is derived from Medjer, because the letter (dej) can be pronounced as (s), so it will be Mesr (Misr). There is another opinion that says the modern name (Misr) was derived from the two words "ms-r," which means "the birth of the word" (spoken word), but I don't agree much with this opinion and agree more with the name Medjer.

The Egyptians and the Arabs, for a long time, especially from the 8th century to the 20th century, used to call Egypt "Misr Al Mahrousa" (المحروسة), which means "Egypt the protected land."

In many cases, they didn't say the official name Misr (Masr) and just said "Al Mahrousa," so people would automatically understand that this name means Egypt.

Het-Ka-Ptah

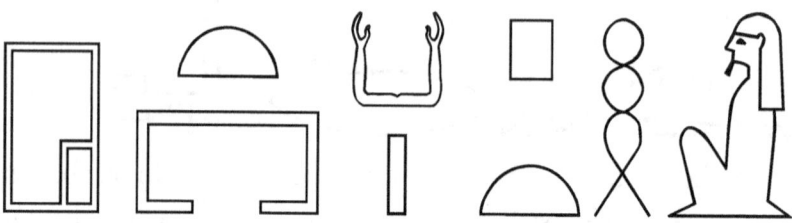

Het-Ka-Ptah is not the name of Egypt during ancient times, but later it became the name for Egypt itself. We pronounce this name as Het-Ka-Ptah, which means "the home of the spirit of Ptah," or in another way, "the Temple of the Ka of Ptah in Memphis." Ptah is a major ntr in Ancient Egypt, and Memphis is his hometown. Ptah is considered as one of the creators of the universe. Memphis was chosen to be the capital of Egypt by the very early rulers of Ancient Egypt, the rulers of Dynasty 0 and Dynasty 1. Memphis was held in very high regard by the Ancient Egyptian rulers, and also by non-Egyptian rulers like Alexander the Great. When he invaded Egypt, he visited Memphis and the Temple of Ptah. The Ptolemaic rulers did the same thing, although they lived in Alexandria and made it the capital of Egypt, but Memphis was highly appreciated.

The Greeks paid much respect to this city, especially Alexander the Great. When the Greeks pronounced the name, they couldn't say it perfectly; they pronounced it as "Et-Ka-Pt" (It-Ka-Pt) and then even shortened the name to "Ecopt"

(Ekopt). This name is the origin of the word "Coptic" (from Copt), which now means "Egyptian Christian," but originally meant "Egyptian" only.

"Ecopt" was pronounced later as "Egopt" (Egypt), and there are some cities in Egypt that still pronounce the letters **Q** and **K** as G or J.

There are some other names for Egypt, but they are not famous or not commonly used, and we can say they were used as titles.

Baket

The name Baket means "the lady" or "the maid," which I think is a way to express the effect of female energy on our lives. We can read this name as Bakah or Bekeh (or Becca), because the letter T at the end of the word could be H.

The holy city for Muslims is called Mecca, and it was mentioned in the Quran as Becca (Bacca). The famous city in Lebanon, Baalbek (Baal-Bek), is known as the city of Baal. In my own opinion, we can say this is a name or title for holy (energetic) cities or lands.

Baket

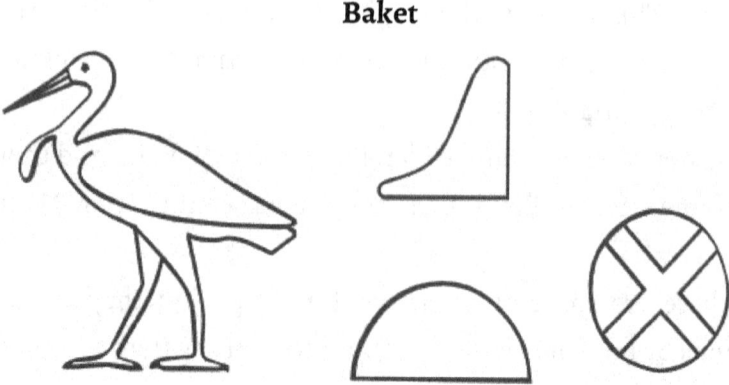

There is another form to write the name Baket; this form has the symbol of the Jabiru bird, which is the symbol of the Ba (soul). So I can say that this name can be translated as "The land of the soul" or "The high land of the soul." The land of Baket is where the soul descended from space and was transplanted into the human body, so I think this name is very clear evidence about the spirituality of Ancient Egypt.

Wadjet

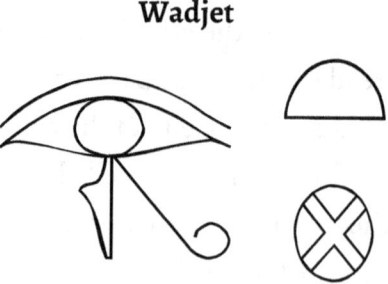

In my opinion, this name means protection, because it was derived from the famous symbol Wadjet, which represents the Eye of Horus, and is also derived from another well-known symbol, Wadjet (the name of the Ancient Cobra, the protector of Egypt). The Egyptians during the Middle Ages used to call Egypt Al Mahrousa, which means The Protected City. In modern days, we may not call Egypt by this name, but we still know and understand that this old name used to be a name or a title for Egypt.

Bia

This name is very strange; first, it means "the two bushes," and in this case, we have a good question: What are the two bushes that can create such a name for Ancient Egypt? We understand that there is a wide Nile Delta at the north of modern Cairo city, a very green land with lots of water because of the many branches of the Nile, but we don't know another part of Ancient Egypt (or Modern Egypt) that can be called bushes. I think this is one of the very old names for Ancient Egypt, perhaps before the dynastic era, to describe the fertile green land of Egypt. So, I think the two bushes were one in the north (the Nile Delta) and the other one in the south (the area between Aswan and Abu Simbel).

There are other words that are pronounced "Bia," and they give very interesting meanings:

1. Bia, which means heaven or firmament, and I can say it is another way to connect Egypt with extraterrestrial dimensions.
2. Bia, which means iron, but not the normal kind of iron; it is the iron of the meteorites, and they called it "bia n pt," meaning the iron of the sky. They paid great attention to the meteorites that were falling from the sky. I can easily say that the two meanings are leading to the concept of "extraterrestrial."

Idebwy

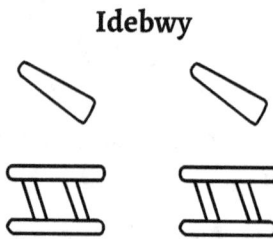

This name means "the two banks," referring to the two riverbanks. The East side of the Nile and the West side of the Nile were not just geographical directions, but they represented the two major stations in the life of the Ancient Egyptians.

Iyabt is the Ancient Egyptian word for East, and it symbolizes the beginning of life and new energies because of the daily sunrise.

Imentet is the Ancient Egyptian word for West, and it represents the end of the first life and the gate to the afterlife journey because of the daily sunset.

Idebwy

There is another way to write the name Idebwy: "the two banks of Horus." In my opinion, they wanted to draw our attention towards the sky (as the hawk always flies at high levels in the sky). Some opinions suggest that the Nile and the Ancient Egyptian sites located on the two sides of the Nile match the shape of the Milky Way. So this could be the meaning of this name, "the two banks of Horus."

We must know that there is a symbol always paired with the name Kemet, this symbol is "**niwt**" (Fig. 8,9), meaning city. It represents the city's main square with the crossroads. I think that when it is attached to the name of the country, it means the civilization of Kemet.

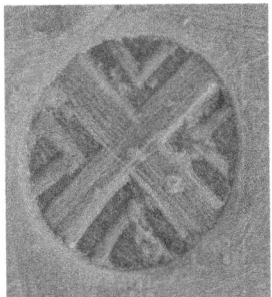

Fig. 8

Fig. 9

The Ancient Egyptians added this symbol next to the names of cities in Egypt. It was not only the Ancient Egyptians who added the "niwt" symbol next to the name of Egypt but also the Persians. There is a statue of King Darius I, and on the sides of the pedestal, there is a list of the countries conquered by the Persians. They made sure to put the symbol "niwt" next to the name Kemet.

The Ancient Egyptians, when they wrote the names of other countries, gave them the symbol "khast" (Figures 10 and 11), meaning mountain, as if they wanted to say these countries were not as civilized as Egypt.

The Ancient Egyptians added this symbol next to the names of the districts and sites located in the desert side of Egypt, either the Western or the Eastern desert, and we can say that all other nations and countries were given the symbol Khast. The statue of the Persian king, Darius I, is a good example of this information. We will understand that adding the symbol "khast" next to the names of all the countries except Egypt was not done by the Ancient Egyptians only; other nations did the same. They gave Egypt the symbol of civilization and the others the symbol "khast." The Persian Empire did the same; on the side of the pedestal, there is a list of the countries conquered by the Persians, and they made sure to put the symbol "khast" next to these countries.

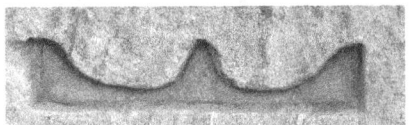

Fig. 10

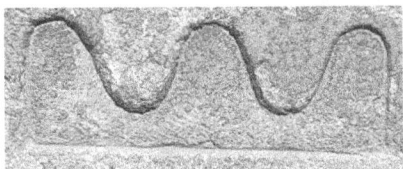

Fig. 11

Kemet *Assyria*
Fig. 12 *Fig. 13*

Religion of Ancient Egypt

Fig. 14

To better know the gods and goddesses of Ancient Egypt, we need first to understand the meaning of a very important symbol in Ancient Egypt, the symbol "ntr" (Fig. 14)

In fact, there are other meanings for this symbol, but first, what does the symbol represent?

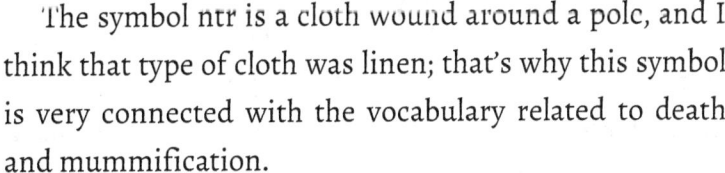

The symbol ntr is a cloth wound around a pole, and I think that type of cloth was linen; that's why this symbol is very connected with the vocabulary related to death and mummification.

When it reads "bd" it means Natron. Natron is a very special type of salt in Egypt, as it was used as an antiseptic for cuts and wounds. However, the main use of natron was during the mummification process to dry and preserve the flesh and the skin of the corpse.

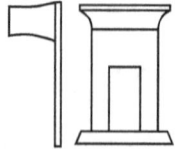 When it reads "sH ntr," it means "an embalmer's workshop." It is the place where the mummification process took place, and the place where they wrap the mummy with layers of linen.

"sH ntr" also means linen, but in my opinion, it refers to the linen used in the booth of Anubis. Anubis is the official embalmer, and that's why the priest must wear the mask of Anubis for a while during the mummification operation.

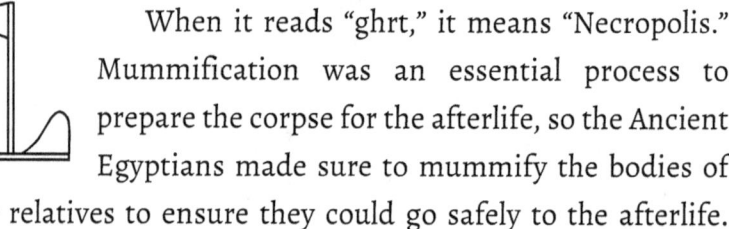 When it reads "ghrt," it means "Necropolis." Mummification was an essential process to prepare the corpse for the afterlife, so the Ancient Egyptians made sure to mummify the bodies of their relatives to ensure they could go safely to the afterlife. However, the quality of mummification depended on how much money they could pay, so we can say that all or most of the dead bodies went to the cemetery wrapped in linen. Therefore, I can say the word "Nether" came from the Egyptian word "ntr," and the term "Netherworld" fits this concept.

  "Ntr" (neter) was explained by almost all Egyptologists as "God," and this is the main reason to call Ra, Horus, Osiris, Amun, and others gods. What caused this misunderstanding and led them to insist that it means "god" is when they saw this symbol next to the symbol of the old man and the symbol of Horus, so they said that the symbol "ntr"

with Horus next to it means "god Horus," and when it has the symbol of the old man next to it, it means "god" in general.

You must know that the right way to write and read the word "ntr" is "nTr" (nTr); we can pronounce it like "net-ther" (net-ser), so I believe this is the word that was taken into the Latin language (naturae), and then it became the English word "nature."

Ntrt (goddess)

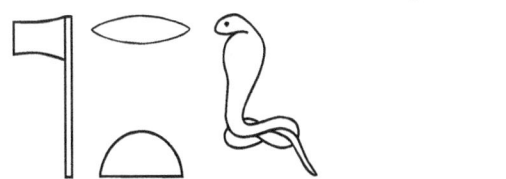

In my opinion, the Ancient Egyptians added the symbol of man/woman to express the nature of a natural element or phenomenon as masculine or feminine. Also, when they added the cobra to the symbol "ntr," it meant feminine, and when it had Horus, it signified the connection between sky and earth, because many of the "ntrs" are from the sky, and others are from the earth.

Ntrs from the sky include
- Atum
- Ra
- Kheper
- Montu
- Aton
- Sekhmet
- Hathor
- Bastet

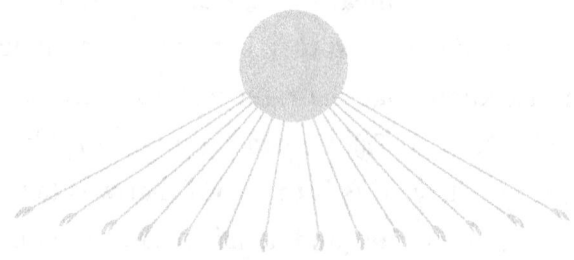

Aton

These ntrs represent different powers of the sun.
- Nut
- Mut
- Tefnut

These ntrts represent the powers of the sky and space.

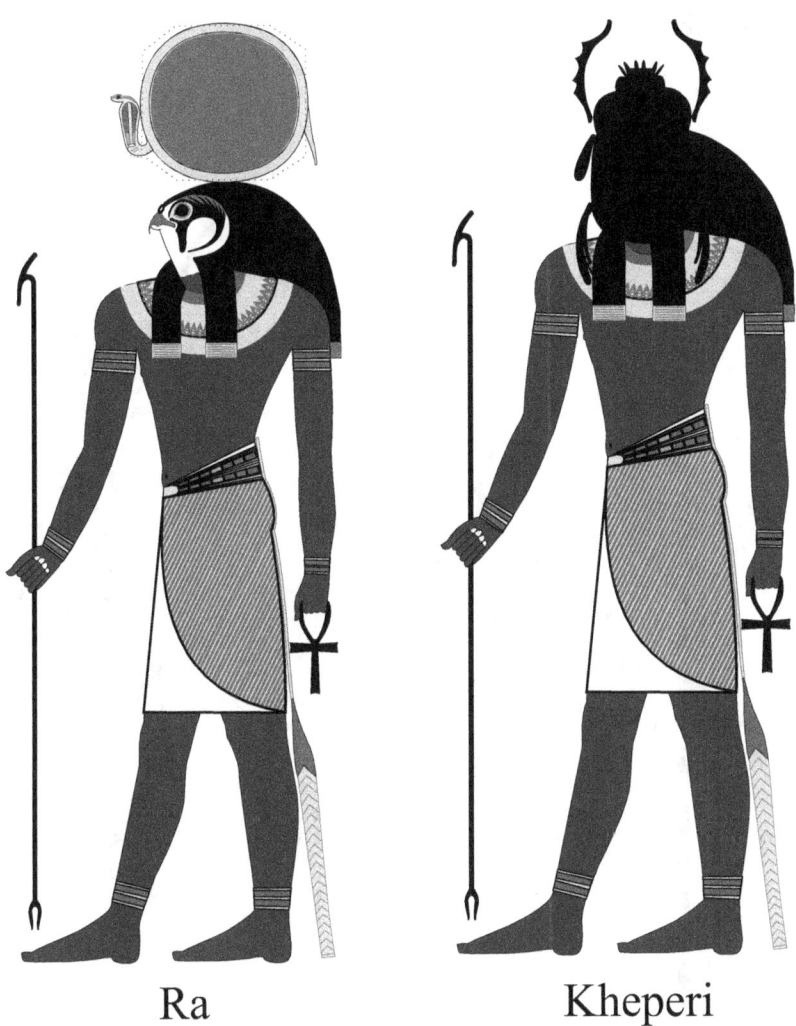

Ra   Kheperi

Other ntrs include
- Thoth
- Ptah
- Sshat

These ntrs represent the power of knowledge and wisdom.

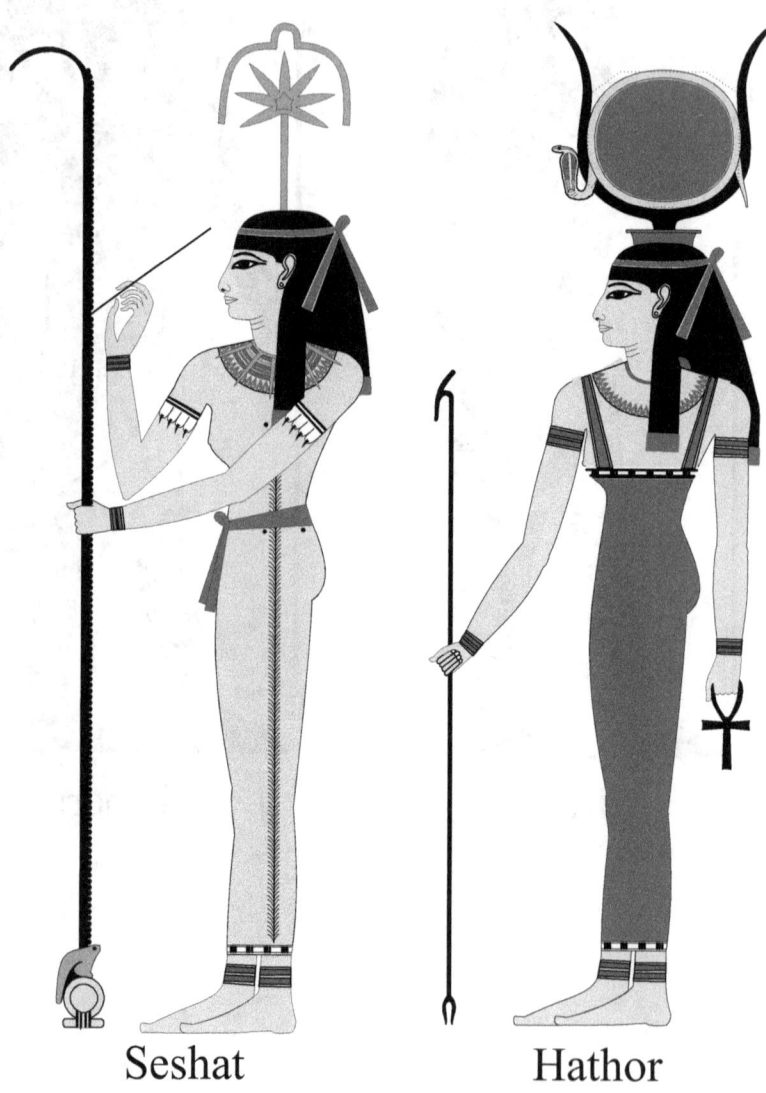

Seshat   Hathor

And other ntrs from Earth include
- Ha-pi
- Ta-wret
- Geb
- Khnum
- Sobek
- Set

These ntrs represent the powers of earth, the power of the Nile, and the power of some of the creatures who live next to the Nile.

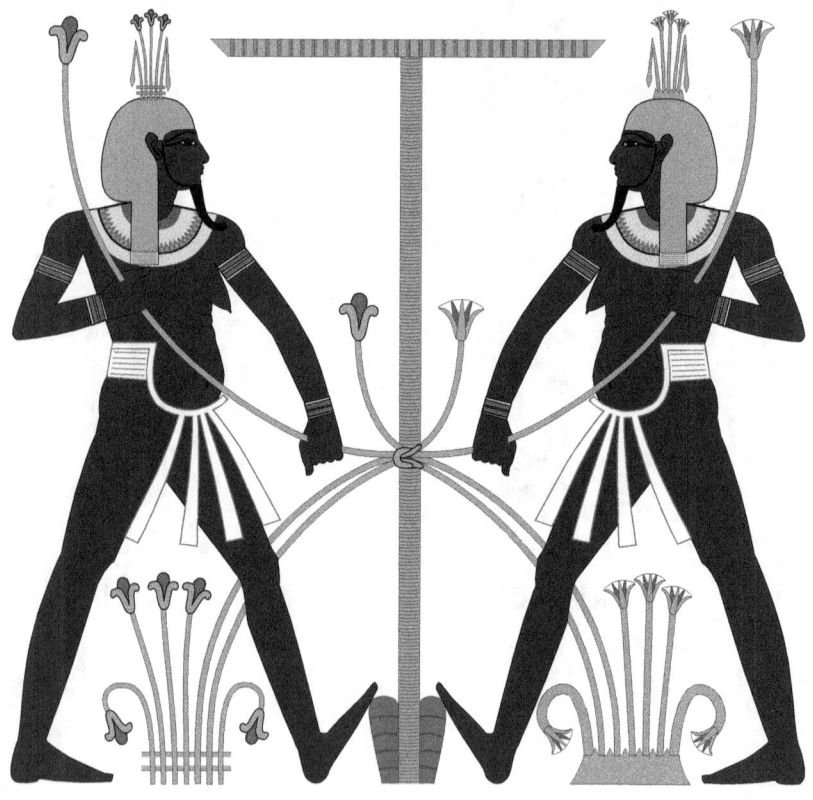

Hapi

Ta-Weret   Sobek

Hwt ntr is a term that Egyptologists have explained as "temple" because Hwt means an enclosure and foundation, and it also serves as "house." Egyptologists explained the word "ntr" as "god," so Hwt ntr means the "house of god" or "temple." However, this is not accurate. As I stated earlier, the word "ntr" means "nature," so Hwt ntr means the "house of nature," and I explain it as an "academy," a teaching academy that could also be a healing center at the same time.

It was an academy for studying and teaching the philosophy and the conditions of the forces of nature. That's why most of these so-called temples are dedicated to one ntr or one force of nature.

If the Hwt ntr is a huge complex, like Karnak Temple in Luxor, it will serve as a university to teach the young students, and it will also function as a healing center. People seeking healing could go every day, but I believe there were certain important, powerful days like the 21st of December at Karnak Temple, especially during the sunrise, and the 21st of June at the Giza Plateau during sunrise.

In the west bank of Luxor, there is a small temple for Isis (Deir el-Shelwit). The locals call it the Temple of the Blood. I was told that the women of the area, when they have issues with bleeding after or during pregnancy or bleeding for other reasons, will immediately go to the temple asking for healing. Of course, there were certain things they would do, but unfortunately, we don't know any details about what they used to do there. What I'm sure about is that the place was active for a long time, at least until 1900 A.D., because the locals who live nearby still remember the function of the site.

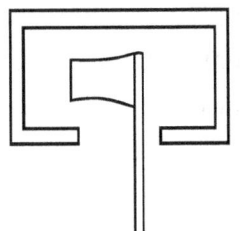
In my opinion, there is another word that can be used instead of Hwt ntr, although it may not be easy to find written on the walls of the temples. This word is pr ntr, where the word "pr" means "house."

I believe Hwt ntr is the name for a large temple, and pr ntr is the name for a small temple.

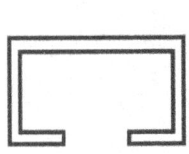 
Pr Ba, in my opinion, is another way to refer to the word "temple" in Ancient Egypt. Many people may not agree with me because we have not found a clear example for such a title, but I think it was a designation for healing temples, as this title means "the House of the soul." The name Para-Be (plural of Pr-Ba) was mentioned by Arab writers and historians like Dhul-Nun al-Misri (9th century) and Ibn Abd al-Hakam (9th century).

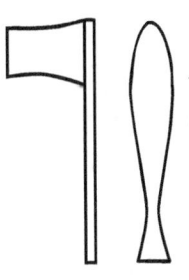
This is one of the most important titles in Ancient Egypt, and it could be the reason for our understanding of the Egyptian civilization. **Hm ntr** is said to mean "priest," "god's servant," and "prophet," and scholars have made classifications for the priesthood, including junior priests, senior priests, and high priests.

There was a very strong female presence in the Egyptian temples. It is likely believed that the title "priestess" was given to the females who served in certain temples dedicated to specific ntrs, like the ntr Hathor and the Temple at Dendera.

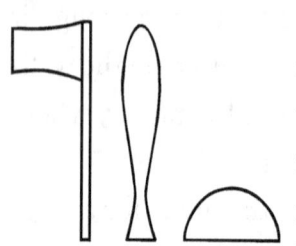

Hmt ntr is the ancient Egyptian word for "priestess." The prevalent idea about the priesthood in ancient Egypt is that it was a male responsibility with limited female presence, and it is strongly believed that the ancient Egyptian priestesses served in certain temples dedicated to specific ntrs.

I stated above that the so-called temples in Ancient Egypt were originally healing centers and teaching academies, and the so-called priest was originally a scientist and healer. But I must explain that during the dynasties, the situation changed, and in order to reap benefits from these structures and this knowledge, they changed the meanings of the ntr, Hwt ntr, and Hm ntr; they became "god," "temple," and "priest."

The priesthood in Ancient Egypt was very powerful, and sometimes, it was more powerful than the king himself, especially after the New Kingdom time. They instituted a very restricted system for education in Ancient Egypt; to go to school, you had to go to the temple, as the temple was the school. To become an accountant or a physician, you had to become a priest first. They wanted to make sure that the knowledge remained in their hands only and to maintain their high positions in Ancient Egyptian society.

Capitals of Ancient Egypt

There are four important cities in Ancient Egypt; their names are related to the most famous stories of creation in Ancient Egyptian mythology.

- Memphis
- Hermopolis
- Thebes
- Heliopolis

According to the Ancient Egyptian language, we can read the 4 names as Men Nefer, Khemnw, Ta Iepet, and Iunu.

These are the same names, but in modern Egypt, they are called: Mit Rahina, Al Ashmunein, Luxor, and Ain Shams.

Memphis

Memphis is the city of the neter Ptah, "God Ptah." It was known as a very old capital of Ancient Egypt and was founded at the beginning of the dynasties, and maybe even older. The city carried several names during Ancient Egyptian history; the oldest name we know for Memphis is Ineb Hedj, which means "the white wall."

We believe that the city was established by King Narmer (Mena) around 3200 BC, and he built a huge white wall around the city; that's why it got its name as the city of the white wall. But the famous name for the city is Memphis or Manf, which is derived from the name Men-nefer, the name of the Pyramid of King Pepi I (6th Dynasty).

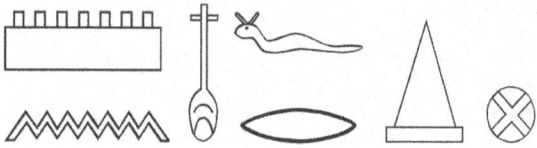

Memphis nowadays is no longer a major city; it is a small village in Badrashien city (my hometown). It lies around 20 km south of Giza and is called Mit Rahina. This name means "the path of the Sphinx avenue." I believe there was a long Sphinx avenue from Memphis to the entrance of the Serapeum at Sakkara, about 15 km.

Ptah is the ntr of Memphis, and he is the main member of the Memphis triad: Ptah, Sekhmet, and Nefertum. Ptah is the patron of craftsmen, including those in metalworking, carpentry, shipbuilding, sculpture, and architecture.

Ptah is always represented as a male figure with a bald head, long straight beard, and wrapped as a mummy. The head is always colored blue, perhaps turquoise, because the head was plated in turquoise. He is holding the Was scepter, the Djed pillar, and the Ankh symbol.

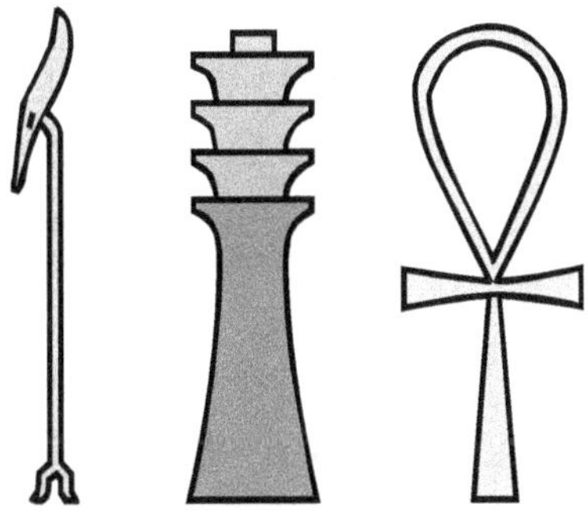

Wass   Djed   Ankh

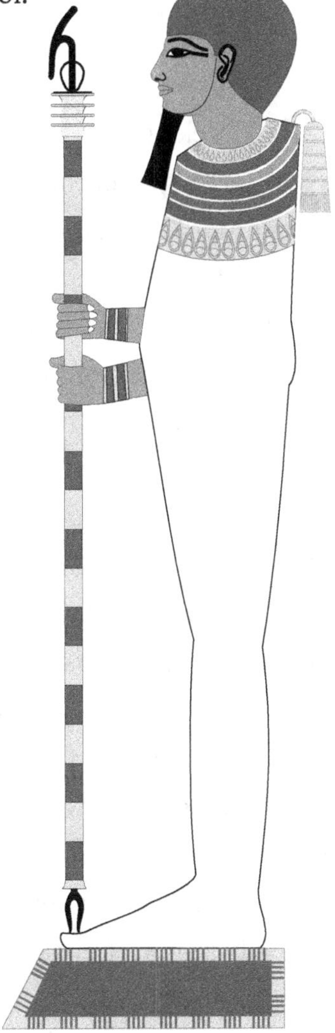

Ptah

Al Ashmunein

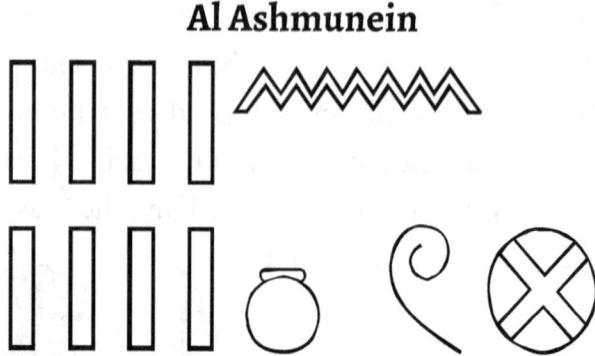

The Greeks called this city Hermopolis, which means the city of Hermes, after they identified Hermes with the Egyptian neter Thoth. This city was the city of Thoth and used to have the biggest Temple of Thoth in Egypt. Thoth was considered the ntr of knowledge and wisdom in Ancient Egypt. His consort is Seshat, the cosmos engineer. His main job was the scribe of the ntrs, and he was the one who started writing and taught the Egyptians how to write.

Thoth has 2 identities, or we can say he is like one coin, but with 2 sides: one side is Thoth, the Ibis bird, and the other side is Djehuty, the Baboon. The Egyptian way to read the name Thoth is T-Hoot.

In some opinions, Thoth is associated with (or considered to be) Enoch, yes, Enoch the messenger. Its name in the Arabic language is Edries because Enoch (Edries) is considered the first human to use the pen to write. It is said that the word "ink" is derived from the name Enoch, and the word "education" (tad-rees in Arabic) is derived from Edries.

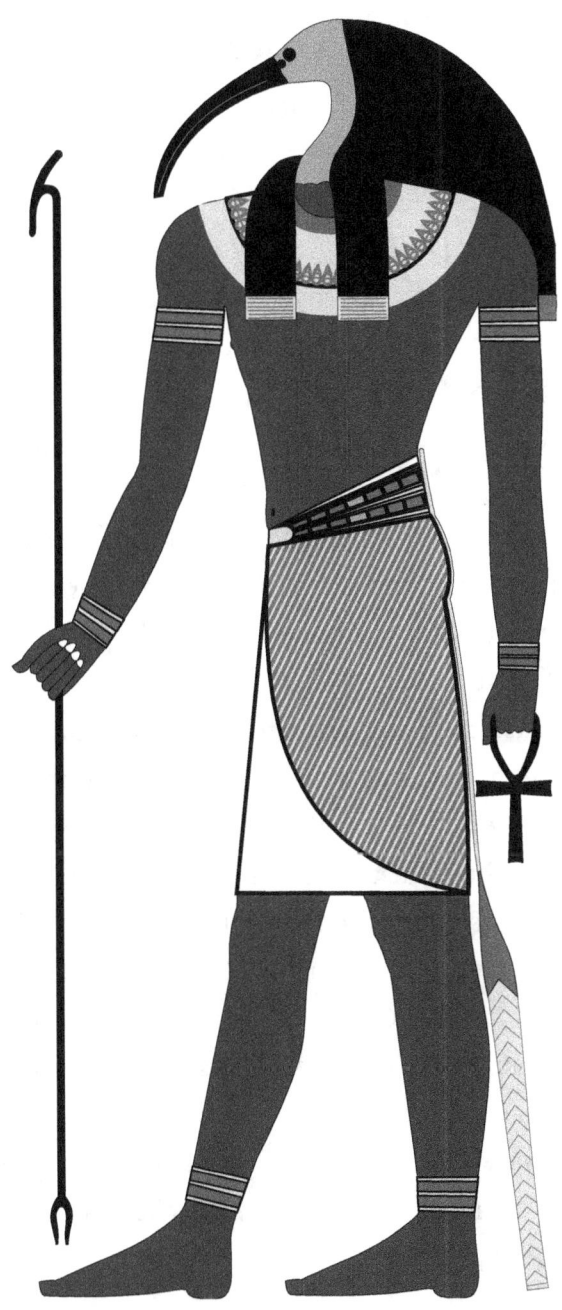

Thoth

Heliopolis

Iunu (Iwnw) is one of the most important cities of Ancient Egypt. It is one of the oldest cities and maybe the oldest city, existing since the predynastic period of Ancient Egypt. The meaning of the name Iunu is "the Pillar" or "the City of Pillars." We still are not sure of the exact meaning, and it may refer to the obelisk because we can still see an obelisk (attributed to King Senusret I from the 12th Dynasty Middle Kingdom, reigned 20th Century BC) standing in the open-air museum of Iunu.

The Greeks called the ancient city Heliopolis (city of the sun) because the city was housing the great Temple of Atum-Ra. There are very few items left in Heliopolis from the great Temple of the Sun, but the most important surviving item is the granite obelisk attributed to Senusret I, the 12th Dynasty.

The Arabs gave it the name Ain Shams, which means "the Eye of the Sun" or "the Center of the Sun." I find this meaning very interesting because it creates a strong relation between the city and the sun.

Iunu is the source of a very important theory in Egyptian history: the Ennead, or sometimes called the Ennead of Heliopolis (Pesdjet).

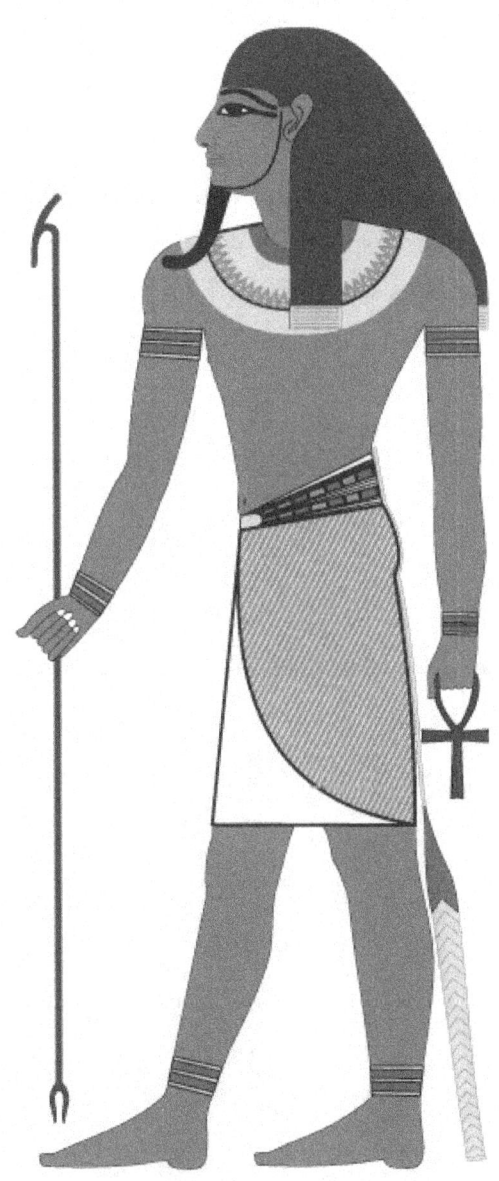

Atum

The ntr of Iunu is Atum. Atum is one of the aspects of the sun, perhaps the main aspect. He was depicted in full human shape, holding the Was scepter and the Ankh. The name Atum came from the Ancient Egyptian word "tm" (Fig. 15), which means "complete" or "perfect."

Fig. 15

Thebes

Wa-set is the ancient official name of Luxor, but there are two more famous names for the same city. The first one is Thebes, which in my opinion is derived from "ta ipt," meaning the land of the Opet festival, and later "ta ipt" was pronounced as Thebes by the Greeks. The second name is Luxor. The Arabs called this city Luxor because when Egypt became a Muslim country in 642 AD, the Arabs went to Thebes and saw these huge temples, thinking they were palaces, so they called it "the city of palaces," Luxor. I believe that the English word "luxury" is derived from Luxor.

Waset is an old city in Ancient Egyptian history, and its main ntr is Montu. But the city gained its political position during the Middle Kingdom time after King Mentuhotep II Nebhepetre. Starting from the New Kingdom time, the city became the most powerful city in Egypt, becoming the capital of Egypt and the capital of the Ancient Egyptian religion under the power of ntr Amun. Amun was considered the most powerful ntr in Ancient Egypt, starting from the New Kingdom; he was called the king of ntrs. In Luxor, there are huge constructions attributed to Amun, like Karnak Temple, Luxor Temple, and Hatshepsut Temple. Amun means "the hidden," and when combined with Ra, to be Amun-Ra, it means "the hidden solar disc," or "the setting sun," the sun from sunset to sunrise.

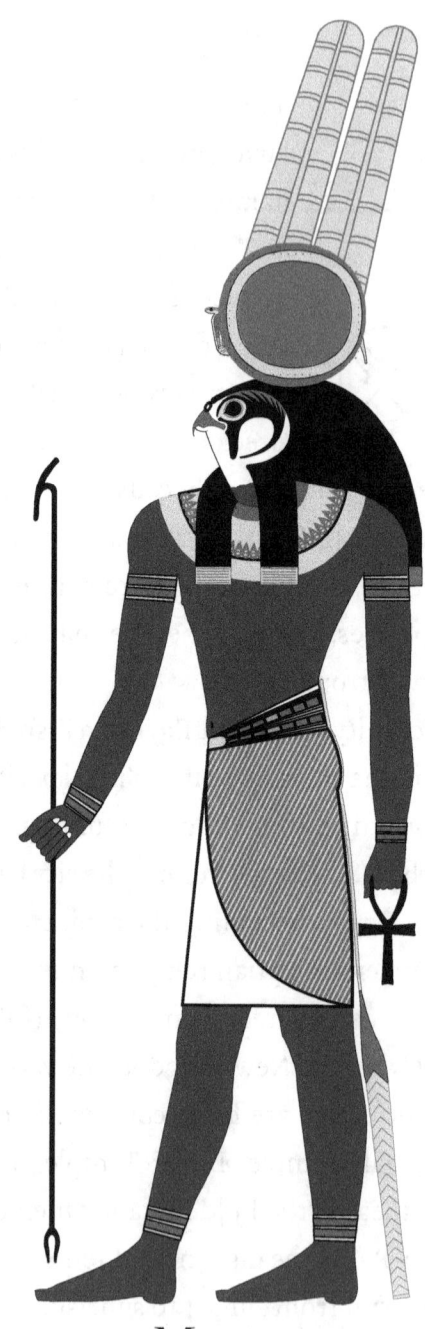

Montu

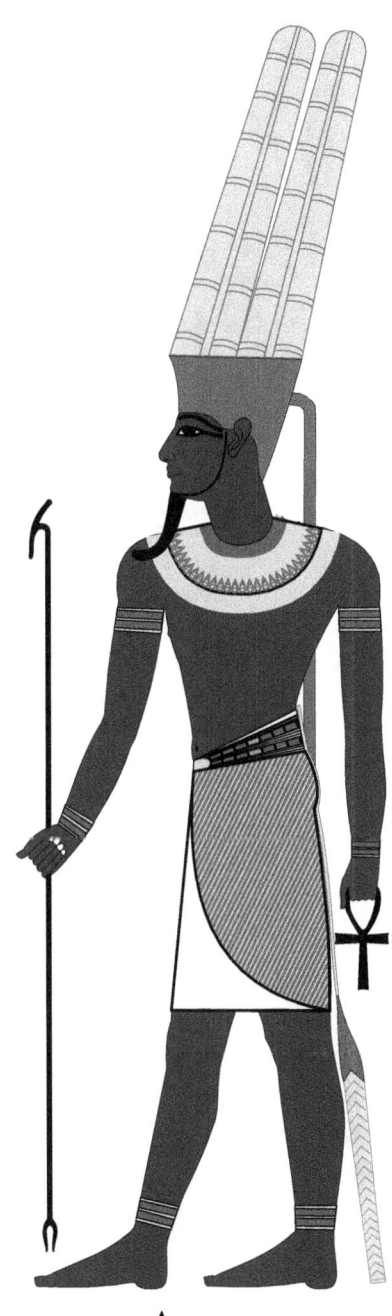

Amun

Theories of creation in Ancient Egypt

The Memphite story of creation (Memphite Theology)

Because of a document transcribed on a stela called the Shabaka stela (Fig. 16) or Shabaka stone (25th Dynasty), we know that Ptah created the world by his will; he conceived the world in his heart and created it through the spoken word. This stone is made of granodiorite and was originally erected at the Temple of Ptah at Memphis. The stone was transported to Alexandria, and it was taken out of Egypt during the 18th century AD; it is now housed inside the British Museum.

Because of the square hole in the middle, we understand that the stone was used as a milestone in later times. Maybe this is the reason the writings are in poor condition, or perhaps the writings were defaced deliberately.

After reading the text, we understand that there are two stories:

The first story is about the unification of Egypt, Upper and Lower Egypt. Horus is accomplishing this mission, but Ptah is the mastermind behind it.

The second story is about creation; in this story, we understand that Ptah is the creator of all things, including the ntrs.

So, we can say, Ptah used the power of his heart and speech to create the ntrs and other beings.

If we replace the letter P in the name Ptah (it is acceptable that some letters can replace other letters) with the letter F, we will read the name Ftah (Phtah). This word in the Arabic language means the opener, the starter, the one who began things.

When I checked the dictionary of the Ancient Egyptian language, I found a word pronounced "ptH" that means "to open."

I need to explain that these theories of creation do not conflict with each other; they complete each other. So, I can say that the work which started by Ptah was completed by Atum using the elements of the Ogdoad.

Shabaka Stone
Fig. 16

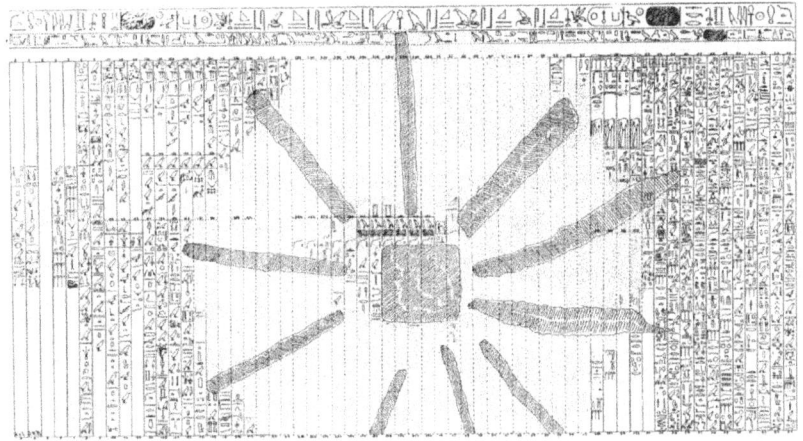

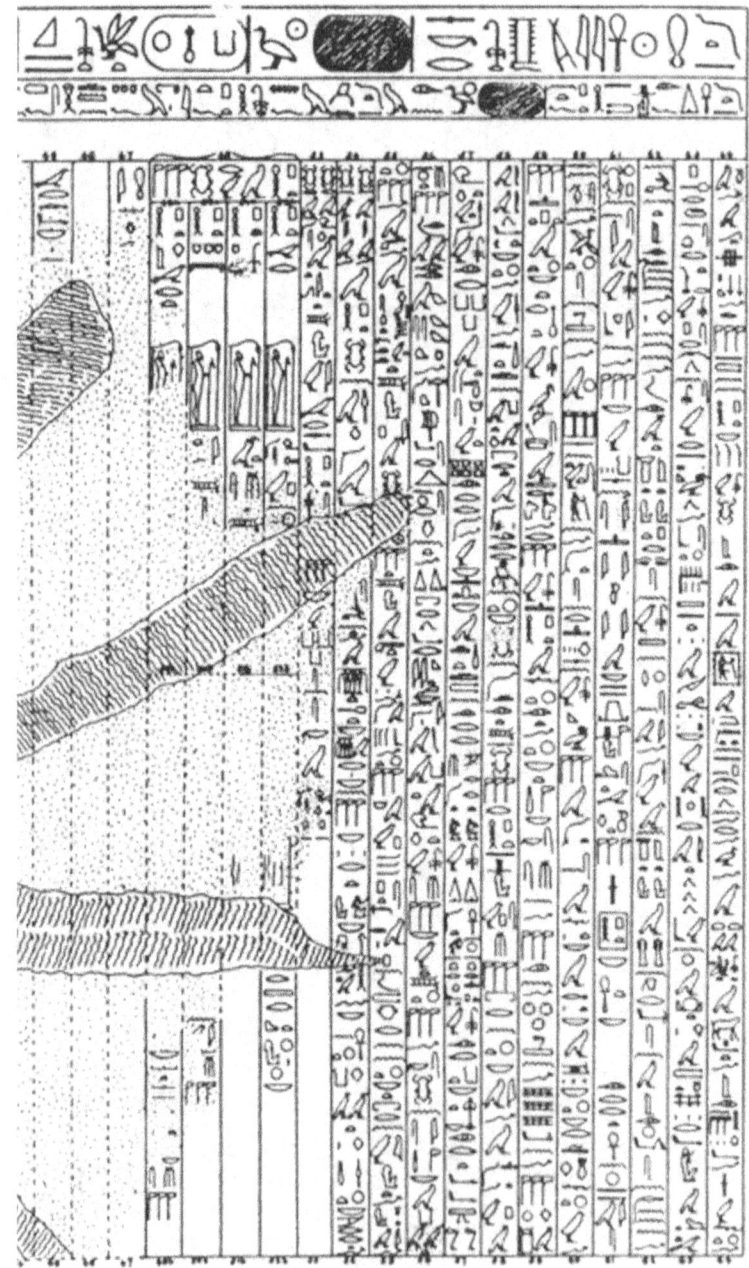

Shabaka Stone

The triad of Memphis is Ptah, Sekhmet, and Nefertum. I can say that the combination of this triad is perfect:
- The will of Ptah (spiritual aspect)
- The power of Sekhmet (physical aspect)
- The harmony of Nefertum (Both Ptah and Sekhmet worked together and produced the beautiful or harmonic creature, Nefertum).

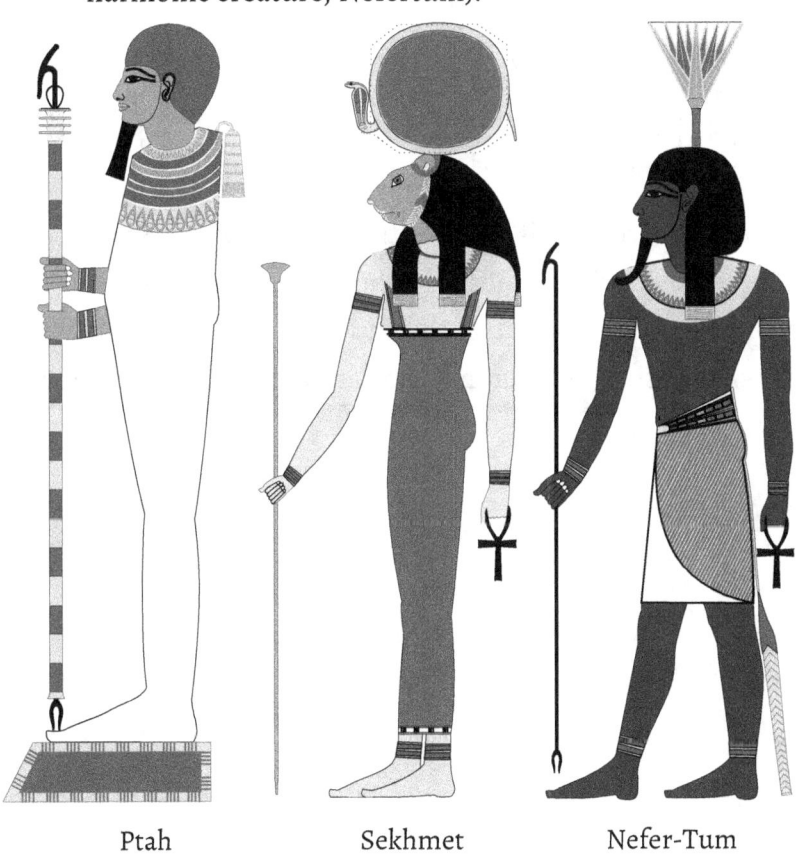

Ptah   Sekhmet   Nefer-Tum

The Story of Creation of Hermopolis (The Ogdoad)

The story talks about eight deities: four males (frogs) and four females (cobras). They were arranged in four pairs, each pair consisting of a frog and a cobra (Fig. 17). Their names are as follows: Nu and Nunet – HeHu and HeHut – Kekui and Kkekuit – GerH and GerHet.

The source of this story is the priesthood of Hermopolis. The word "Ogdoad" means eight (8), and the origin of this word is the Greek word "okto." In some sources, we can read a very interesting title for the neter Tuth; this title is "the creator of the Ogdoad."

Fig. 17

Nun and Naunet

It is possible that they are symbols of the primordial water, because we have the sign for sky (pt) and the sign for water (mu), so they may represent the primeval ocean, Nu. They could also represent a link between the story of the Ennead and the story of the Ogdoad (Fig. 18).

Nu / Nun

Naunet / Nut

Nu/Nun is the male (frog)

Nut/Naunet is the female (cobra)

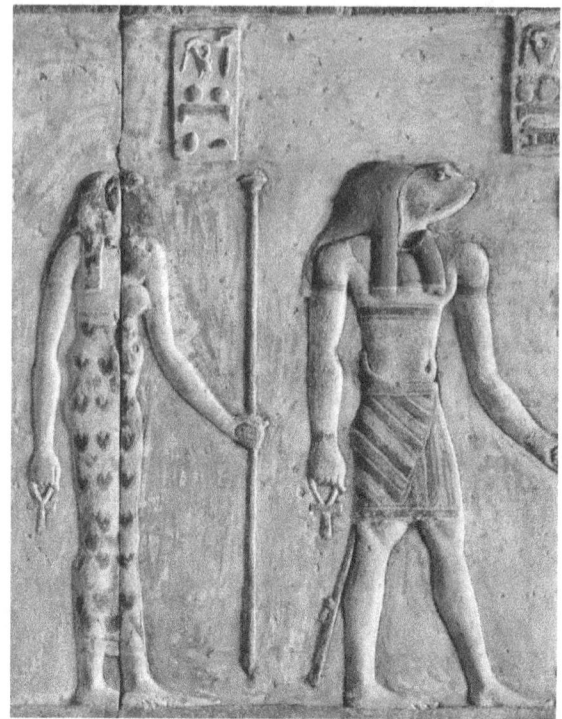

Fig. 18

Hehu and Hehut

It is possible that they are symbols of the primordial time because they may have been derived from the word HeH, which means endless time (millions of years) (Fig. 19).

HeHu is the male (frog)
HeHut is the female (cobra)

Fig. 19

Kekui and Kekuit

It is possible that they are symbols of space because it has the symbol for the sky during the night, so it may refer to space and the universe (Fig. 20).

Kekui   Kekuit

Kekui is the male (frog)
Kekuit is the female (cobra)

Fig. 20

QerH and QerHet

It is possible that they are symbols of darkness because they could be derived from the word grh, which means night.

GerH   GerHet

gerH is the male (frog)
gerHet is the female (cobra)

This last couple was replaced by another famous couple: Amun and Amunet.

Amun and Amunet

We know for sure that they are symbols of invisibility because they could be derived from the word imn, which means "the hidden" (Fig. 21).

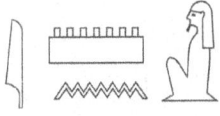
Amun

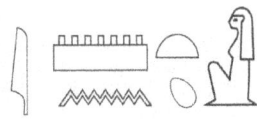
Amunet

Amun is the male (frog)
Amunet is the female (cobra)

Fig. 21

Theban theology

Explaining this theory is not easy due to its complexity. This is the latest theory of creation after the Memphite story, the Ogdoad story, and the Ennead story. Amun is mentioned only in the Ogdoad theory, and not as the solo creator, but rather as having partners.

The priests of Amun explained that Amun wasn't part of the Ogdoad, but he encompasses them and the Ennead as well. He is also the sound of the spoken word in the Memphite story. According to the story, Amun represents the Unseen Powers, and his invisibility is the foundation of all the ntrs (deities). His act of creation occurred when he disrupted the stillness of Nun (the primeval ocean) with the scream of the goose.

The goose was one of the representations of Amun, alongside the human and ram images. The triad of Thebes (Luxor) consists of Amun, Mut, and Khonsu. However, in some depictions, they show Amunet instead of Mut. Amunet is the female aspect of Amun, and Mut represents the sky, specifically the sky during the night.

Amun himself has 3 main identities;
- Amun
- Amun-Ra
- Amun-Min

Sometimes, they add an extra title to AmunMin to be Amun-Min-Kamutef.

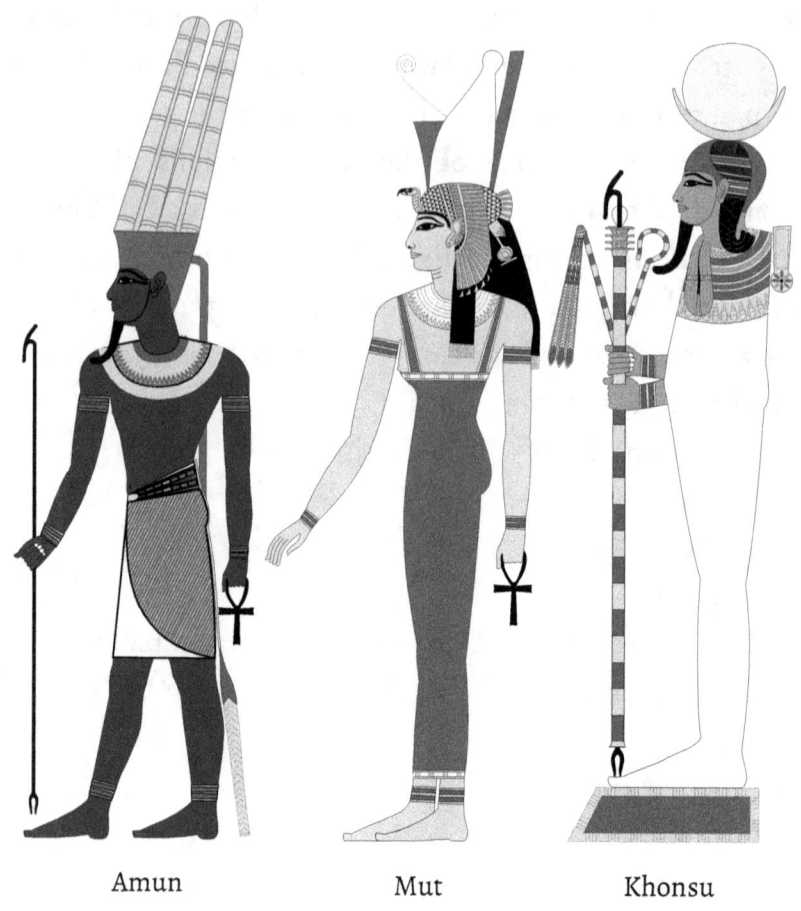

Amun Mut Khonsu

The Story of Creation of Heliopolis (The Ennead)

The Ennead story talks about the nine deities who were worshipped in Heliopolis. The word "god" or "deity" is the translation of the Ancient Egyptian "neter" (originally written without vowels as "ntr"). However, "neter" as I understand it means nature or force of nature. So, Ra is not the sun god; Ra is the sun energy, and Khonsu is not the moon god; Khonsu is the moon's power.

The Ennead story is the story of creation, not the creation of mankind, but the creation of the universe or what we can call the "Zep Tepi" (Sep Tepi). "Zep Tepi" means the creation moment or the first time.

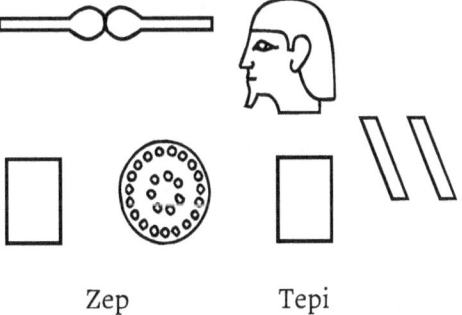

Zep   Tepi

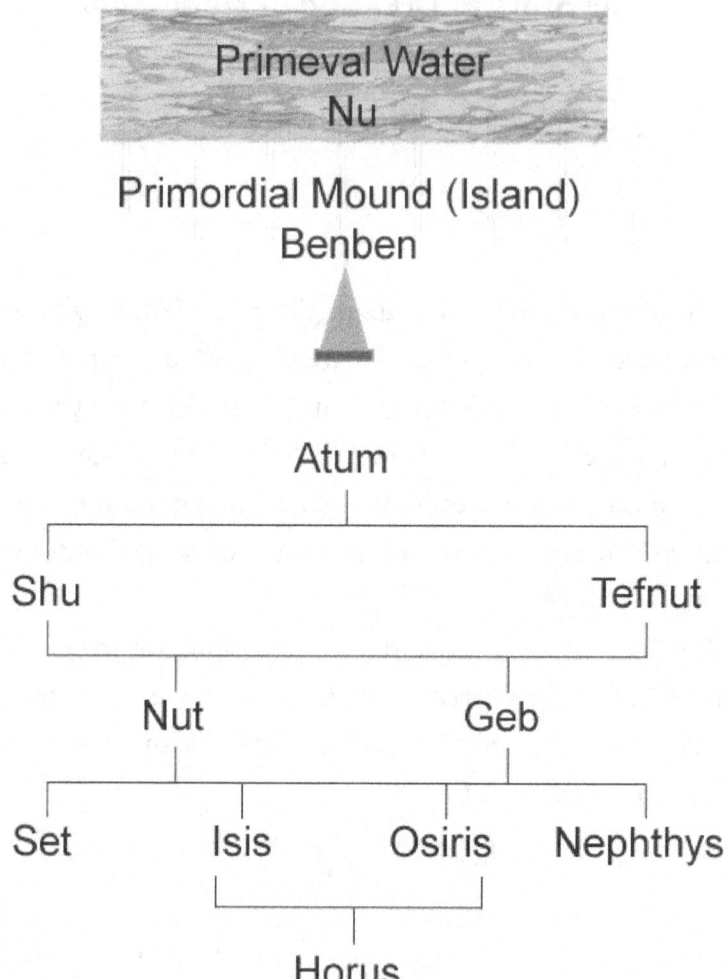

The Ennead story explains that there was a great ocean, or what we can call the primordial waters. The Heliopolitan priests called it Nun. Most explanations of this story say that Nun is a pre-creation element, but in my own opinion, Nun is the first element that was created. In the beginning, Nun was completely silent water.

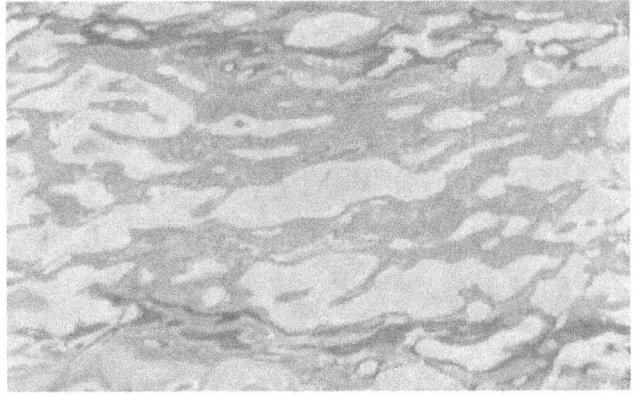

There was no movement, but then the water started to vibrate and a mound (island) arose from Nun. In my opinion, this primeval mound was a pyramid or very close to the pyramid shape.

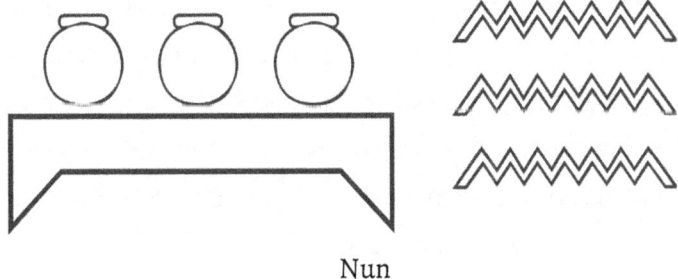

Nun

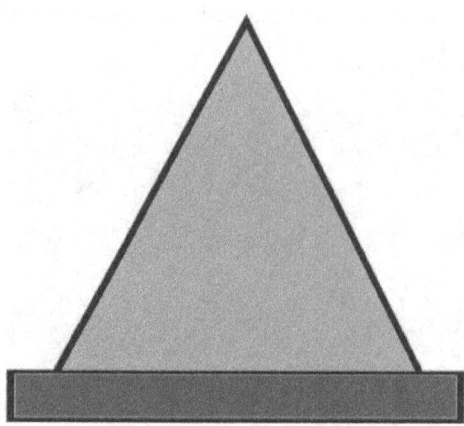

On top of the primeval mound, Atum was created. In the Ancient Egyptian language, Atum means "the complete one" or "the perfect one." Some opinions suggest that Atum is Adam (remember that we mentioned earlier that we are sure about vowels in the Ancient Egyptian language). Also, the letter "T" can be replaced with the letter "D." For instance, the name of our beloved queen Cleopatra is written as Cleopadra. As you can see, I can prove that Atum is Adam from a linguistic point of view. However, I don't agree that the identity of Atum is the same as that of Adam because we are still discussing cosmic powers and not the human level yet.

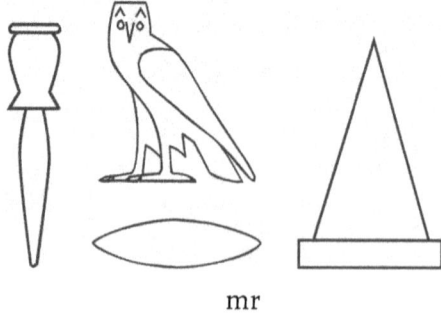

mr

Egypt Before the Written History

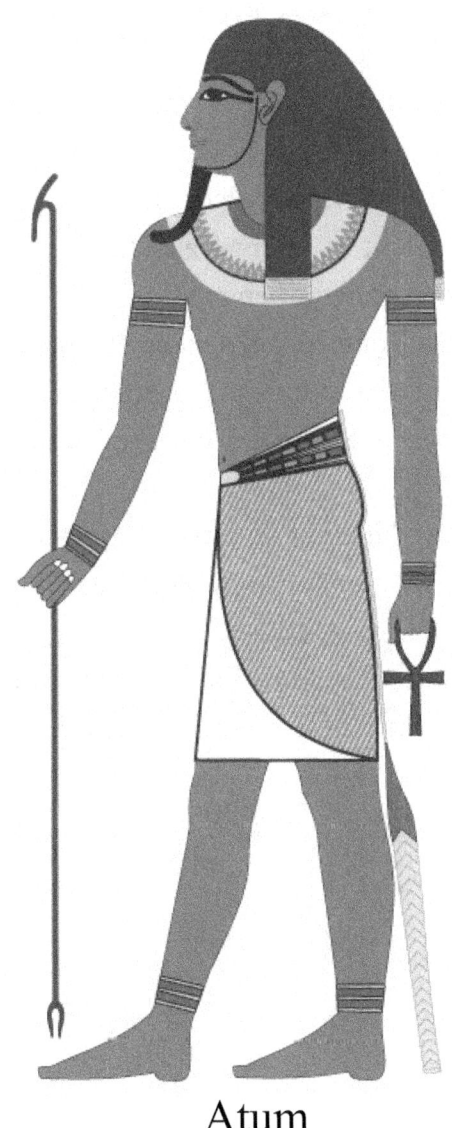

Atum

There is another suggestion that says Atum is Atom. I agree more with this suggestion because when we say Atum is the complete one, we are not necessarily talking about megalithic volumes; it could be the opposite completely. The Atom is extremely small, but it is "complete." Therefore, we can say that neutral or ionized atoms compose all the known elements in our universe (except living beings).

Atum is usually depicted as a complete human holding the Was scepter in one hand and the Ankh in the other. Sometimes he wears the royal head-dress (Nemes) or the double crown of Egypt.

The story of the Ennead was written in many eras in Egyptian history. The oldest known source for it is the pyramid text of the 5th and 6th dynasties.

The story states that Atum either masturbated, spitted, or sneezed to create two neters, Shu and Tefnut.

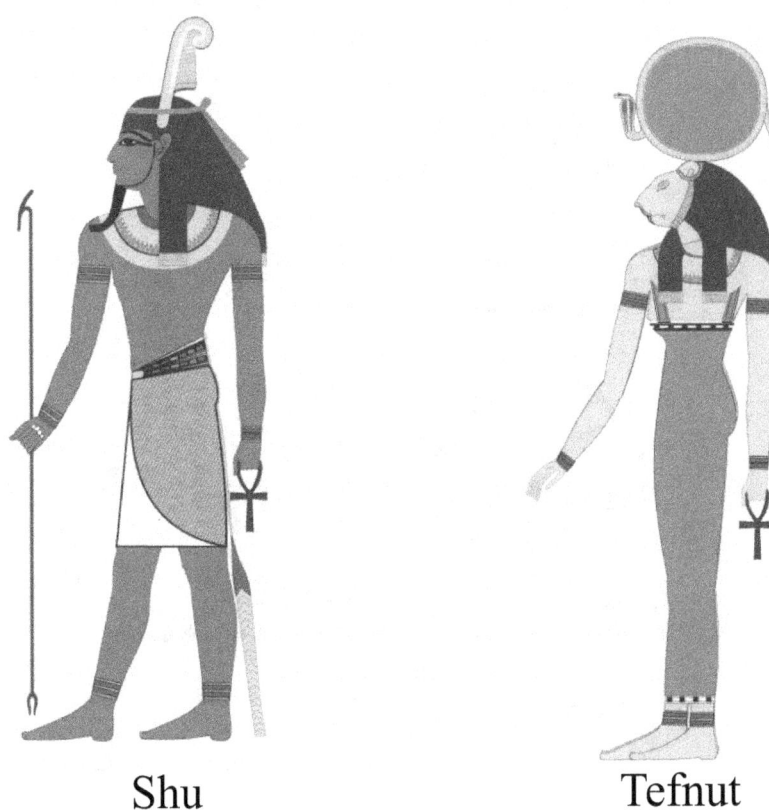

Shu   Tefnut

Shu is air with a feather above the head, while Tefnut represents moisture and is depicted as a woman with the head of a lioness. Together, they are known as the rwty and were symbolized as two recumbent lions or "Sphinxes." This information will later help us understand that the Great Sphinx at the Giza Plateau was originally a complete lion or lioness. However, I will explain this story in another book.

I need to clarify that there is an opinion that suggests the meaning of the name Tefnut is "the spit of Nut" (Tef = spit, nut = Nut). This opinion is incorrect. According to the Ancient Egyptian story, Tefnut is the spit of Atum.

rwty

Shu and Tefnut got "married" and Tefnut gave birth to two important neters: Geb and Nut.

Geb represents Earth. It's important to note that in the Ancient Egyptian Language, feminine words must have the letter "T" at the end of the word. If there is no letter "T" at the end of the word, it signifies a masculine word. Therefore, in this case, Earth is masculine, not feminine, as indicated by the name Geb.

Geb   Nut

Geb also could mean the deep layers of the ground, caves, and underground shafts.

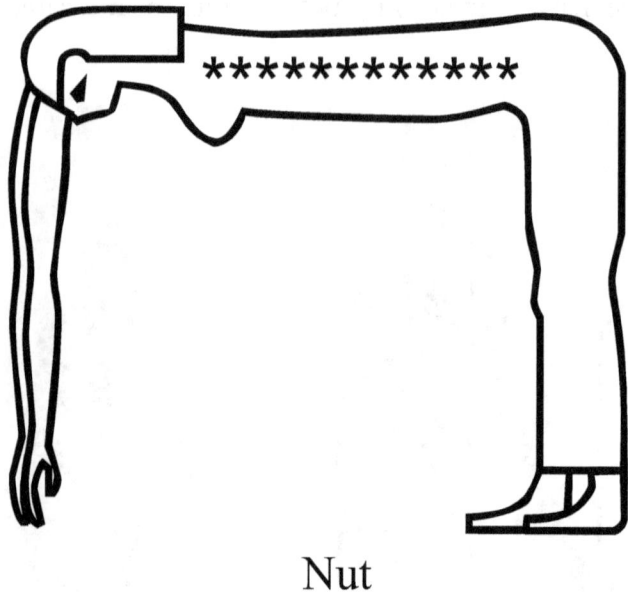

Nut

Nut is the sky, the sky we see during the day, while there is another ntr called Mut who represents the sky at night. Geb and Nut "get married," and Nut becomes pregnant. I understand it may seem like a childish story, but this is how it was written. The story explains that Atum was quite angry due to this marriage, perhaps it was arranged without his consultation. As a result, he sent Shu to separate Nut and Geb (Fig. 22).

As the delivery day draws near, Atum tells Nut that he owns the 360 days of the year and he doesn't permit Nut to give birth on any day of his year. A new ntr emerges in the story who doesn't belong to the Ennead; this ntr is Ptah. Ptah is the manifest, and he is the master of architects and craftsmen. Ptah manifests 5 magical days to help Nut give birth, which is why there are 365 days in the year in Ancient Egypt. Nut gives birth to 4 children, two boys and two girls, in two separate times.

Fig. 22

Nut was often depicted as a woman with a long body, her form enveloping the ceilings of certain temples, such as the Dendera temple. She gave birth to Set (Seth) and Nut first, and later she gave birth to Osiris and Nephthys.

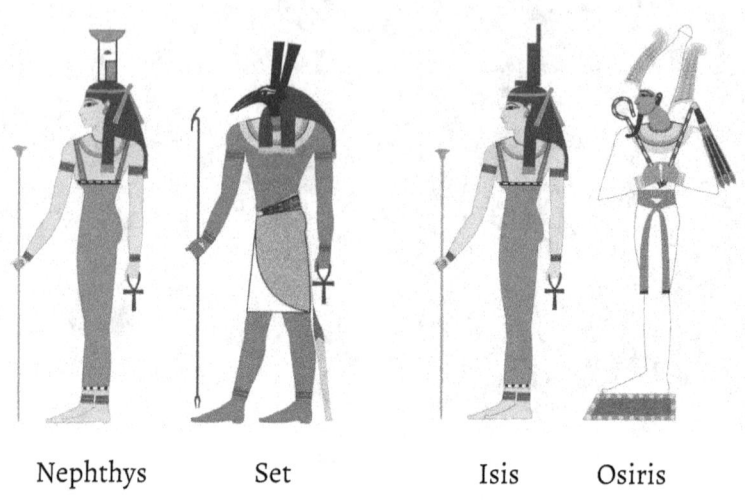

Nephthys   Set   Isis   Osiris

Seth, also known as Set or Sotekh (though I prefer to refer to him as Set), is a crucial member of this family; he is the elder brother of Osiris. When Osiris married and aligned with Isis, he became grounded, stable, and became the ruler. On the other hand, when Set married "associated with" Nephthys, he moved beyond the gate, moved outside (the desert). As a result, he became associated with the wrathful aspects of nature. Set embodies the spirit of the desert, heat waves, and sandstorms, which is why the color associated with Set is red.

The symbol of Set is an unidentified animal. Some suggest it might be the aardvark, while I believe it closely resembles the tapir. However, the true identity of Set's symbol remains uncertain.

Set

One of the strange titles I found connected with Seth is the title wer hekau, which means the great of magic. Previously, I thought this title was resevred for Isis.

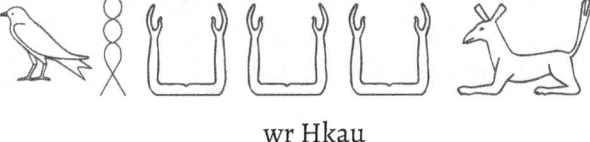

wr Hkau

Isis is the throne (chair), the base, the power of the woman. When we read her name, Isis, we read it according to the Greek way, but her name, according to the Ancient Egyptians, is **Iset** (Aset, Uset, or Eset). Meanwhile, the word chair in the Ancient Egyptian language is st (set). If you see a woman is represented with this symbol above her head, she will be Isis without a question.

I read her name Es-set, which means the lady in modern Egyptian, so when she was married to Osiris, she gave him this power, she gave him the throne, and he became the eternal ruler of Egypt.

Isis's main talent is MAGIC, and one of her main titles is Weret Hekau, which means "the great of magic" (the one who does great magic).

wrt Hkau

One of the things she uses while doing her magic is what we call the Tyet knot, or sometimes we call it Isis's blood.

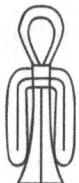

Tit or Tyet

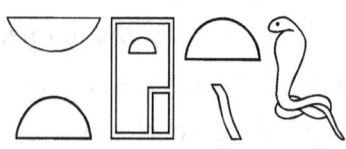

Nephthys, her name means the lady of the house, and this is the Greek way of pronouncing her name. According to the Ancient Egyptian writings, her name is **nbt het** (Nebet-Het). I read her name as Napheysa, which means the precious, the jewel of the house, but according to the symbol above her head, I call her the portal or the gate.

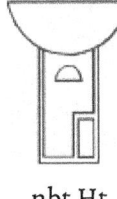

nbt Ht

There are few details about Nephtys, but I understand that she is very important to the family, as she is mentioned as helping Isis with restoring the body of Osiris. Some opinions suggest that Anupis is the son of Nephtys and Osiris.

 **Osiris.** Once again, the Greek pronunciation of his name doesn't carry the intended significance. To grasp the meaning of his name, we must interpret it through the lens of the Ancient Egyptian language: As-Ier. Some individuals read it as Aus-Ier, signifying "to be," "to exist," and "to act." Osiris is often symbolized by the color green, representing the fertile land of the Nile valley. In certain instances, the color black is employed to symbolize the land of Kemet. In the later stages of Ancient Egyptian civilization, he was referred to as wen-nefer, connoting "the beautiful existence" or "the harmonious existence."

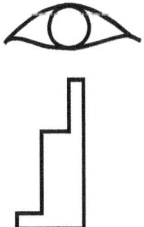

The story unfolds dramatically and explains that Set (Seth) was dissatisfied with this situation and resolved to alter it.

To claim the position of Osiris, he plotted to kill him. Various versions of the story exist, each describing a distinct manner in which Seth killed Osiris. One narrative recounts that Set cunningly enclosed his brother in an elaborate wooden coffin and cast it into the Nile River. The swift current carried the coffin to the Mediterranean Sea and eventually to Jebel in Lebanon. Another rendition suggests that Seth dismembered his brother's body into 42 pieces and scattered them across Egypt. Each location that received a piece of Osiris' body came to be known as Bu-Osir (Abusir). Despite the variations, all the stories concur that Isis managed to reassemble her husband's body and, through a miraculous conception, gave birth to her only son, the formidable falcon Horus—an influential deity in Ancient Egypt. Horus had to fight his uncle Seth in order to avenge his father and to return the throne, which was previously usurped by Seth.

Horus symbolized the eternal ruler of Egypt, and all Egyptian rulers governed under his authority.

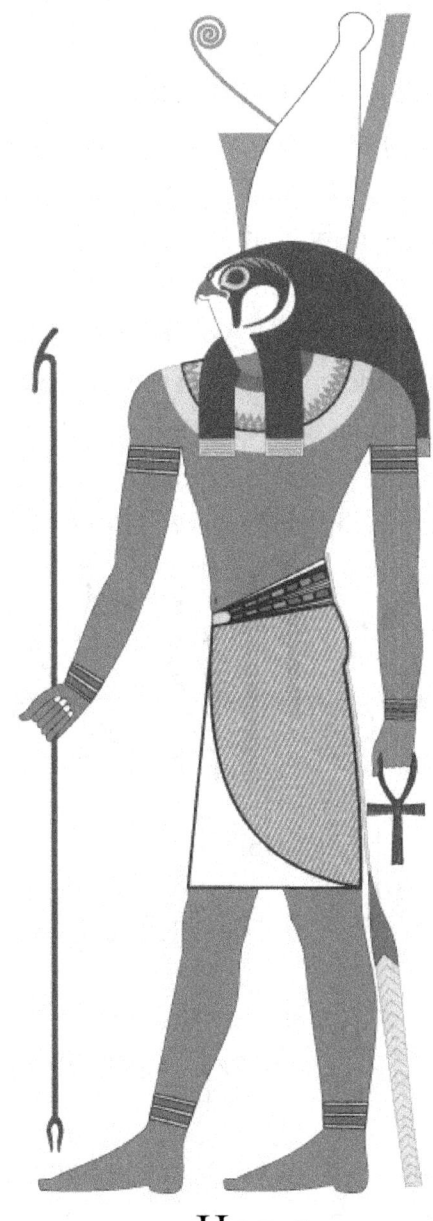

Horus

After Osiris, Horus assumed the role of the eternal ruler of Egypt—a powerful monarch on the Egyptian throne. Some suggestions propose that the Ennead's creation culminated in Horus; their existence paved the way for Horus' presence.

According to the Turin King List, a papyrus compiled during the 19th Dynasty containing the names of 223 rulers of Ancient Egypt, the list commences with certain ntrs as the initial rulers of prehistoric Egypt, including Ra, Geb, Osiris, Seth, Horus, and others. Following the ntrs, a group of rulers known as 'the spirits' or demigods is listed. Preceding the well-known dynastic kings, there is a group of early rulers known as Shemsu-Hor, signifying "followers of Horus."

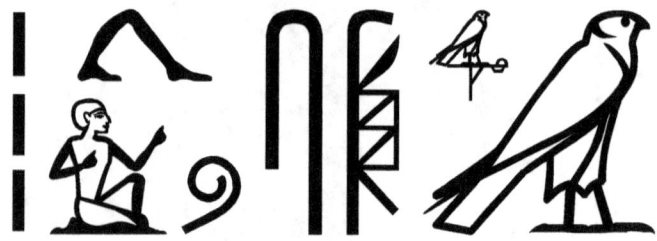

This is the title shemsu-Hor

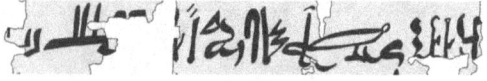

This is a part of the papyrus with some details.

This is a reconstruction of the picture above, and we can read that the shemsu-Hor ruled for 23200 years.

The initial design was created to accommodate the names of Ancient Egyptian rulers; this is what we refer to as the "serkh."

Above this design, they positioned a falcon – symbolizing Horus – atop the façade of the royal palace.

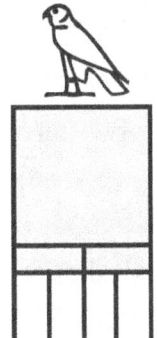

This name, which we refer to as the "Hr name" (Horus name), originated during the pre-dynastic period. Many of these serkhs were empty but featured a falcon on top of them. At times, the serkh had two falcons. It was during the times of Dynasty 0 and Dynasty 1 that we began to witness the standardized form of the serkh. This design endured throughout all Ancient Egyptian dynasties, persisting until the conclusion of Egyptian civilization. An illustration of the Hr name for the second king of the 4th Dynasty, King Khufu, can be seen within the serkh. This name is read as "Medju."

After the Shemsu-Hor, the reign of the human kings started (the dynasties), and they kept their connection with Horus and kept the Hr name (Hr title). Although, they used some new other important and famous titles (Fig. 22):

- Nswt-Bit title (king of Upper and Lower Egypt).
- Sa Ra title (Son of the Sun).

They developed a new design to contain the name of the king rather than the serkh; this design is called Shen. However, the modern name for it is Cartouche.

Fig. 22

The Geology of Egypt

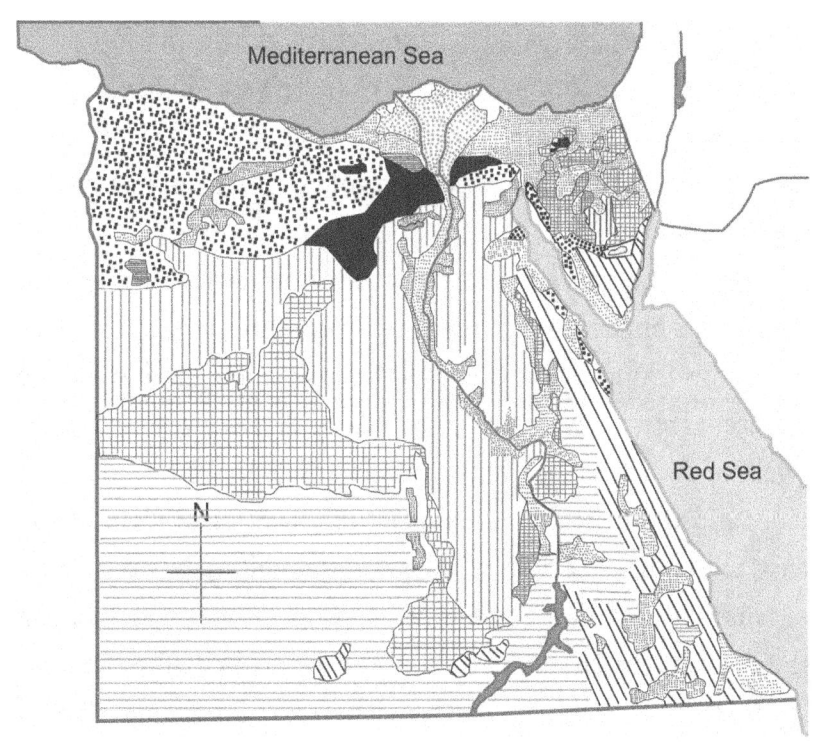

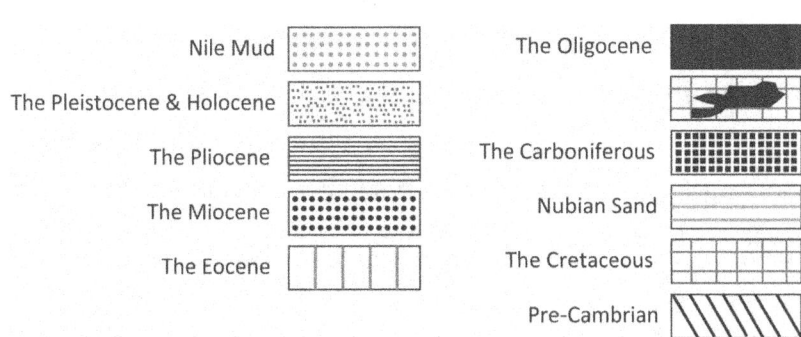

Geological Map of Egypt

I always say that the best way to understand the Ancient Egyptian Civilization is to have a big group of scientists working together, scientists of different fields and different types of science.

This group must include Egyptologists, engineers, physicists, alchemists, zoologists, anthropologists, and geologists.

In this first section of the chapter, I will delve deeper into Egypt's geology, focusing on the nature and formation of its surface. In the second part of this chapter, you will have a good idea about the pre-historic cultures of Egypt, and I will try to explain what kind of tools they had and what kind of techniques they developed.

Egypt was completely different from nowadays. The Egyptian desert was once under the sea for a long time, and once it was green for a long time. This was because the climate was very different from age to age. The Nile flowed in the western desert (west of its actual location). Its water flowed into the Faiyum lake, and then the current shifted the location slightly to the east, to its current position. The Nile gradually deposited fertile silt on its two banks in the south and north of Egypt, creating the delta of the Nile. The level of the ground changed at least 2 times. The first instance was when the limestone plateau sank and the sea submerged the Egyptian land up to Esna. The second change occurred when the level of the limestone plateau rose again, and the sea retreated to its current position in Alexandria. As time passed, rainfall diminished significantly, causing Egypt to lose its green surface, and the eastern and western deserts began to emerge.

The Nile carved its channel through the North African Limestone plateau in ancient times, creating 8 terraces (8 levels of banks). In the first four terraces, we didn't find things related to humans, but in the fifth terrace, we found tools made by man.

Let's delve into the deep history of the geology of Egypt so we can gain a more profound understanding of the shape of Egypt's surface, which was, "again," very different from today. The size of the land mass, in comparison to the water size, underwent changes from one period to another.

Through the presence of hundreds of billions of scattered seashells on hills, mounds, and plateaus in Egypt, we discern that they were beneath the sea level during ancient geological epochs. However, we can assume that the configuration of Egypt's surface has remained unchanged over the last 5000 years.

Examining the geological deposits found within the Egyptian landscape, we discover formations from all geological eras, with a few exceptions.

For instance:
- We won't encounter any deposits from the Paleozoic era except those from the Carboniferous age. Thus, we deduce that the Egyptian surface remained dry throughout most of the Paleozoic era, except during the Carboniferous age.
- Similarly, there are no deposits from the Mesozoic era, except for the Jurassic and the Cretaceous periods.

The Precambrian

> The Arckeozoic (2500 million years ago - 1000 million years ago)
> The Proterozoic (1000 million years ago - 600 million years ago)

The stones which formed in these 2 time periods were plutonic and volcanic stones, and they occupy almost 10% of the size of Egypt.

These stones can be observed in the mountains of the eastern desert, the mountains of South Sinai, and they cover a vast area to the south of Egypt, including Aswan and the southern borders of the western desert.

Stones like granite and gabbro (Fig. 23) from this period lack fossils. Additionally, other types of stones existed during this time, some of which are metamorphic stones like schist and gneiss. These were originally Sedimentary Stones, but after being exposed to the lava of a volcano, they changed to metamorphic stone and all the fossils disappeared or were destroyed.

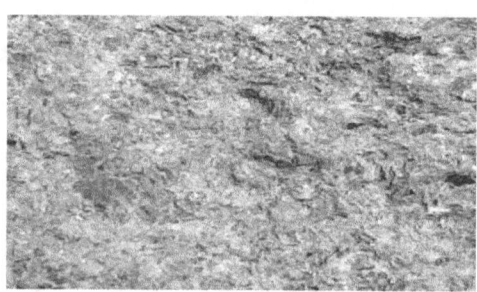

Rose Granite from Aswan. Fig. 23

The Paleozoic

> *The Carboniferous (358 million years ago - 298 million years ago)*

The deposits of the Carboniferous age are located in 3 sites in Egypt.

- West of Sinai
- Araba Valley in the eastern desert
- El Uweinat mountain in the western desert

During that era, Egypt experienced warm and humid weather accompanied by substantial rainfall, creating favorable conditions for the growth of massive trees. The Carboniferous age saw much of the Egyptian land covered by the sea.

> *The Permian (298 million years ago - 251 million years ago)*
> *The Triassic (251 million years ago - 201 million years ago)*

The weather in Egypt underwent a transformation; it was no longer warm, humid, and rainy. Instead, the atmosphere turned cold. Additionally, the land's elevation surpassed that of the water level, leading to the retreat of the sea to the north of Egypt. This shift also gave rise to new stone types, such as conglomerates (Fig. 25) and breccia.

In the Triassic age, dinosaurs made their first appearance. However, no fossils of dinosaurs from this era have been discovered in Egypt.

Conglomerate. Fig. 25

The Mesozoic

> *The Jurassic (201 million years ago - 145 million years ago)*

Deposits from this era are visible in Jabal al-Maghara, North Sinai, and Gabel El Galala in the eastern desert. The rocks of this era primarily consist of sandstones and limestones. Notably, these rocks contain minimal seashells and fossils. In Abu Rawash, we have discovered Jurassic limestone located at significant depths beneath the ground.

Easily dubbed the "age of dinosaurs," this era lacks dinosaur fossils found within Egyptian territories.

> *The Cretaceous (145 million years ago - 56 million years ago)*

The deposits of this age cover around 40% of Egypt. The predominant stones during this period are sandstone and limestone. Notably, the renowned sandstone quarries in Nubia, Egypt, were formed during this epoch.

During this era, the sea covered a significant portion of Egypt.

Numerous dinosaur fossils have been found in Egypt, including Aegyptosaurus, Bahariasaurus, Carcharodontosaurus, Deltadromeus, Inosaurus, Mansourasaurus, Paralititan, and Spinosaurus. The initial discoveries of dinosaur fossils in Egypt date back to this era, with the Mansourasaurus fossils being the foremost examples.

The Cenozoic and Modern Ages

> *The Eocene (56 million years ago - 34 million years ago)*

The Eocene deposits cover around 20% of Egypt. They are primarily located in the high grounds of the Egyptian desert and the high edges of the Nile Valley from Cairo to Luxor.

> *The Eocene (56 million years ago - 34 million years ago)*

The deposits from this era cover roughly 20% of Egypt's terrain. During the Eocene epoch, modern mammals began to emerge. The name of this age, "Eocene," translates to "New Dawn," alluding to the advent of modern mammals.

The sea encompassed nearly the entirety of Egypt, extending from the north to Aswan in the south. Limestone deposits stretch from Cairo to Qena on both sides of the Nile. Some limestone hills reach heights of approximately 500 meters. The Eocene limestone is abundant in seashells and marine fossils, earning it the moniker "Nummulites limestone."

The Ancient Egyptians extensively utilized various types of limestone, including the Nummulites limestone (Fig. 26). In contemporary times, it's referred to as Qurashy limestone due to the word "qersh," meaning "piaster" (coin), resembling the round seashell in shape.

Nummulitic stone. Fig. 26

> *The Oligocene (34 million years ago - 23 million years ago)*

The deposits of the Oligocene cover 1.5% of Egypt. They span the desert region between Cairo and Suez, extending around 200 km to the southwest of Cairo. Predominantly composed of sand and sandstone, these deposits lack fossils. However, they do contain petrified wood (you can visit the Petrified Forest in the east of Cairo). Additionally, in the Faiyum area, these deposits hold remains of large animals such as elephants (ancestors of modern elephants) (Fig. 27).

The cost line was at running at south of Cairo and north of Faiyum, so we understand that the ground level of Egypt in the Oligocene was higher than the ground level during the Eocene.

Fig. 27

This might be the age when the Red Sea formed, and mountain ranges emerged on its sides.

We understand that an older river than the current Nile River existed. This river ran parallel to the modern river but further to the west, either ending at Faiyum lake or crossing Faiyum and extending further north.

> *The Miocene (23 million years ago - 5 million years ago)*

Deposits from the Miocene era are present in the east and west of Cairo and to the north of Egypt. These deposits consist of sandstone, limestone, and mud layers, containing seashell fossils. The Nile river, as we know it, likely formed during this age.

> *The Pliocene (5 million years ago - 2 million years ago)*

Pliocene deposits can be found in Wadi El Natron (Natron's Valley) in the western desert, as well as in the northern parts of the western desert. These deposits contain seashells, coral, and urchin fossils. In other Pliocene deposits, remains of elephants, rhinos, giraffes, and crocodiles were discovered. This suggests the possibility that the Nile's current might have initially flowed west of the modern Nile during the Oligocene age.

> *The Pleistocene (2 million years ago – 11700 years ago)*

The Pleistocene, also referred to as the Ice Age and the modern age, covers nearly 15% of Egypt. Before the Pleistocene, the water level in the Red Sea was about 100 meters higher than the current level. However, during the Pleistocene age, the ground level of the land overlooking the Red Sea and Suez Gulf (east of Egypt) rose, becoming approximately 100 meters higher than the sea level. Conversely, the northern coast of Egypt saw a different shift, as the water level in the Mediterranean Sea was around 43 meters lower than the current level. This indicates that Egypt's coastal line was 10 km further north.

We used to believe that humans did not exist at the beginning of the Pleistocene and emerged during the mid-Pleistocene. However, new evidence suggests that humans existed at the beginning of the Pleistocene or even before.

> *The Holocene (11700 years ago– until now)*

The Holocene began immediately after the last glacial age. Its name, Holocene, signifies "whole new" or "entirely new." It is the era we presently inhabit. The Holocene marks the onset of known human civilizations during both ancient and modern times. Due to stable climate conditions, humans were able to establish numerous civilizations worldwide.

Certainly, humans existed before the Holocene, but the crucial question revolves around civilization: Were they merely primitive hunters and cave dwellers? Or were there great civilizations before the Holocene?

Cultures of the Stone Ages in Egypt

Before 1869, there was no mention or expectation of an earlier civilization or culture preceding the dynasties that began around (perhaps) 3200 BC. Most archaeologists didn't believe in the existence of the Stone Ages in Egypt and erroneously assumed that the dynasties emerged and developed suddenly. Any ancient tools made from stone found in Egypt were often attributed to the dynasties without question, possibly because these tools were considered cheap implements crafted during that time.

In 1869, during their expedition above the hill of the Valley of the Kings in Luxor, Ernest Hamy and François Lenormant documented in their diaries that they discovered numerous flint tools. This discovery could be evidence of the existence of the Stone Age in Egypt.

Flint was the primary material used during the Stone Ages, although early humans also employed other types of stones such as obsidian, quartz, granite, and diorite. Beyond stones, they utilized materials like wood, bones, ebony, and more.

In order to survive and meet their needs, humans crafted tools for various functions. They created large axes, small axes, knives, drills, and later progressed to crafting microlithic tools.

In English, we use the terms "flint" and "chert," while in French, there's a single word for this stone ("silex"), and the same applies in Arabic ("zalat" زلط).

- Chert is the silica deposits inside the limestone layers.
- Flint is the silica deposits inside the cretaceous layers.

Flint is a very good material because when it shatters, it creates sharp blades, which are excellent knives.

If we talk about Pre-historic Egypt from a geological perspective, we will talk about 3 main geological eras:

- Paleolithic
- Mesolithic
- Neolithic.

But before we talk about these geological eras, we must understand that there are other classifications to explain the development through the Egyptian stone ages in a good way. The stone industries of the stone ages and its development, so there are some definitions needed.

> *Acheulean Industry (1,760,000 BC – 160,000 BC)*

Stone tools were discovered at a site in France known as Saint-Acheul. Flint hand-axes were unearthed there (fig. 28), fashioned in an oval shape, or one could liken their form to that of a pear. Acheulean tools were found in conjunction with the remains of Homo erectus.

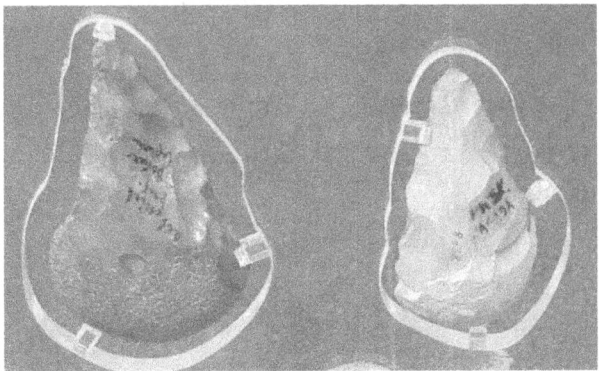

Fig. 28

> *Chellean Industry (600,000 BC – 400,000 BC)*
> *Abbevillian industry (600,000 BC – 400,000 BC)*

Stone tools were discovered in a suburb of Paris known as Chelles. These tools bear a striking resemblance to others found in a French town called Abbeville, which is why both are referred to as the Abbevillian industry. Initially utilized by archaic humans, the Abbevillian tools were subsequently adopted by Homo erectus (Fig. 29).

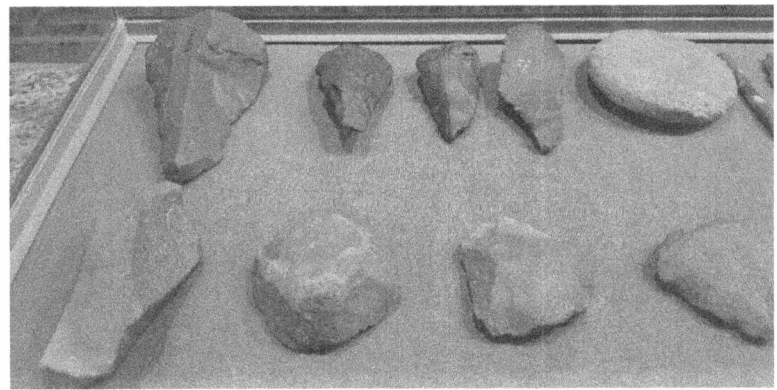

Fig. 29

> *Mousterian industry (160,000 BC – 40,000 BC)*
> *Levalloisean Technique*

Stone tools were found at a French site called Le Moustier. The Mousterian industry is associated with the Neanderthals in Europe. Flint tools were found in a suburb of Paris called Levallois-Perret (Fig. 30).

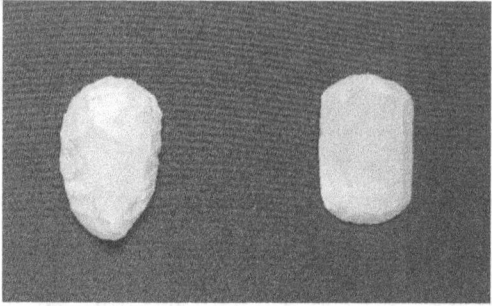

Fig. 30

Paleolithic (Stone Age)
(700,000 or 500,000 - 8000 BC)

> *Wadi Halfa*

This location lies in the far north of Sudan, near the borders of Egypt. Archaeologist Waldemar Chmielewski discovered small structures there in a site named Arkin 8. He dated these structures to 100,000 BC. Hand axes crafted from flint cores were also uncovered from this era.

In 1994, near Dendera, a site called Taramsa yielded a significant find. The Belgian University of Leuvenin discovered the skeleton of a child, estimated to be around 8 years old. Professor Pierre Vermeersch, upon examining the skeleton, dated it to approximately 55,000 BC (Fig. 31). Evidently, the child was engaged in a flint workshop.

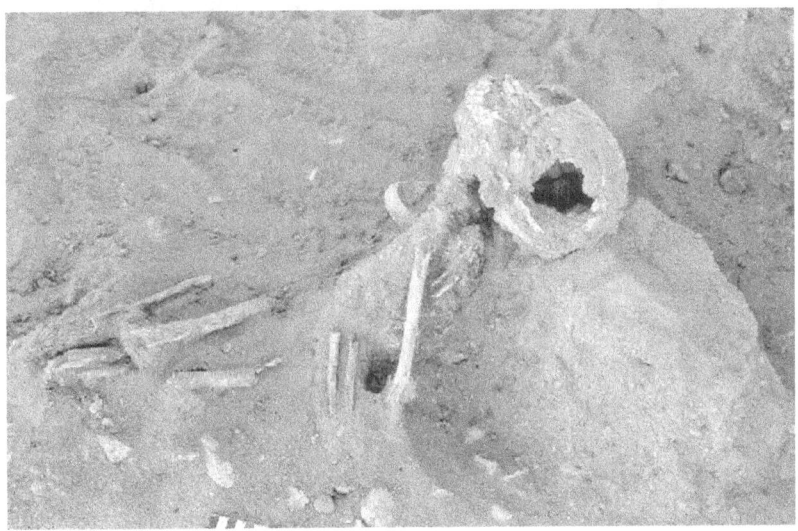

Fig. 31

> *Aterian Industry*

The name Aterian is related to the type of tools that were found in Algeria near a site called Bir El Ater, south of Tébessa city. Evidence of the Aterian Industry has been discovered in various locations beyond Algeria, spanning North Africa, Saudi Arabia, Oman, northeast Africa, and the Thar Desert. Notably, certain tools found in Egypt have been attributed to the Aterian industry, dated to around 40,000 BC (Fig. 32, 33).

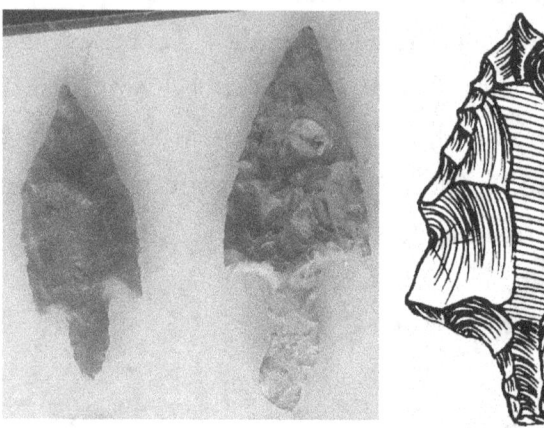

Fig. 32, 33

> *Khormusan Industry*

The Khormusan industry (Khor Musa) thrived in Egypt and Sudan from around 42,000 BC to 18,000 BC. This industry derives its name from the type site 1017 located at Khor Musa, south of Wadi Halfa, Sudan. In Egypt, tools crafted from stones, animal bones, ivory, and hematite have been associated with this industry. Additionally, a collection of arrowheads has been linked to the same industry. Interestingly, these arrowheads bear a resemblance to those used by Native Americans. Despite the discovery of numerous arrowheads, an intriguing mystery remains: no bows from that era have been found (Fig. 34).

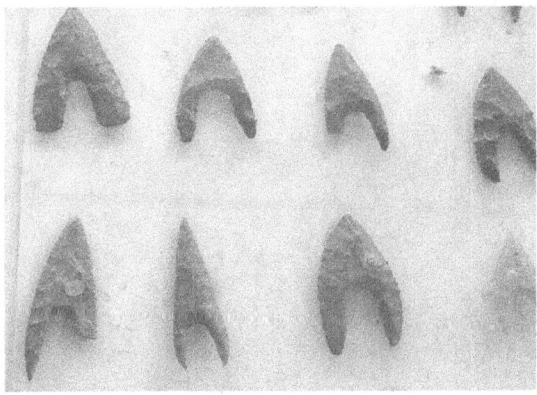

Fig. 34

> *Late Paleolithic (30,000 BC – 12,000 BC)*

In 1980, the Belgian University of Leuvenin discovered a skeleton in Nazlet Khater in Sohag. Nazlet Khater is situated in the city of Tahta, within the Sohag province. It's in proximity to Abydos. The skeleton was transported to Belgium for analysis and dating purposes. Carbon dating was conducted on the skeleton, resulting in a date of 35,000 BC (Fig. 35). This skeleton belongs to an adult male (modern human) and shares anatomical resemblance to the skeletons found at Jebel Sahaba and Wadi Halfa.

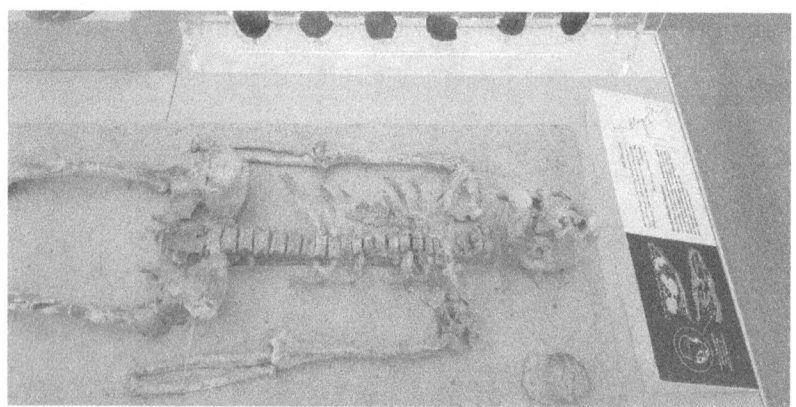

Fig. 35

Mesolithic (26,000 BC – 8,000 BC)

> *Halfan and Kubbaniyan cultures (26,000 BC or 22,000 BC)*

These two cultures were very similar to each other. Halfan is located at the northernmost part of Sudan, near the Nile River, while Wadi Kubbaniya lies northwest of Aswan. In 1982, Fred Wendorf and Romuald Schild discovered a skeleton (Fig. 36).

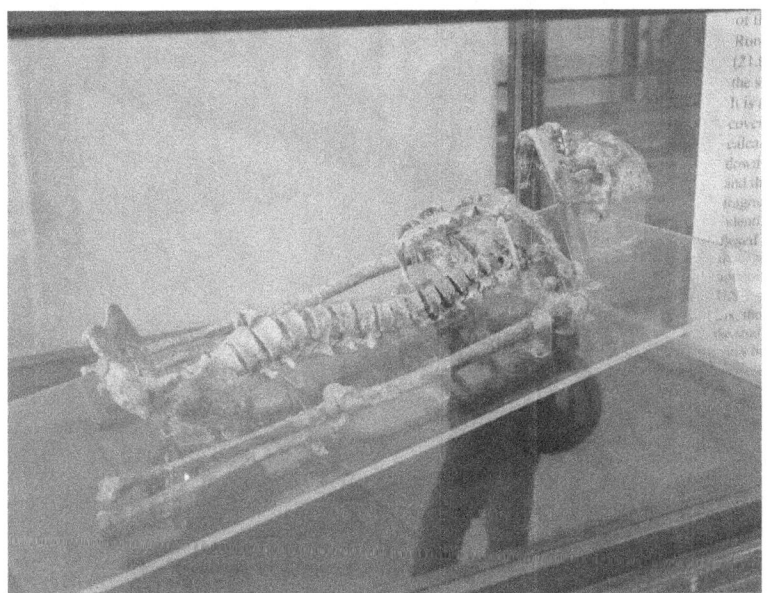

Fig. 36

> *Sebilian Culture (13,000 BC – 10,000 BC)*

Also referred to as the Esna culture, this culture thrived alongside the Nile River at the 10-15 feet terrace. It was there that Sebilian tools were uncovered. Among these tools, there are the characteristic levallois diorite implements. Additionally, another type of tools belonging to the microblade industry were discovered.

Microblade tools!? I've always been curious about the purpose behind crafting such tiny tools - those minute blades (Fig. 37). And I think the answer is: they needed these small blades to make precise cuts.

Fig. 37

> *Qadan culture (13,000 BC – 9,000 BC)*

There are many sites belonging to this culture, spanning from the 2nd cataract to Tushka near Abu Simbel (approximately 250 km south of Aswan).

It appears that a substantial community of tribes relied on agriculture during this period, as evidenced by the abundance of grinding stones found from this culture.

In 1964, American archaeologist Denver Fred Wendorf discovered 61 skeletons in a location known as Jebel Sahaba (Mountain of the Companions). This site straddles the border between Egypt and Sudan, now submerged beneath Lake Nasser.

Carbon dating revealed that one of these skeletons was almost 13,000 years old. It is highly suggested that these skeletons were victims of a conflict between two or more tribes, implying the existence of multiple human communities in Qadan and nearby locations.

> *Harifian Culture (9,000 BC or 8,000 BC)*

It appears that the Harifian culture was interconnected with the Faiyum cultures, and for an unknown reason, groups from this culture migrated to northeastern Egypt, Sinai, and the Levant (giving rise to the Natufian culture). This is likely why many artifacts discovered in the Negev Desert bear a striking resemblance to tools associated with the Harifian culture (Fig. 38, 39, 40, 41, 42, 43).Evidence points to their domestication of animals and a lifestyle centered around camps. They notably advanced the creation of arrows featuring compact heads.

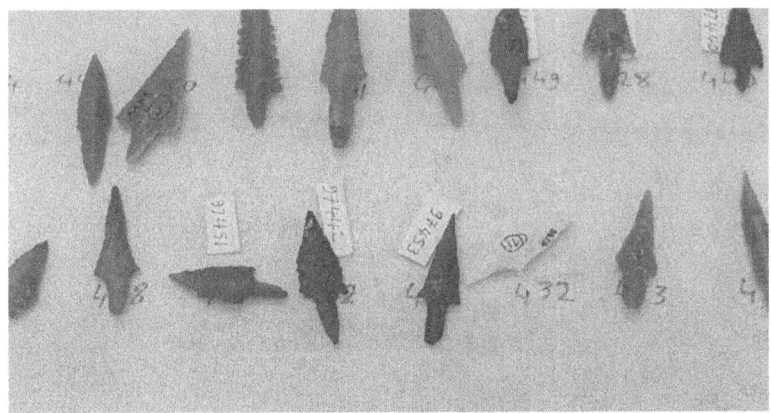

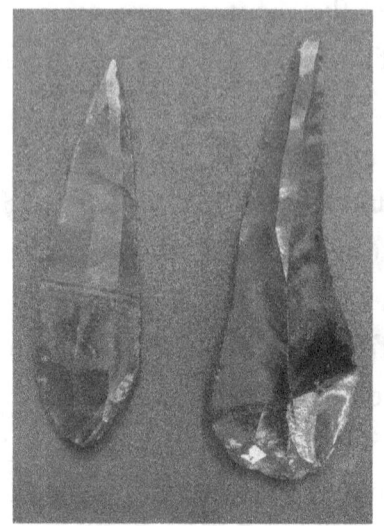 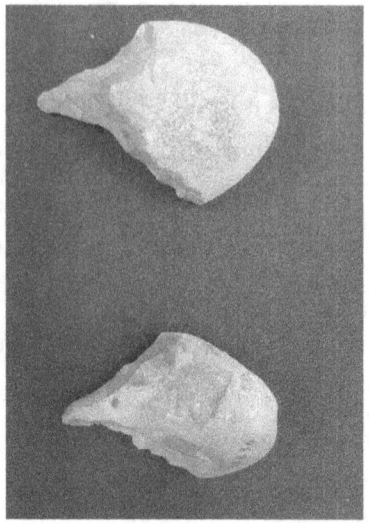

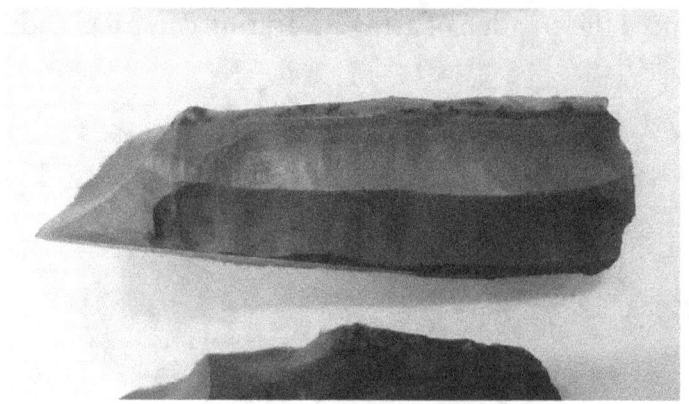

Fig. 38, 39, 40, 41, 42, 43

Pre-Dynastic Egypt

The Ancient Egyptian history didn't start in 3200 BC as commonly mentioned in history books. No, this perspective is entirely mistaken. Dating the Ancient Egyptian Civilization at 3200 BC reflects a significant oversight in interpreting ancient sources that mention the rulers and reigns of ancient Egypt.

According to written sources like Manetho's history (Aegyptiaca Book) and the Royal Canon of Turin (Turin Papyrus), Ancient Egyptian history dates back to more than 30,000 BC. I'd venture to say that this conservative estimate could even be much earlier, given the gaps and missing data in these sources. Both Manetho and the Turin Papyrus encompass legendary rulers (including gods and semi-divine beings) like the Shemsu-Hor, as well as human kings from various dynasties.

For instance, the Turin Papyrus notes that the Shemsu-Hor ruled for 23,200 years. Furthermore, based on Manetho's chronology and the Royal Canon of Turin, the first ruler of the dynasties might have emerged around 5000 BC. This is due to our lack of comprehensive information about many of the Ancient Egyptian rulers, particularly those from the Old Kingdom.

So, what preceded the dynasties? Before the dynastic period, there existed the pre-dynastic era, which potentially spanned around 4000 years prior to what is traditionally considered the start of Ancient Egyptian history, and it could be even older.

Research into the pre-dynastic era is a relatively modern undertaking, and regrettably, it's quite challenging due to the limited number of pre-dynastic sites, many of which are situated in densely populated areas of Egypt. Understanding the remnants of pre-dynastic people demands a high level of expertise and long-term investigative efforts.

In 1894, Sir Flinders Petrie discovered thousands of tombs in the ancient site of Naqada. His findings included numerous vessels, jars, combs, spoons, and various objects crafted from diverse materials. This discovery led scholars to acknowledge the existence of pre-dynastic cultures, with Jacques De Morgan being among the first to embrace this realization.

However, it's crucial to recognize that the tools unearthed in places like the Valley of the Kings' hills, while similar in appearance, don't pertain to pre-dynastic Egypt but rather belong to prehistoric Egypt.

Predynastic Egypt thrived between 9000 BC and 3200 BC, encompassing diverse cultures situated in both the northern and southern regions of the country. This era can be referred to as Neolithic Egypt or the New Stone Age in Egypt.

Cultures of pre-dynastic Egypt

Lower Egypt

- Faiyum A culture (9,000 BC – 6,000 BC)
- Merimde culture (5,000 BC – 4,200 BC)
- El Omari culture (4,000 BC)
- Maadi culture

Upper Egypt

- Tasian culture (4,500 BC)
- Badarian culture (4,400 BC)
- Naqada culture (4,400 BC - 3,000 BC)
- Amratian culture (Naqada I) (4,000 BC)
- Gerzean culture (Naqada II) (3,500 BC)
- Protodynastic Period (Naqada III) (3,200 BC)

We must appreciate the great efforts and work of Sir Flinders Petrie in this field. He established a very precise system to study the tombs of Naqada, Abydos, and another place called Al Abdiah, and he created for us what we call it The **S**equence **D**ates.

Fig. 44, 45

This system was designed to show us the differences between the different kinds of the vessels (poetry, Alabaster and other materials) (Fig. 44, 45, 46, 47), and how their designs evolved from simple forms with plain surfaces to intricate patterns adorned with paintings and colors. I must admit that this system was effective when considering pottery jars.

However, it fell short in providing insights into objects crafted from stone, such as slate, alabaster, granite, and granodiorite.

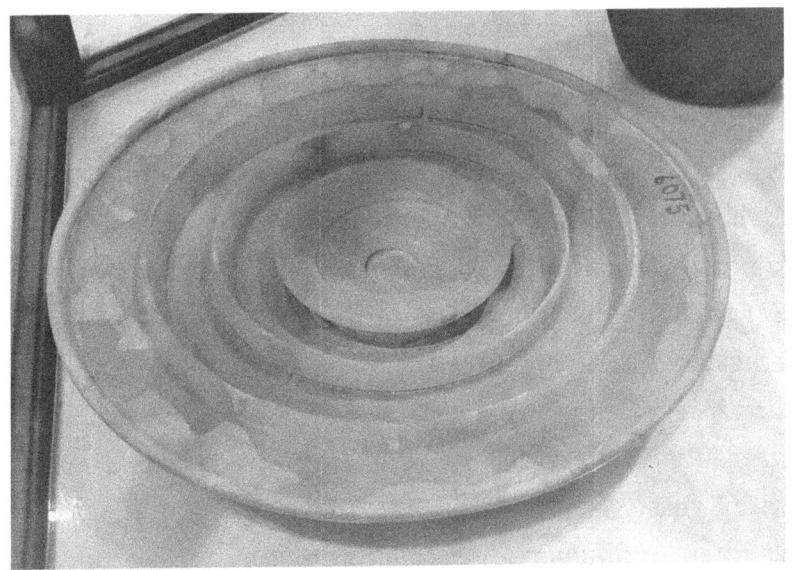

Fig. 46

Fig. 47

The first discoveries of the pre-dynastic cultures were in the south of Egypt, and by the beginning of the twenties century more locations were discovered in Upper Egypt (south), and later in Lower Egypt (north).

According to the famous story, Ancient Egypt was divided into two kingdoms: one in the southside of Egypt (Kingdom of Upper Egypt), and one in the northside of Egypt (Kingdom of Lower Egypt). These two kingdoms were separate entities, each with its own capital, deity, crown, and king. The two kingdoms were united by King Narmer (Mina), and Ancient Egypt became one kingdom ruled by one king. This king is considered the founder of Dynasty 01, and according to the king lists, we can say there were 30 dynasties that ruled Egypt from 3100 BC to 331 BC, starting with Dynasty 01 and ending with Dynasty 30.

After continuous work and effort to learn more about pre-dynastic Egypt, archaeologists discovered many pieces of evidence proving the existence of earlier rulers before Narmer (Mina). As a result, Egyptologists had to add Dynasty 0 to the beginning of the king's list. Another surprising revelation emerged as more evidence indicated the presence of even earlier rulers than Dynasty 0. This led to the necessity of adding Dynasty 00, which was initially met with skepticism by most Egyptologists. However, as the evidence accumulated and became undeniable, they accepted its validity and began to show increased interest in the pre-dynastic era. Some of them even initiated scientific expeditions to learn more about the early rulers of Ancient Egypt.

There is a significant debate surrounding the identities of rulers during the time between the Naqada II culture and

Naqada III culture (3500 BC – 3220 BC). When discussing the pre-dynastic era, several important questions arise. However, there are three main questions that stand out about the rulers of pre-dynastic Egypt:
1. Are they dominant rulers or did they used to be local chiefs or mayors?
2. Also are they different entities, or are these names just titles for one or two kings.
3. Are they real rulers (human beings)? Or are they symbols and powers?

Günter Dreyer worked as an Egyptologist at the German Archaeological Institute. In 1988, he and his colleague Werner Kaiser started an excavation in Abydos. Dreyer published the information about the discovery of the huge tomb in Abydos, Umm el-Qaab (it is called tomb U-j) (Fig. 48).

This tomb was attributed to King Scorpion I. Also, some graffiti were found at Gebel Tjauty (west of Luxor) with the name "Scorpion." This graffiti was explained, as usual, to depict a scene of victory where the Thinite king (Scorpion I) defeated the king of Naqada (Falcon) (Fig. 49).

Fig. 48

Ivory tags were found at the tomb U-j.

Fig. 49

Thinis was one of the very important cities in Upper Egypt (south). The location of Thinis is not identified yet, but it is strongly believed to be located near Gerga in Sohag governorate.

According to Manetho, the Egyptian historian during the time of Ptolemy II, Thinis was the hometown of the rulers of the first Dynasty. The ancient Egyptian name for Thinis is Tinu or Tini.

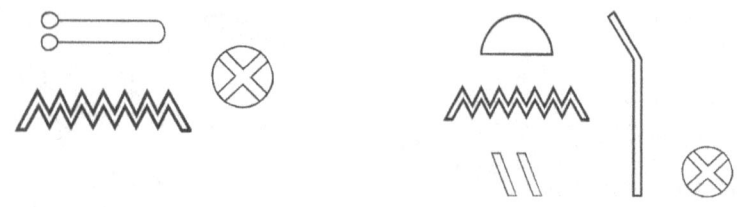

Tini

In the tomb U-j, they found thousands of pottery jars. Among these jars, around 700 jars have what we can call a Syrian and Palestinian style. However, we must understand that the Syrian and Palestinian style of jars appeared after the Ancient Egyptian jars, so we shall say that these jars are of Egyptian style.

Egyptologists managed to figure out some of the names of those earlier rulers of Ancient Egypt from "Dynasty 0" due to some evidences and sources.

Ivory tags: These tags were attached to some jars to prove that these jars were the property of the king whose name is inscribed above the tag (Fig. 50, 51).

Fig. 50

There are thousands of similar examples from the dynastic time.

Fig. 51

In one of these ivory tags, we found the name of the ruler Elephant.

Rock inscriptions: I believe there are thousands of rock inscriptions from the predynastic era, but we haven't found most of them yet. This is due to many reasons, like erosions and the rough weather conditions of the desert. Some are still buried under sand, and we haven't discovered them yet. It's possible that these very ancient sites were re-used by the dynasties over time.

In Gebel Tjauti (Theben desert road in the western desert near Luxor), they found a graffiti that may depict a military scene. It shows a falcon, a scorpion, and a human with the head of a bull near what we can consider as a prisoner (Fig. 52).

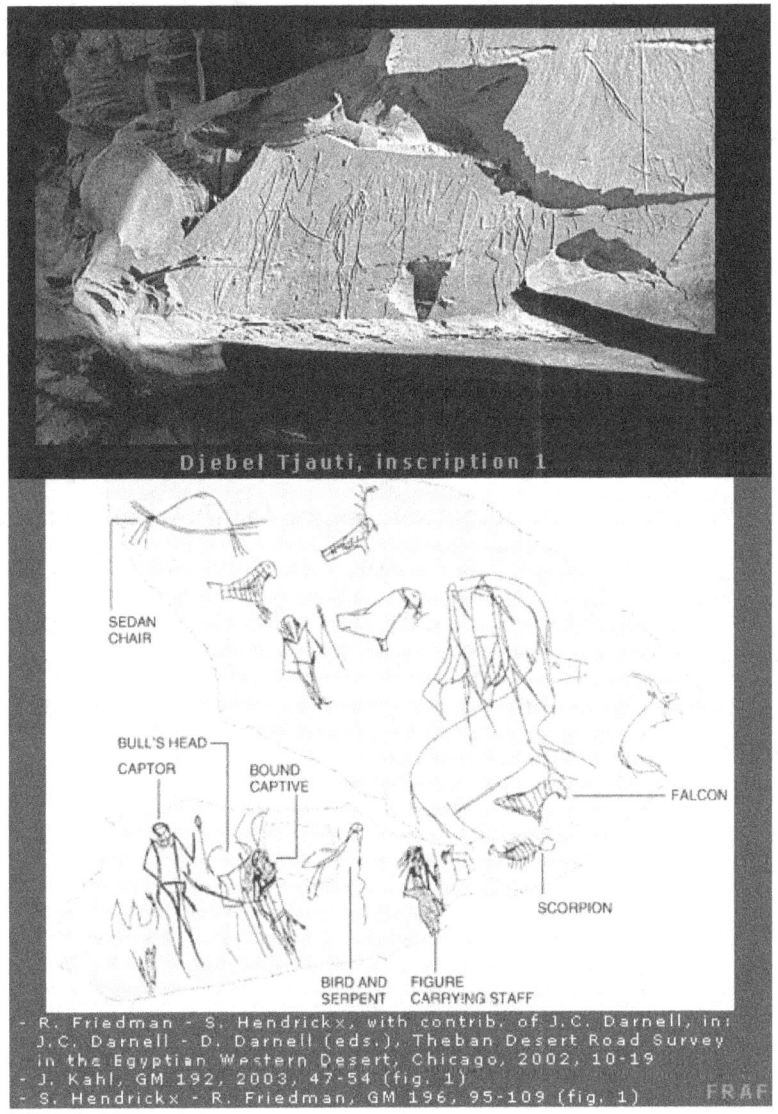

Fig. 52

There is also a carving next to the prisoner of a bird pecking a serpent. This same scene of a bird pecking a serpent was found on a painted vessel from Qustul tomb L23 at Qustul and Gebel Sheikh-Suleiman.

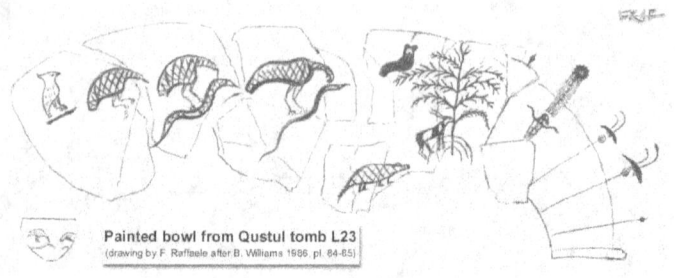

Painted bowl from Qustul tomb L23
(drawing by F. Raffaele after B. Williams 1986, pl. 84-85)

There is another important source for the names of the rulers of Dynasty 00, it is a statue was found by Petrie in the Temple of Coptos (The Colossus of Min) in 1894. In 1995, Dreyer suggested that the graffiti on the statue were the names of rulers older than King Narmer, and Narmer is the last one to add his name to this king list.

Egypt Before the Written History

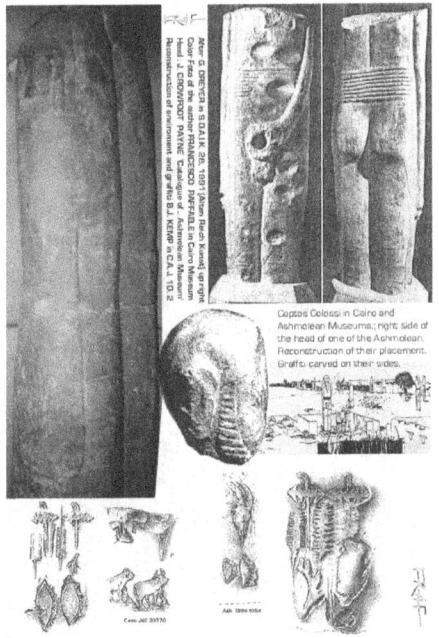

Some of the kings of Dynasty 00 (Fig. 53)

- King Falcon
- King Elephant
- King Bull
- King Lion
- King Scorpion

Fig. 53

Dynasty 0

In 1900, J. Quibel suggested that the owners of the tombs in Umm el-Qaab B are forming what we can call "Dynasty ." They ruled Egypt before Dynasty one, and before the Scorpion king II and King Narmer.

I agree with the opinion that the final unification success, which happened in Dynasty 1, was achieved because of the efforts of the rulers of Dynasty .

Most of the names of those rulers were found above jars made from pottery and other materials. Their names were written in a design called a Serkh (srx). This Serkh was explained to be the shape of the front part of the palace or the royal house, and the falcon (Horus) is standing above it.

Some of the kings of Dynasty

- Ny Hor
- Hat Hor (Hatj Hor)
- P Hor
- Hedj Hor (Hedjw Hor)
- R Hor (Iry Hor)
- Ka (Ka Hor)
- Crocodile
- Scorpion II

One of the very famous examples of these objects is the so-called Narmer Palette, which was found in Hierakonpolis (Nekhen) in Upper Egypt. According to the well-known interpretation, it depicts the unification between the south and the north of Egypt after a final battle led by King Narmer, the king of Upper Egypt, against the ruler of Lower Egypt. He defeated the army of Lower Egypt and became the sole ruler for both Upper and Lower Egypt (Fig. 54).

We started to collect more information about the era before the dynasties and we could understand that there were two main kingdoms in Ancient Egypt: one in the northside (Lower Egypt) and the other in the southside (Upper Egypt). Both had a similar group of symbols and traditions but in different colors or designs.

Narmer Palette
Fig. 54

The Kingdom of Lower Egypt (North Egypt)

I think that this kingdom existed in the area from north Cairo until the Mediterranean Sea, or we can say it occupied the area of the Nile Delta.

It is called Lower Egypt because the ground level of northern Egypt is lower than the ground level of the south of Egypt; that's why the Nile runs from south to north.

The land of the north was called in the Ancient Egyptian language as "mhw" (Mehw or Meho), which represents a clump of papyrus.

mHw

The capital of the kingdom of the north (lower Egypt) was called Buto (Dp or P). Buto could be the place called Tell El Faraein, which is the location of the modern city Desouk, in Kafr El Sheikh Governorate.

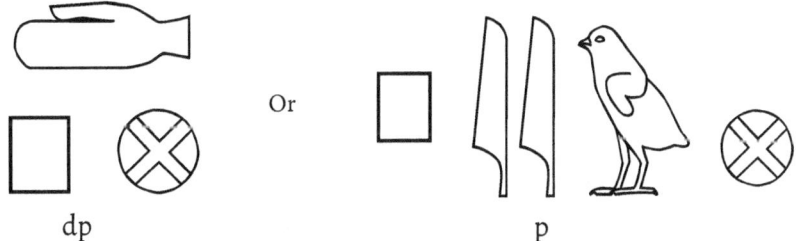

dp   p

There are some opinions that suggest Dp and P were two individual towns, and they were united and became one big city. I think they were two cities or two sides of the city (east and west).

The main symbol, or we can say the main ntr, was the cobra (wadjet). In some cases, the name of the city was Pr Wadjet.

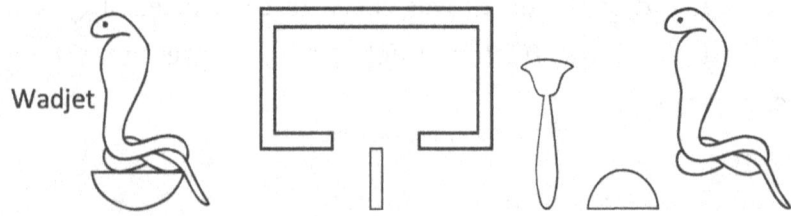

The crown of the ruler of the North was the red crown (deshret)

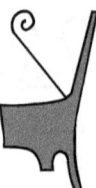

The title of the ruler of the North was bity (the red crown above the symbol nb (neb), which is half a circle, but originally the title bity or the word bity is the honeybee.

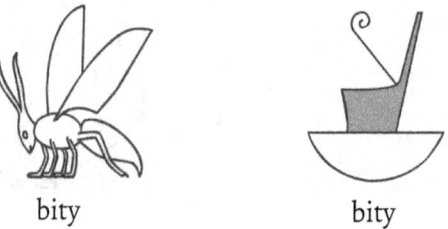

bity   bity

The people who lived in Buto were called the Depu (Depw)

So, the name Depu is the name of the people of Buto, but what about the name of the people who live in Lower Egypt in general?

The name for them is Bityw, whic means people of North Egypt, people of Lower Egypt, as well as the beekeepers.

Honey was widely produced in Lower Egypt, which is why Lower Egypt was famous for the industry of sweets. This was the case in ancient times and still continues in modern times.

The word "bity" also means honey.

Honeybee

Papyrus plant is the plant or the symbol of Lower Egypt.

Kingdom of Upper Egypt (South Egypt)

The capital was called Nekhen (the Greeks called it Hierakonpolis, which means the city of Hercules, so we understand that the city was connected with Horus). The modern name of Nekhen is Kom el-Ahmar, located in Edfu city, Aswan Governorate in southern Egypt).

The main symbol, or we can say the main ntr, was the vulture (Nekhbet).

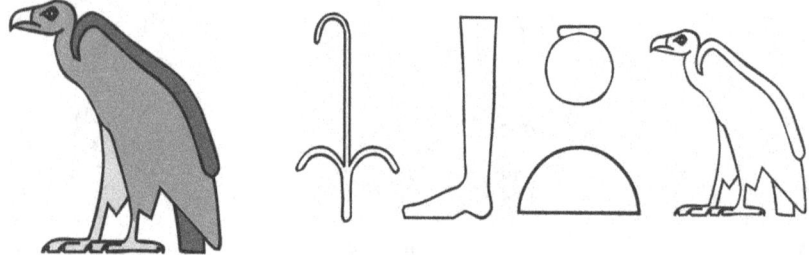

The crown of the ruler of the North was the white crown (hedjet)

Lotus flower was the plant symbol of Upper Egypt.

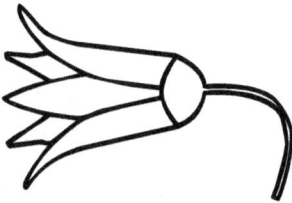

The title of the ruler of the South was nsw (the white crown above the symbol nb (neb), which is half a circle, but originally the title nsw or the word nsw is the rushes on the Nile banks.

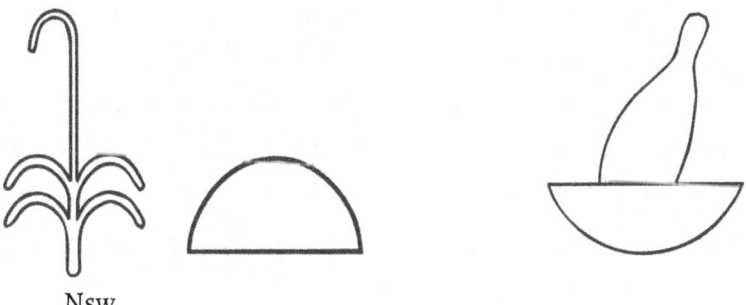

Nsw

The people who lived in Nekhen were called the Nekheny (or Nekhenite).

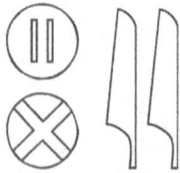   

Nekheny

I don't believe that there was a kingdom of Upper Egypt and a kingdom of Lower Egypt. I believe both cities were important for Egypt, one in the north and one in the south, because both kingdoms are identical. Yes, I know that the symbols are not the same, of course, but it is the same idea, the same concept, and the same style. So maybe the kingdoms were actually two parts of one country (north and south), or the two kingdoms were originally one kingdom, and because of political reasons, they split and became two separate kingdoms with two separate rulers and administrations.

According to the famous story, King Narmer (king of the south) led his army against the king of the north (whose name we don't know). He defeated the army of the north, and Egypt became one kingdom once more. The white crown of the south was put inside the red crown of the north.

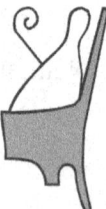

The title of the south and the title of the north were put together before the name of the King of Egypt.

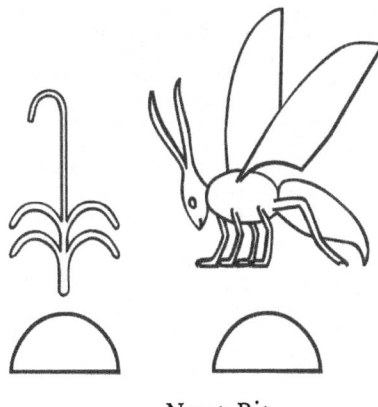

Nswt-Bit

Mohamed Ibrahim Elbassiouny

Dynastic Egypt

According to most Egyptologists, the first Dynasty was established by King Narmer (or Mina) around 3100 BC. The chronology they have put for Ancient Egyptian history explains that Ancient Egypt was ruled by 30 dynasties between 3100 BC and 332 BC. Egyptologists like Nicolas Grimal, Jaromir Malek, Rolf Krauss, Erik Hornung, and Jürgen von Beckerath have contributed to this understanding. I prefer to refer to this history as Dynastic Egypt.

The main sources for Ancient Egyptian history are the transcriptions of the book "Aegyptiaca" by Manetho, fragments of the Palermo Stone, and the Turin Papyrus.

The title "Dynasty" was chosen instead of the title "royal family" because some dynasties included members who were not part of the royal family. For example, the 18th Dynasty includes King Horemheb, who was not a member of that family. This is also the case in many instances in the Old Kingdom and Middle Kingdom.

Thus, the rulers of each Dynasty were organized according to various features such as religion, art, politics, and the social system. The 30 dynasties were also divided into three main kingdoms: Old, Middle, and New Kingdoms. Between these kingdoms, there are three eras of civilization's collapse known as the First, Second, and Third Intermediate Periods.

The Archaic Period (Dynasty 01 and Dynasty 2)

The expression "Archaic periods" refers to Dynasty 01 and Dynasty 02. In some newer classifications, they are included as part of the Old Kingdom of Egypt. However, I prefer to use the old classification and refer to them as the Archaic period.

The preparation of dynastic Egypt and the distinctive style of Ancient Egyptian civilization began during this time. Egypt was a unified country, encompassing both the north and south, under the rule of one ruler during the Archaic period. The rulers of this period established a system for the Ancient Egyptian government and policy, both internal and external. Throughout the Archaic period, Ancient Egypt had a relatively well-structured government system. There were viziers for the north and south, as well as mayors for each city. While this system might not have been completely stable, efforts were made to implement it, rectify mistakes, and make necessary adjustments. Additionally, the main aspects of the Ancient Egyptian religion were established during this period. Religious structures were built for major gods, initially using simple designs and materials like mudbricks and wood. During the Archaic period, they began to use various types of stones in their artwork and construction, and their techniques and tools improved. Burials and the concept of the afterlife were of great importance, leading to the development of tombs and associated burial elements.

Dynasty 01

It is not easy to claim that we know much about the first Dynasty, as not all of their tombs and structures have been found, resulting in many missing pieces of information about this period. We are uncertain about the identity of the founder of the 01st Dynasty. According to king lists, he was King Menes (Mni), but based on certain objects like the Narmer Palette, he was King Narmer.

According to the famous story, King Mni established a new capital for Egypt known as Inb-Hdj (Ineb-Hedj), meaning the white wall. Later, it became Mn-Nfr (Men-Nefer) and was eventually pronounced as Memphis. There was a long debate between two teams regarding King Meni and King Narmer. The first team believed that King Meni and King Narmer were the same person. The second team argued that they were two different kings. I support the second team's argument because there is no reliable evidence proving that King Meni is King Narmer.

A seal made of mud was discovered in Sakkara, bearing the name of King Qa'a. This seal contains a list of the rulers of Dynasty 01: Narmer, Hor-Aha, Djer, Djet, Den, Adjeb, Semerkhet, and Qa'a. Notably, the name Meni was never mentioned. The list starts with the title Khenti-Amneti followed by the names of the rulers. This same list appears on another seal related to King Den, but the name Meni is absent. Therefore, I do not agree that King Narmer and King Meni are the same person. I believe the name Meni was invented during the New Kingdom period. We have found many artifacts bearing the name Narmer.

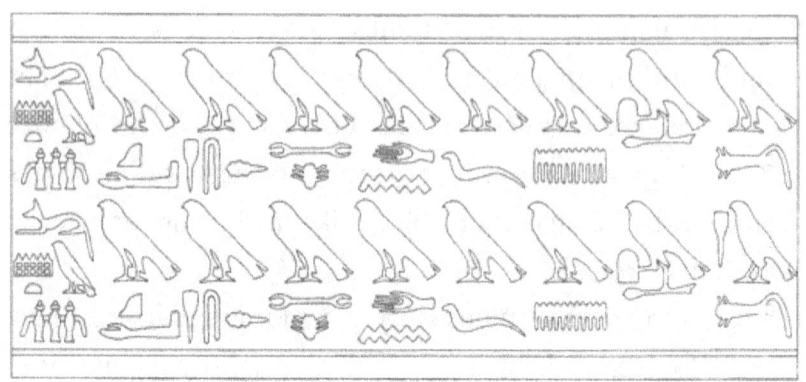

Seal impressions from the time of King Qaa

Seal impressions from the tomb of Horus DEN (Umm el Qaab - Abydos)
from W. Kaiser in M.D.A.I.K. 43, 1986 p. 115-119
(cfr. also G. Dreyer in M.D.A.I.K. 43 p. 33-43 + plates)

Another seal was found, this time from the reign of King Den, and it supports the same idea. However, there is still a possibility that the name Meni could be an alternative name for King Narmer or possibly another name for Hor-Aha.

mn

Because the symbol mn was repeated in 2 labels, one belongs to Narmer and the other belong to Hor-Aha, the word mn means stable or stability, so mni (Meni) may mean (the stable one).

Narmer　　　　　　　　　　Hor-Aha

According to what we have found and the king lists, we can identify 9 or 10 rulers of the 1st Dynasty. They ruled Egypt from a location known as Thinis (located in southern Egypt, in

Sohag). The tombs of these rulers were discovered in a site near Abydos called Umm el-Qaab. In the Umm el-Qaab necropolis, we have found inscriptions containing the names of the rulers of the 1st Dynasty, such as:

- King Narmer, tomb B17-B18
- King Aha, tomb B10-B15-B19
- King Djer, tomb O 326
- King Djet, tomb Z 174
- Queen Merytneith, tomb Y 41
- King Den, tomb T 121
- King Adjib, tomb X 63
- King Semerkhet, tomb U 69
- King Qa'a, tomb Q 26

But in 1938 and 1958, Egyptologists found another cemetery for the rulers of the 1st Dynasty, but this time in the north of Egypt; the cemetery is located at north Sakkara, very close to Abusir pyramids.

We found the same names inside the tombs except for Aha and Semerkhet. There is a strong opinion suggesting that the tombs at Sakkara are the actual tombs, and the tombs of Umm el-Qaab are symbolic tombs. However, there is another opinion suggesting the opposite: the actual tombs are the ones at Umm el-Qaab, near their hometown, and the cemetery at Sakkara is the symbolic one. I don't care which cemetery is the real one and which is the symbolic one; I care about the locations and why Abydos and Sakkara?

In my opinion, the answer will be linked to our understanding of the main neter (deity) of each site. The primary neter of

Abydos is Osiris (Ausir). The Ancient Egyptians considered Osiris as the lord of the afterlife. According to their beliefs, the deceased would go to the hall of judgment (the court of Osiris), where Osiris serves as the judge.

There are various opinions about the presence of an older neter in Abydos called Khenti-Amentiu. His name means "Foremost of the Westerners," and it has been suggested that Khenti-Amentiu was a distinct god from Osiris, with his own position and cult center. I, however, believe that Khenti-Amentiu is an epithet for Osiris, and both deities represent the same neter.

The main neter of Sakkara is Seker (Soker). He is also associated with the afterlife, much like Osiris. One of his titles is "Lord of the Rostau." Seker is often depicted as a mummified hawk, or sometimes a hawk's head emerging from a mound. This imagery relates to his title, symbolizing his role as "the one above his sand."

In my interpretation, Seker is closely connected with the pathways to the afterlife or, in other words, he is the neter of the tunnels and galleries beneath the ground. As such, I speculate that there is an ancient connection between Abydos and Sakkara, and that over time, the two neters of Abydos and Sakkara, along with Ptah (the neter of Memphis), became united in the form of one neter called Ptah-Soker-Osiris.

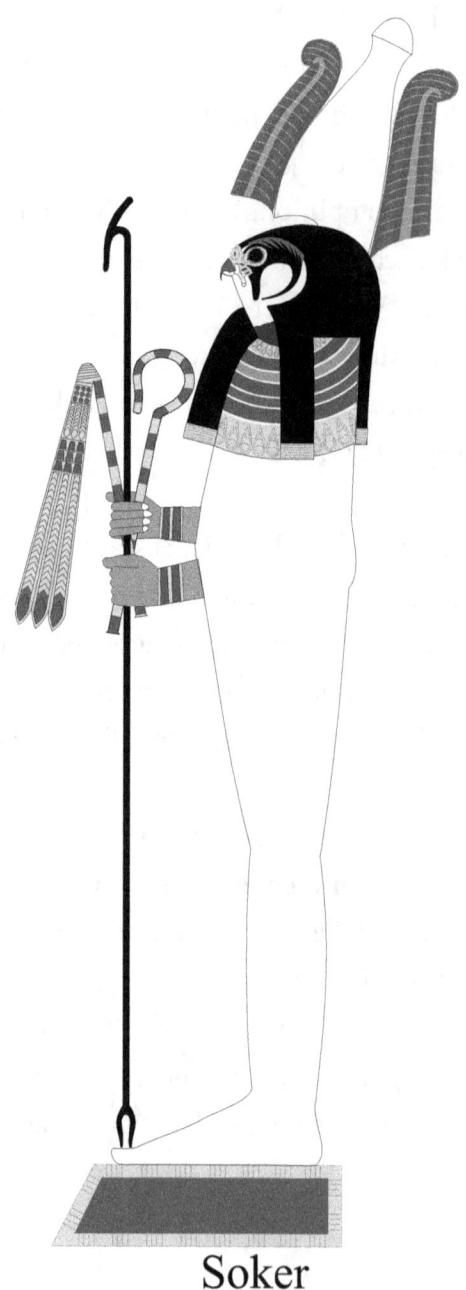

Soker

Dynasty 02

We don't know much about the 2nd Dynasty, so we rely on our suggestions and presumptions to explain the history of this Dynasty. This is due to the lack of archaeological evidence and historical facts. As I mentioned before, there aren't many records or items left from this Dynasty, and we lack information about how the transition of the throne occurred. Manetho's writings provide an interesting perspective on this Dynasty. He mentions that it consists of 9 kings who ruled for 302 years. However, this story is highly questionable among Egyptologists.

In addition, we are not entirely certain about the accurate sequence of rulers. Nevertheless, we do possess substantial information about two kings: Hotepsekhemwi and Khasekhemui.

It's worth noting that some of the rulers of the 2nd Dynasty chose to build their tombs in Sakkara, rather than Abydos.

- King Hotepsekhemwi
- King Reneb
- King Nineter (Ninetjer)
- King Weneg
- King Senedj
- King Neferkare
- King Neferkasokar
- Hudjefa
- King Peribsen
- Khasekhem
- Khasekhemwi

King Khasekhem and King Khasekhemwi could be the same person. It has been suggested that the unity of Egypt fell apart after the first Dynasty, and he is the one who reunited both kingdoms again, so the name Khasekhem could be his first title before the unification (it means the rise of the power) and Khasekhemwi could be his his title after the unification (it means the rise of the 2 powers). By the end of the second Dynasty and the beginning of the third Dynasty, Egypt stepped into a new era of civilization, this era is called the Old Kingdom of Ancient Egypt.

Old Kingdom (Dynasty 3-6) 2686 BC - 2181 BC

The German Egyptologist Baron von Bunsen, in 1845, categorized the Ancient Egyptian dynasties into 3 golden ages: the Old Kingdom, Middle Kingdom, and New Kingdom.

The Old Kingdom of Ancient Egypt encompasses dynasties 03, 04, 05, and Dynasty 6. This period is often referred to as the age of the Pyramid Builders. The rulers of the Old Kingdom constructed pyramids spanning from Abu Rawash (north of the Giza Plateau) to Meidum (south of Giza). The capital of Egypt during the Old Kingdom was Ineb Hedj, also known as Memphis.

Dynasty 03

So far, we have 6 kings in Dynasty 3, but I expect that there were more kings in this Dynasty, but we haven't discovered their tombs yet. It's uncertain what happened at the end of Dynasty 2 and how the throne was transferred to Dynasty 3, but we understand that it was a peaceful transition. The star of this Dynasty is King Djoser, whom many people believe was the first ruler or the founder of Dynasty 3. However, according to some sources including the Abydos king list and the Turin Papyrus, the first ruler of Dynasty 3 is King Sanakht, who might be the elder brother of Djoser. Their mother is Nimaat-Hap (Nimaathap), the wife of Khasekhemwy.

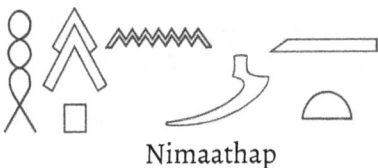

Nimaathap

Many pyramids were built during the time of Dynasty 3, but most of these pyramids are unfinished or not in good condition. The only one that remains in great shape is the Step Pyramid of King Djoser.

The unfinished pyramid at Zawyet El Aryan may be related to Sanakht, as the name Nebka was found there, according to the Italian Egyptologist Alessandro Barsant

King Djoser (Zoser) built the Step Pyramid at Saqqara. However, you may come across other sources that mention King Netjerikhet as the builder of the Step Pyramid at Saqqara. It's important to note that both names refer to the same person, as indicated by writings from the Middle Kingdom.

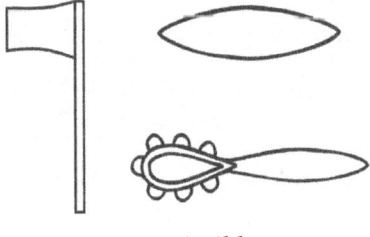

Netjerikhet

When discussing King Djoser and the Step Pyramid, it's essential to mention Imhotep. The name "Imhotep" translates to "he who comes in peace," although I like to interpret it as "he who comes in power."

The brilliant Imhotep served as the chancellor and architect of King Djoser. The design and construction of the Step Pyramid are attributed to him.

King Sekhemkhet also constructed a pyramid in Saqqara, located southwest of the Step Pyramid; this pyramid is known as the Buried Pyramid.

King Khaba built a Step pyramid at Zawyet El Aryan, which is referred to as the Layer Pyramid.

King Huni is closely associated with the construction of the Meidum Pyramid.

- King Sanakht (Nebka)
- King Djoser (Netjerikhet)
- King Sekhemkhet
- King Hudjefa
- King Khaba
- King Huni

Dynasty 04

King Sneferu is the founder of Dynasty 4, not only the founder but also the father and grandfather of the rulers of this Dynasty. I can say that the transition from Dynasty 3 to Dynasty 4 was very peaceful; it seems that Queen Hetep-Heres is the key to understanding this transition.

The Egyptian administration was very effective and extended all over the Egyptian region. The kings of Dynasty 4 sent their workers to Sinai to bring turquoise. Egypt had very good relations with its neighbors, sending the Egyptian fleet to Lebanon to acquire cedar wood.

The completion of the Meidum Pyramid is attributed to King Sneferu. Additionally, the two pyramids at Dahshur—the Bent Pyramid and the Red Pyramid—are also attributed to him.

The iconic construction of Dynasty 4 is the Great Pyramid, built by King Khufu, with Hemiunu as its architect (Hemiunu is the cousin and architect of Khufu).

King Djedefre altered the family plans and moved away from the Giza Plateau to a nearby plateau in an area called Abu Rawash, where he built his pyramid.

King Khafre (Khafra) erected the second pyramid at the Giza Plateau, and the Great Sphinx is attributed to him.

King Nebka could possibly be the builder of the unfinished pyramid at Zawyet El Aryan (the northern pyramid). Some scholars believe so, suggesting that this pyramid is similar to the one built by his father Djedefre.

King Menkaure constructed the third pyramid at the Giza Plateau. However, his son, King Shepseskaf, did something very unusual—he built a mastaba tomb, and not even on the Giza Plateau, but rather at Sakkara.

The second peculiar thing at the end of this family's rule is that the daughter of Shepseskaf, Queen Khentkaus, built a small pyramid for herself on the "Giza Plateau."

- King Sneferu
- King Khufu

- King Djedefre
- King Khafre
- King Ba-Ka ?
- King Menkaure
- King Shepseskaf
- Queen Khentkaus

Dynasty 05

It's not clear how the transition to Dynasty 5 happened, but according to a story attributed to the time of Dynasty 4 called "Khufu and the Magicians," the end of this story suggests that the royal family of Khufu would lose the throne, and a priest would marry one of Khufu's descendants, leading to his children becoming the new rulers of Egypt.

Even though the first king of Dynasty 5 built his pyramid at Sakkara, and a few rulers of this Dynasty followed suit, Abusir is considered the center of the pyramids of Dynasty 5. I can also mention that the power of the priest of Ra increased to higher levels than before.

When discussing Dynasty 5, we must also mention their unique constructions—the Sun Temples.

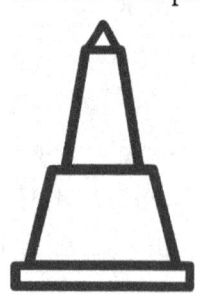

King Userkaf built his pyramid at Sakkara, but he built his Sun Temple at Abu Gorab (part of Abusir); his sun temple was called Nekhenre.

King Sahure built his pyramid at Abusir; his sun temple was called Sekhetre.

King Neferirkare Kakai built his pyramid at Abusir; his sun temple was called Setibre.

King Neferefre built his pyramid at Abusir; his sun temple was called Hetepre.

King Shepseskare maybe he built a pyramid at Abusir; his sun temple was called Hotepibre.

King Nyuserre Ini built his pyramid at Abusir; his sun temple was called Shesepibre.

King Menkauhor Kaiu built his pyramid at Sakkara; his sun temple was called Akhetre.

King Djedkare Isesi built his pyramid at Sakkara; we don't know if he built a sun temple or not.

King Unas built his pyramid at Sakkara; we don't know if he built a sun temple or not.

King Unas started something very unique for the development process of the pyramids. In the Unas Pyramid, we see what we call the Pyramid Texts—no pyramid has had texts like these before.

- King Userkaf
- King Sahure
- King Neferirkare Kakai
- King Shepseskare
- King Shepseskare

- King Neferefre
- King Niuserre
- King Menkauhor
- King Djedkare Isesi
- King Unas

Dynasty 06

The end of Dynasty 5 witnessed weakness in many aspects, including the economy and the power of the palace. The authority of the priesthood increased to higher levels from the time of King Neferirkare Kakai. It seems that the rulers of Dynasty 6 also suffered from the same weakness, which eventually led to the end of the Old Kingdom after Dynasty 6.

The transition from Dynasty 5 to Dynasty 6 was peaceful. Egyptologists strongly believe that Iput, the wife of King Teti (the founder of Dynasty 6), was the daughter of King Unas. This makes Teti the son-in-law of Unas.

Rulers of Dynasty 6 ruled from Memphis and showed great respect for the deity Ptah (the god of Memphis). This is evident in the title of the founder of this Dynasty, King Teti. His title is "Teti Mery N Ptah" (Teti, Beloved of Ptah).

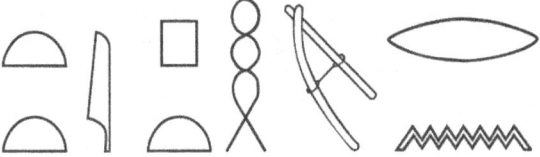

Rulers of Dynasty 6 built their pyramids at Saqqara, and their high officials also constructed impressive mastabas there, such as Kagemni and Mereruka.

King Teti constructed his pyramid at Saqqara and named it "Djed Iswt." This pyramid includes the Pyramid Texts, much like Unas Pyramid.

The kings of Dynasty 6 built their pyramids at Saqqara, but there are some kings about whom we know very little, like King Userkare.

King Pepi II ascended to the throne of Egypt when he was just 6 years old and lived to the remarkable age of 100 years, ruling Egypt for nearly 94 years.

The conclusion of Dynasty 6 remains rather unclear. We are uncertain whether the last ruler of the Dynasty was male or female. There is a high possibility that the final ruler was Queen Nitocris (Nitekreti), and perhaps the name "Neterkare" in the Abydos king list refers to her name in a male form.

- King Teti
- King Userkare
- King Pepi I
- King Nemtiemsaf I (Merenre I)
- King Pepi II
- King Nemtiemsaf II (Merenre II)
- King Nitekreti or queen (Nitocris)

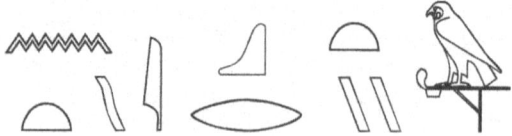

By the time of the Old Kingdom, the Ancient Egyptian kings had 5 titles (5 royal titles).

1. Hor name (Horus name)

This name means "who belong to Horus," or "who rule under the power of Horus." This is the oldest title for the Ancient Egyptian rulers, and it began in the pre-dynastic era, lasting until the end of the Egyptian civilization.

2. Hor-Nub name (Golden Horus name)

This name means "who belong to golden Horus," or "who rule under the power of golden Horus." This name could also mean "the victorious Horus," because we can see Horus above the nwb sign, which belongs to the deity Seth. Therefore, it could be a metaphor.

3. Nebty name (The Two Ladies name)

This name means, "who belong to the 2 ladies" (Nekhbet and Wadjet), or "who rule under the power of the 2 ladies."

4. Sa-Ra name (Son of Ra name and Birth name)

This name means "son of Ra" or "the child of Ra"; this name is the birth name for the king.

5. Nsw-bity name (Throne name)

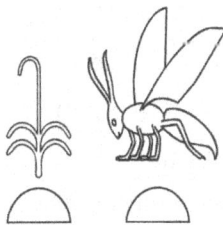

This name means "who belong to the Honeybee and the Reed plant." This is the title of the king after coronation.

First Intermediate period

This is the time when the Ancient Egyptian Civilization collapsed. The glory of the Old Kingdom ended with the conclusion of Dynasty 6, and chaos ensued at the outset of Dynasty 7.

There are very few monuments discovered from this era, but we know about these rulers because of the Abydos king list, Turin Papyrus, and Manetho's history.

During this period, two main powers were competing against each other:

The rulers of Heracleopolis (the modern name is Ihnasiyyah, Beni Suef in Upper Egypt).

The rulers of Thebes (Luxor)

The First Intermediate period includes Dynasty 7, 08, 09 and Dynasty 10.

Dynasty 07

We don't know much about Dynasty 7 or Dynasty 8 because of the lack of structures and sources.

We know that they ruled Egypt from the capital of the previous dynasties, Memphis.

The Egyptian priest (historian) Manetho mentioned that 70 kings ruled for 70 days, which is very difficult to understand!

Maybe the 70 kings were a council ruling Egypt, but it didn't last more than 70 days.

The name Neferkare Tereru was mentioned clearly as a king in Abydos king list, but we know nothing about him.

- King Netjerikare

- King Menkare
- King Neferkare
- King Neferkare Neby
- King Djedkare Shemai
- King Neferkare Khendu
- King Merenhor
- King Sneferka
- King Nikare
- King Neferkare Tereru
- King Neferkahor

Dynasty 08

The capital of Ancient Egypt during Dynasty 8 was Memphis, and it seems that the rule of this Dynasty was very short (20-45 years)

- King Neferkare Papisneb
- King Neferkamin Anu
- King Qakare Ibi
- King Neferkaure
- King Neferkauhor
- King Neferirkare II

Dynasty 09

It seems that there was a conflict between the rulers of Dynasty 7 (Memphis) and the rulers (high officials) of Heracleopolis. At the end of Dynasty 7 and the beginning of Dynasty 8, the capital was changed to Heracleopolis (Ihnasiyyah).

- King Khety I (Akhtoy I)

Dynasty 10

Dynasty 10 were from the same origin as Dynasty 9. Heracleopolis (Ihnasiyyah) was the capital during the rule of Dynasty 10.

The ancient name of the city was Gwt-nn-nswt, which means "child of the king."

As Heracleopolis was the opponent of Memphis and Dynasty 7 and 08, Thebes became the opponent of Heracleopolis and Dynasty 9 and 10.

- King Khety V (Akhtoy V)

Middle Kingdom

The Reunification (2040 - 1782 BCE)

I can call the Middle Kingdom time "The Rise of the Ancient Egyptian Civilization," as if the Phoenix arises from dust (ashes).

After the collapse of the Old Kingdom, the rulers of three cities were struggling together to control the throne of Egypt. The rulers of Memphis ascended to the throne first, and then they were overthrown by the rulers of Heracleopolis. The rulers of Thebes joined this struggle, but finally, king Mentuhotep II from Thebes managed to put an end to this struggle and united Egypt under one power: the Theban rulers.

The capital during the Middle Kingdom was Thebes (Luxor), and the rise of the deity Amun started with the time of the Middle Kingdom.

The Middle Kingdom includes Dynasty 11 and Dynasty 12.

Dynasty 11

Many rulers from the beginning of Dynasty 11 engaged in battles with the rulers of Dynasty 10. King Mentuhotep II ended this long fight after defeating the last king of Dynasty 10. Therefore, I can say that king Mentuhotep II is the real founder of Dynasty 11 and the Middle Kingdom.

- King Intef I
- King Mentuhotep II Nebhepetre

Dynasty 12

The founder of this Dynasty is King Amenemhat I. We don't know much about him before ascending the throne. Also, we don't know the circumstances which led to the transition from Dynasty 11 to Dynasty 12, but it seems to be a peaceful transition. Maybe Amenemhat was a vizier (minister) to king Mentuhotep IV, who perhaps died without an heir.

Dynasty 12 is the pearl of the Middle Kingdom. No other Dynasty had its power and achievements during the time from the Old Kingdom to the New Kingdom.

For an unknown reason, king Amenemhat I changed the capital. He chose a city south of Cairo near Faiyum, but we don't know the exact location of this city. It was called Iti-Tawey (Iset-Tawy), and maybe it is at the location of the modern town El Lisht.

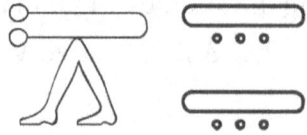

The state of Egypt was very strong during Dynasty 12. The Egyptian army engaged in battles at the south and northeast of Egypt. The economy was in great shape, and the rulers of Dynasty 12 initiated numerous agricultural projects like dams and water canals.

The kings of Dynasty 12 are the last Egyptians who built pyramids.

Queen Sobekneferure is the last ruler of this Dynasty, and I can say she was the last ruler of the Middle Kingdom.

- King Amenemhat I
- King Senweseret I (Sesostris I)
- King Amenemhat II
- King Senweseret II (Sesostris II)
- King Senweseret III (Sesostris III)
- King Amenemhat III
- King Amenemhat IV
- Queen Sobekneferure

Second Intermediate Period

The golden age of the Middle Kingdom was suddenly stopped. After queen Sobekneferure, who maybe didn't have an heir, a group of weak rulers ruled Egypt as Dynasty 13 and Dynasty 14. The Egyptian administration was weak, but I think the economy was good, so many Middle Eastern people immigrated to Egypt. Due to famines in the Middle East and surrounding countries (Minor Asia), Egypt became a shelter for many refugees. If this had happened during the Old Kingdom or the Middle Kingdom, it would have been manageable. However, because of the weak administration and the lack of strong kings, many of those immigrants and refugees became employees and eventually high officials. Many of them were also hired in the Egyptian army and attained high positions. All of these factors led to one fact: these groups of foreigners suddenly found themselves controlling Egypt. They named one of them "king of Egypt" and started Dynasty 15. The Ancient Egyptians called them Heka-Khaswt, which means the rulers of foreign land (I say it means the shepherds of the land behind mountains).

The earliest representation for the Hyksos was a painting in the tomb of the high official Khnumhotep from Dynasty 10 (Beni Hasan tombs).

In my opinion, the main reason for the collapse of the civilization after the Middle Kingdom is the strong houses (families) of different cities who held the throne of Egypt at one point, like Memphis, Iti-Tawey, Ihnasiyyah, and Thebes.

This time of weakness was a great opportunity for refugees in Egypt (from the Middle East and nearby countries) to obtain jobs in the government and the Egyptian army. With time, they started to receive promotions and became commanders.

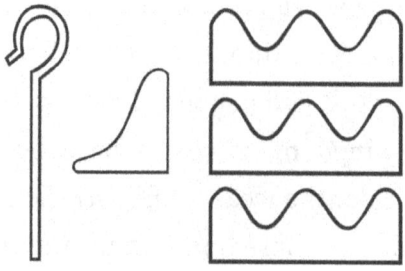

Heka-Khasut

Dynasty 13

Despite the large number of rulers included in this Dynasty, we have very little information about them.

The most famous kings in this Dynasty are King Khendjer who built a small pyramid south of Sakkara and King Hor who made that beautiful Ka statue at the Egyptian museum.

- King Ugaf
- King Ameni Kemaw (Sehetepibre)
- King Amenemhat VI
- King Sebekhotep I
- King Hor I
- King Khendjer
- King Didumes

Dynasty 14

The history of this Dynasty is very difficult to track and understand. The capital was moved to the northeast of Egypt, and we are not sure why. Some Egyptologists suggest it was because of the Canaanite origin of the rulers of Dynasty 14. Some of their names are Canaanite or similar. Another question about this family is the name of one of the kings, Nehesi, which means "the Nubian" (belonging to Nubia). So, I'm not sure if this Dynasty was composed of one group of rulers or many groups. However, like Dynasty 13, this Dynasty includes many rulers who reigned for short times.

We are confused about the capital during this Dynasty: was it Xios or Avaris?

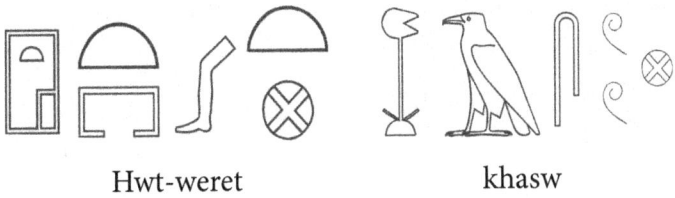

Hwt-weret   khasw

- King Nehesi

Dynasty 15 (Hyksos Rulers)

This is the Dynasty of the Heka-Khaswt, the Hyksos. The capital of Egypt during the Hyksos time was Avaris. We understand king Salitis is the founder of Dynasty 15. I believe he wasn't the first Hyksos ruler, but maybe he was the first strong ruler who put an end to all the struggles and ruled Egypt as one kingdom. I must add to this information that the house (local rulers) Abydos were the opponents of the Hyksos first, but the local rulers of Thebes were the true opponents of the Hyksos. They considered themselves the true kings of Egypt.

The Hyksos rulers and people took Sotekh (Seth) as their deity and gave him the title Neb-Hwt We'e ret (lord of Avaris).

- King Salitis
- King Sheshi

- King Yakobner (Yakobher)
- King Khian
- King Apopi
- King Khamudi

Dynasty 16 (Hyksos Rulers)

There are tens of names for rulers that were attributed to Dynasty 16. Some names are not Egyptian, like Aper-Anat and Semqen, while other names are Egyptian, such as Nebmaatre. I think there were two thrones during the time of Dynasty 16: the main throne of Egypt at Avaris and another throne with another local Dynasty at Thebes. It seemed that the power of the Theban family was getting stronger over time.

- Ruler Anat-Her
- Ruler Aper-Anat (User-Anat)
- Ruler Semqen

Dynasty 17 (Egyptian Rulers)

We don't know much about this Dynasty, especially its beginning, but we do have some strong speculations about the relationship between the Hyksos and the house of Thebes. It is strongly believed that Thebes was paying tributes to the Hyksos king, whose name was mentioned on a papyrus from the Ramesside period as Apophis. At the same time, their power and influence were increasing. Thus, the rulers of Dynasty 17 started to put their names inside the cartouche preceded by royal titles like Nsw-Bity. By the time of King Seqenenre Tao II, they felt that they could initiate a liberation war against the Hyksos. Again, we don't know much about the beginning of this war, but from the severe condition of the mummy of Seqenenre Tao II, we understand that it was a tough battle for both sides. After the killing of Seqenenre, his son Kamose took on the leadership of the army and continued the war against the Hyksos. I should mention that some women played an important role in this war by encouraging and supporting their husbands and sons, like Queen Tetisheri and Queen Ahhotep.

- King Intef V
- King Sebekemsaf I
- King Nibiraw I (Nibirierawet I)
- King Intef VI (the Elder)
- King Snakhtenre Tao I
- King Seqenenre Tao II (The Brave)
- King Kamose

New Kingdom

This was the time for Egypt to rise again and start one of its greatest eras. King Ahmose was chosen to be the founder not only of Dynasty 18 but also the founder of the New Kingdom.

The Egyptian army defeated the Hyksos troops and followed them outside Egypt until they reached Sharuhen.

The New Kingdom can also be called the time of the Ancient Egyptian Empire, as Egypt expanded its territories and conquered many of the surrounding lands. We refer to the Old

Kingdom as the pyramid builders and the New Kingdom as the era of military achievements.

The kings of the New Kingdom produced great art, constructions, and improved many of the Ancient Egyptian industries and techniques. The New Kingdom witnessed a serious conflict between Amun-Ra and Aton. I can say the priests and followers of Amun-Ra were against the king and the followers of Aton. This conflict ended with the victory of the priest of Amun-Ra and his followers.

Kings of the New Kingdom didn't build pyramids, but they constructed great temples like Karnak temple, Luxor temple, Hapu temple, Hatshepsut temple, and Abu Simbel temple.

Dynasty 18

This Dynasty is known for its great rulers, builders, and warriors. As mentioned earlier, it was the House of Thebes (Luxor) that led the effort to liberate Egypt, which is why Thebes was chosen as the capital. It served as both a political and religious capital since the deity Amun of Luxor became the main god of Ancient Egypt, with temples dedicated to Amun built all over the country. The Egyptian kingdom expanded into an empire, particularly during the reign of King Thutmose III.

The rulers of this Dynasty didn't build pyramids, but they constructed grand temples and erected huge obelisks. The end of this Dynasty was marked by the revolutionary reign of King Akhenaten, who aimed to change the beliefs of the Ancient Egyptian community, especially those related to Amun and Osiris. King Horemheb, the military leader, brought an end to this sudden change brought about by the Amarna Family.

- King Ahmose (The Victorious)
- King Amenhotep I (Amenophis I)
- King Tuthmosis II
- Female King Hatshepsut
- King Tuthmosis III
- King Amenhotep II (Amenophis II)
- King Tuthmosis IV
- King Amenhotep III (Amenophis III)
- King Akhenaten (Amenhotep IV)
- King Semenkhkare
- King Tutankhamun
- King Ay
- King Horemheb

Dynasty 19

King Horemheb, as the army leader, saw the danger posed by the policy of the rulers of Amarna not only to Egypt but also to the countries under Egyptian control. He assumed power and declared himself king of Egypt. After his rule, his friend or assistant general Ramses became the ruler under the name King Ramses I. Dynasty 19 includes the legendary King Ramses II. During this time, there were two important cities, Memphis and Thebes, that served as capitals of Ancient Egypt. However, Ramses II established a new city called Pr-Ramisw (House of Ramses), which became the real capital of Egypt.

- King Ramesses I
- King Seti I
- King Ramesses II
- King Merenptah

- King Seti II
- King Amenmose
- King Siptah
- Queen Taweseret

Taweseret

Dynasty 20

The transition from Dynasty 19 to Dynasty 20 was peaceful. It seems that Sethnakht was a descendant of Ramses II. After Queen Taweseret's death, he proclaimed himself king of Egypt. The rulers at the beginning of this Dynasty were considered the last great rulers of Ancient Egypt. Ramses III marked the end of this chain of great rulers. After Ramses III, there were eight more kings named Ramses, but none reached the greatness of Ramses II or III.

King Ramses III built a huge beautiful temple on the west bank of Luxor called the Hapu temple.

- King Sethnakht
- King Ramesses III
- King Ramesses IV
- King Ramesses V
- King Ramesses VI
- King Ramesses VII
- King Ramesses VIII
- King Ramesses IX

- King Ramesses X
- King Ramesses XI

Third Intermediate Period

After Dynasty 20, particularly after King Ramses III, Egypt had weak rulers and began to lose power. Due to this weakness, Egypt became vulnerable to nations like Kush, Persia, Assyria, and some Libyan tribes from the west. The capital changed multiple times during this era, moving between Tanis, Bubastis, Heracleopolis, and Sais.

The Third Intermediate Period encompasses dynasties 21, 22, 23, 24, and 25.

No significant construction was done during this time.

Dynasty 21

By the end of Dynasty 20, the Egyptian state lost control over Thebes due to the increasing power of the Amun priest. Consequently, the capital was moved to Tanis in the northeast of Egypt.

The Amun priest ruled the south of Egypt, while the king of Egypt ruled the north.

- King Smendes
- King Amenemose
- King Pasebakhaienniut I (Psusennes I)

- King Amenemopet
- King Osorkon the Elder
- King Siamun
- King Pasebakhaenniut II (Psusennes II)

Dynasty 22

Sometimes we refer to this Dynasty as the Libyan Dynasty. A series of immigrations from Libya to the northeast of Egypt occurred at the end of the New Kingdom. These immigrants were members of the Libyan tribe called Meshwesh, and they settled in the city of Bubastis.

King Sheshonq I, the founder of this family, is assumed to be the biblical king known as King Shishak.
- King Sheshonq I
- King Nimlot
- King Osorkon I
- King Sheshonq II
- King Takelot I
- King Osorkon II
- King Horsiese I
- King Takelot II
- King Sheshonq III
- King Pimai (Pami)
- King Sheshonq V
- King Osorkon IV

Dynasty 23

I can say that Dynasty 22, Dynasty 23, and the Amun-Ra priests were ruling Egypt at the same time but from different cities. Dynasty 23 ruled Egypt from Bubastis, the center of the goddess Bast. Hence, I can say that the political situation in Egypt was not stable at all during this era.

- King Padibastet I (Petubastis I)
- King Iuput I
- King Sheshonq IV
- King Osorkon III
- King Takelot III
- King Amunrud (Rudamon)
- King Iuput II
- King Sheshonq VI
- King Peftjauawybast
- King Nimlot (4)
- King Djehutiemhat

Dynasty 24

Tefnakht, the mayor of Sais, was trying to unite the struggling cities and families of Egypt and consolidate Egyptian powers under one ruler, the power of the Egyptian throne. He managed to unite the western and eastern Delta (north of Egypt) and marched with his army to the south, to

Thebes. However, a sudden turn of events occurred when he found the Army of Kush marching north towards Egypt. The Kushite king Piye defeated Tefnakht's army, putting an end to his ambitions

saw

- King Tefnakht
- King Bakenrenef (Bokchoris)
- King Padinemti

Dynasty 25 (The Kushite Dynasty)

Sometimes the kingdom located to the south of Egypt is called the Kushite kingdom, and sometimes it's referred to as the Nubian kingdom. It was called the Nubian kingdom because this region is considered Nubia. Nubia is a vast region extending from Kmo Ombo (north of Aswan) to Meroe (south of Napata). Many Egyptian priests, including Amun priests, escaped to Napata due to conflicts with Akhenaten and economic challenges after King Ramses IX. This external migration led to the development of a strong civilization outside Egypt. This kingdom later invaded Egypt. The primary deity for the Kushites was Amun. The Dynasty came to an end due to the Assyrian invasion of Egypt.

- King Alara (Alula)
- King Kashta

- King Piankhi (Piye)
- King Shabaka
- King Shabataka
- King Taharqa
- King Padibastet II (Petubastis)
- King Neferkare
- King Tenuetamun

Late Period

The power of the Assyrians increased in the Middle East, and they aimed to expand their kingdom, which led to invasions of various Middle Eastern kingdoms, including Egypt. The Assyrian kings Esarhaddon and Ashurbanipal conquered Egypt twice and defeated King Taharqa on both occasions. The first rulers of Dynasty 26 were essentially appointed by the Assyrians when they designated Nekau I as ruler of Sais, followed by his son Psametik. The late period includes dynasties 26, 27, 28, 29, and Dynasty 30.

Dynasty 26

Dynasty 26 marks the last powerful Egyptian Dynasty to rule Egypt. It represents the final renaissance of Ancient Egypt. Although brief, the rulers of this Dynasty managed to revive some of the features of the great civilization. King Psametik I is the true founder of Dynasty 26. The Dynasty's control over Egypt resulted from the Assyrian invasion, and its end came due to the Persian invasion.

- King Nekau I
- King Psametik I

- King Nekau II
- King Psametik II
- King Apries
- King Amasis
- King Psametik III

Dynasty 27

It's natural for nations to rise and fall. During this time, the Persian nation emerged with dreams of building a vast empire, leading to many battles and invasions under their rulers. Cambyses II defeated King Psamtik III at the Battle of Pelusium, resulting in Egypt being invaded once again. However, a curse seemingly followed Egypt's invaders. Cambyses faced a tragic fate and ultimately took his own life. The destruction of Memphis and Heliopolis is attributed to the Persians.

- King Cambyses II
- King Petubastis III
- King Darius I (The Great)
- King Xserxes I
- King Artaxerxes I (Longhand)
- King Darius II
- King Artaxerxes II Mnemon (Arsaces)

Dynasty 28

Amyrtaeus, possibly the mayor of Sais, rebelled against the Persians. While there was a previous rebellion led by Inaros against the Persians, it was not successful. The rule of King

Amyrtaeus was short-lived, as General Nefaarud rose against him and emerged victorious.

- King Amyrtaeus

Dynasty 29

General Nefaarud ended Dynasty 28 by defeating and executing King Amyrtaeus. Nefaarud became the king of Egypt and founded Dynasty 29. Mendes served as the capital during this Dynasty's time.

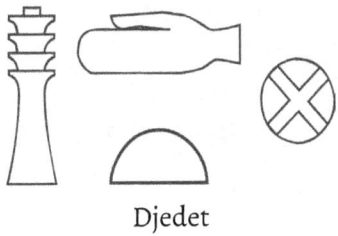

Djedet

- King Nefaarud I (Nepherites I)
- King Psammuthis
- King Akhoris
- King Nefaarud II (Nepherites II)

Dynasty 30

General Nectanebo, hailing from Sebennytos, took actions similar to those of King Nefaarud I (Dynasty 29) against King Nefaarud II (the last ruler of Dynasty 29). However, it is uncertain whether General Nectanebo killed King Nefaarud II or simply dethroned him.

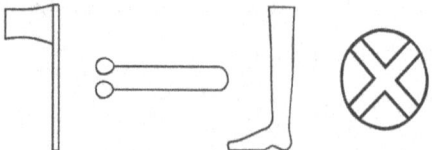

The Persians attacked Egypt during the time of Dynasty 30. There is a well-detailed story about Artaxerxes III's unsuccessful attempt to conquer Egypt.

- King Nectanebo I
- King Djedhor (Takhos, Teos)
- King Nectanebo II

Dynasty 31

The Persians made persistent efforts to reconquer Egypt. King Artaxerxes III led an invasion in 350 BC, but the campaign failed due to a high flood that coincided with the invasion, inundating the Delta. Eventually, the Persians succeeded in their attempts, and King Artaxerxes III invaded Egypt. The last king of Dynasty 30, Nectanebo II, disappeared during this invasion.

During the time of this invasion, we found that one of the mayors of Upper Egypt, called Khababash, claimed himself as the king of Egypt. He added the royal titles to his name and wrote it inside the cartouche. There is a granodiorite box in the Serapeum at Sakkara bearing the name of Khababash in the traditional royal style of Ancient Egypt.

- King Khabash

Khabash

The Primitive Techniques and Tools of the Pre-Dynastic and the Archaic Periods

When I discuss the tools and products of the predynastic Egyptians and the first two dynasties (Dynasty 1 and Dynasty 2), I'll organize them into classifications based on the materials used. Then, I'll explain the techniques employed by each craftsman.

The materials utilized by the predynastic Egyptians and the first two dynasties include flint, ivory, wood, leather, gold, clay, turquoise, lapis lazuli, and certain types of stones such as granite, granodiorite, and alabaster.

It's evident that the oldest culture in Egypt from the Neolithic era is the Faiyum A culture (9,000 BC – 6,000 BC). This culture emerged as the first after the cataclysm that occurred around 9,700 BC at the end of the last Ice Age. From Faiyum A culture to Naqqada III culture, a plethora of artifacts has been discovered across numerous sites in Egypt, both in the south and north. This extensive presence indicates that we are discussing a significant nation, not merely a small tribe striving to survive.

During the pre-dynastic period, Egyptians used flint stones and other types of hard stone to create blades. These blades served as weapons, such as arrows, as well as daily use tools like knives.

Fig. 55

Pottery

The Predynastic Ancient Egyptians recognized a significant need for containers to store liquids and perhaps various types of food. It's conceivable that they initially invented leather bags for this purpose. However, these leather bags might not have proven sufficient to fulfill their requirements. Consequently, they explored alternative solutions and successfully developed pottery jars.

The Egyptian environment boasts abundant sources of mud and clay, found both in the Nile River valley and the eastern and western deserts. This availability rendered these materials highly suitable for the pre-dynastic Egyptians to fashion into jars.

The Ancient Egyptian word for clay is Sint (Sent)

The Ancient Egyptian word for jar is Hnw (Henou)

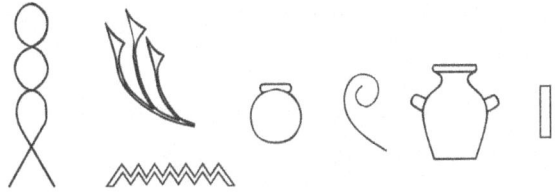

The Ancient Egyptian word for pottery is QrHt (Qerhet)

According to the widely accepted belief about human evolution, it's understood that humans began to settle and form agricultural communities by the end of the Stone Age. This suggests that the Ancient Egyptians likely began crafting pottery around the same time. They created jars, vessels, and plates for various purposes, including cooking, eating, and preserving food. Additionally, pottery was utilized as containers for items placed within tombs alongside the deceased.

Earlier, I mentioned Egypt's abundance of mud and clay. I want to clarify that Ancient Egyptians did not use mud or Nile silt to produce pottery. Instead, they utilized marl and Nile clay for this purpose. Along the Nile River, there's a high-quality supply of Nile clay, while the eastern and western deserts offer good-quality marl.

Clay, being a sticky substance, required careful manipulation. Ancient Egyptian potters had to blend this clay with sand, hay, straw, and sometimes even animal dung, especially cow dung. There are two main types of clay used as raw materials:

Pure and soft clay: Employed for crafting delicate jars and vessels.

Rough and dry clay: Utilized for creating larger jars and vessels that didn't demand high quality.

Another classification of pre-dynastic pottery products is based on the clay's composition:

- Clay with a high concentration of dung, iron compounds, and sand. When fired, this type takes on brown or red hues.
- Clay rich in calcium carbonate, with little to no dung and possibly some iron compounds. When fired, it exhibits black, yellow, or orange colors; a shorter firing time results in a red hue.

Before using the clay, it needed to be cleansed of small stones, gravel, or impurities. Water was added, and the mixture was kneaded to achieve the desired texture. The shaping was done by hand. Notably, designs from the early jars and vessels indicate that the pre-dynastic Egyptians did not initially invent or employ the pottery wheel (Fig. 55). It's believed that this development came later. Initially, they might have used a rudimentary form of the pottery wheel, rotated by hand. After shaping, the jar's sides could be smoothed using a substance akin to mud paint (mixture of mud and water). This aided in sealing the pottery's pores and enhancing its appearance. After shaping, the jar was left to dry in the sun or a sheltered area. Perhaps before complete drying, flint, shells, or other items were used to polish the external surface of the jar, ensuring a higher quality finish.

In a few instances, they created carvings or drawings of animals or geometric shapes on some pottery items. These were allowed to dry completely before use.

Fig. 5

Moving on to finished pottery, two types existed: polished surface and rough surface.

1. Polished Surface: This pottery was polished before it fully dried, smoothed either by hand or a tool. This type emerged due to the pre-dynastic Egyptians starting to fire pottery using kilns. Many of these polished jars and vessels were found empty, suggesting they might have been made for decorative purposes. Over time, some of these items were further embellished with carvings

and drawings. These decorations ranged from simple and small to more intricate designs that covered larger areas of the jar.

2. Rough Surface: This type of pottery was crafted by hand, without efforts to polish it. These jars and vessels had not only rough surfaces but also thicker walls. Such pottery was used for cooking and storing water or other liquids (Figure 56).

Ancient Egyptian potters mixed clay with water and shaped jars or vessels by hand, allowing them to dry in the sun. However, this type of pottery wasn't very durable. The technique was refined later, involving the use of ovens (fire). After sun-drying, the items were placed in the oven again to become solid. Some pots had black stains due to the presence of burnt ashes, indicating that fire dried the pottery and changed its color.

The typical color of pottery is brown, but the firing process could alter this. Cooking in a smoky fire led to blackening, while a short firing could result in red hues. Before using clay, impurities were removed, water was added, and the mixture kneaded to reach the desired consistency. The pottery was shaped by hand, and initially, the potter's wheel was not used extensively, though a rudimentary form might have been employed.

After shaping, the jar was sun-dried, often with external smoothing. Flint, shells, or other materials were sometimes used to polish the exterior while still not completely dry. This enhanced the quality of the pottery. The diversity of pottery from the pre-dynastic era and the first two dynasties of Ancient Egypt reveals a rich cultural and artistic history.

Jar
Rim
Neck
Body
Base

Bowl
Rim
Body
Base

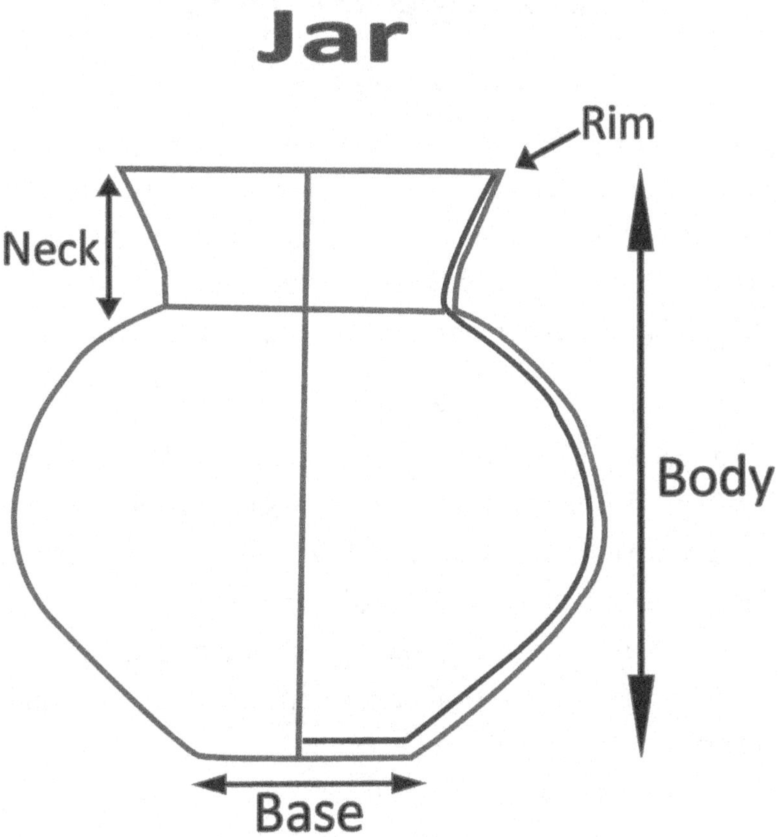

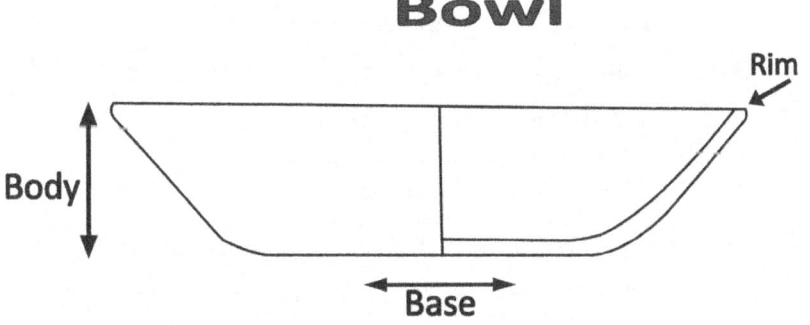

Upper Egyptian Cultures

Fayum A

The pottery of Fayum was made of low-quality clay containing lots of straw. Fayum jars and vessels were unicolor, red only or black only, but most of these objects were red. It was made totally by hand. The rim is not straight, there is no neck, and the walls of the jar are not symmetrical or harmonic.

Merimde

The pottery of Merimde is primitive and could be older than Fayum pottery or at least from the same era. Merimde jars and vessels were unicolor, red only or black only, but most of these objects were red. It was made totally by hand.

The rim is not straight, there is no neck, and the walls of the jar are not symmetrical or harmonic. But there are some unique features with Merimde pottery:

1- In many jars and vessels there are handles.

2- In some jars and vessels, there are pierced knobs (it takes the shape of a button) below the rim.

3- Some pots had two compartments.

The rim is not straight, there is no neck and the walls of the jar are not symmetrical or harmonic.

Omari

The pottery of Omari was made of marl and clay, they added some organic materials and sometimes it contained minerals. Omari jars and vessels were unicolor, red only or black only, but most of these objects were red. It was made totally by hand.

Omari pottery is very close to Fayum pottery and Merimde pottery. Omari pottery was made by hand, but it seems that they used some techniques, like coiling techniques, and they used something to concave the inner surface of the base.

Some of the Omari pottery has knobs below the rim, and there are no decorations on the walls of the jars, but we started to see jars with necks from Omari culture.

Badari

I can say the pottery industry in the Badari culture was much better than the earlier cultures; the Ancient Egyptian potter became more qualified and more talented in making pottery.

The pottery of Badari was made of good quality clay which contains organic materials like chaff and straw.

I can say that the Badarian pottery was also handmade, but it had some new features than the earlier pottery:
1. The surfaces of the jars and vessels are smoothed.
2. The rim was blackened (shiny black color).
3. The pots were usually burnished surfaces.
4. The surfaces of the pots started to have decorations.

The decoration above the Badarian pottery was wavy lines made in a good shape; these wavy lines were etched on the surfaces with a good order. It's most likely that the tool which was used to create such wavy lines was a kind of a comb or a fishbone.

There is another culture in Upper Egypt called Tasa Culture, and because the Tasian pottery is very close to the Badarian pottery, I didn't include it as a separate title.

A special type of vessel was found in the Tasian tombs; this type is called the Bell-Shaped vessel, and it has horizontal lines and wavy lines as decoration. The surfaces of this type of vessel were black polished, and the decorations were filled in white color.

Naqada I

The pottery industry of Naqada I culture developed in many ways, and we can recognize the artistic touch on the surfaces of the jars and vessels. Naqada pottery was made from clay with organic materials and clay without organic materials (marl), and it was made totally by hand.

There were 3 types of Naqada pottery according to the color:
- Polished red surface, without decoration.
- Polished red surface with black rim.
- Polished red surface with black rim and decorated.

I can say that the most important pottery from Naqada culture is the pottery decorated with geometrics and shapes (human, animals, birds, and more). Flinders Petrie called it the Pottery with white crossed lines. When this white color was analyzed, they found that it is white clay, and it seems that Naqada was an important place for this type of pottery. There is another type of Naqada pottery that was decorated with 3D designs (mainly animals like elephants, crocodiles, and lizards).

Naqada II

Jars and vessels, Naqada II pottery was made from clay with organic materials and clay without organic materials (marl), and it was of better quality than the clay used in the previous cultures. In Naqada II, they produced what we can call the pottery with red drawings and the pottery with wavy handles. Both were made of smoothed red pottery but not polished.

The pottery of Naqada II was made by hand, but the firing technique (kilns) was developed in a better way. Naqada II pottery is full of "decorations". There are so many drawings of boats, animals, birds, humans, geometric shapes, and wavy lines. In some cases, the jar itself was designed in the shape of a bird or an animal. This makes Naqada II pottery a great source of information about Naqada culture.

Naqada III

Naqada III was almost the same like Naqada II, the only difference or what I can call it development is that the potter of Naqada III maybe used the Potter wheel, I think it was the beginning of potter wheels which was developed later during the dynasties, so that wheel was slow wheel was rotated by hand.

During the Naqada cultures, potters imitated the designs and colors of the jars, vessels, and pots made of stones (basalt, alabaster, granite, and other types of stones).

Lower Egyptian Cultures

Buto - Maadi

Pottery of Lower Egypt was made from clay with organic materials, clay without organic materials, and marl (we understand that this marl is from Upper Egypt because there is no marl in Lower Egypt). There are two types of pots from Lower Egypt Cultures:

1. Pottery was produced by hand.
2. Pottery was produced by the slow pottery wheel.

I can say that many features from the pottery of Upper Egypt Cultures exist in the pottery of Lower Egypt. The surfaces were done well, polished, and painted with decorations. Some decorations were painted in white color. Also, there were knobs under the rim in many jars and vessels. We can see that many of the jars had short or long necks. Some of the jars had inside decorations. The pottery of Lower Egypt had red color and brown color. There are some claims saying that some of the pottery of Lower Egypt has Palestinian origin (Palestinian style) or Syrian origin, but I disagree with these claims. From all the above details in this chapter, we can understand that the Predynastic Egyptians invented and developed the pottery industry from scratch.

Archaic Period

Pottery of the Archaic Period (Dynasty 1 and Dynasty 2) was mainly made from Nile silt. They also used marl, but not as much as the silt. The manufacture of the pottery of the Archaic Period was similar to the techniques of the previous eras. Maybe the potter's wheel was more developed than before because in some vessels, we can see regular lines decorating the external surfaces and sometimes the internal surfaces. But we must know that the potters of the Archaic Period didn't stop producing handmade pottery, as thousands or tens of thousands of handmade pottery were found from this era. The pottery during this era was red and brown in color. The surfaces were smoothed and polished well. The strange thing about the pottery of the Archaic Period is the decoration. I can say it is rare to find jars or vessels from this era with decorations on the surfaces like the ones of Naqada cultures, but some jars had big handles.

Many of the pottery items from the Archaic Period were large storage jars and tall jars for wine and beer. Some jars were made in a special style called "tapering body," where the size of the body decreased from bottom to top or the opposite. Some jars were made with the ovoid style and the globular style. In many of these jars, we can see the serkh, which includes the name of the king, inscribed on the shoulder of the jar.

Ivory

There are big collections of different products from ivory that were made during the predynastic era. The source of the ivory in Ancient Egypt was the tusks of elephants and the teeth of hippos. We understand that hippos used to live in Egypt, and maybe more so in the south of Egypt, but what about elephants? Most opinions, if not all, will tell you that the Ancient Egyptians used to import ivory from nearby African countries. I don't agree with this story. I believe that there were elephants in Ancient Egypt for two main reasons:

1. We have an island in Aswan called Elephantine Island, and the Ancient Egyptian name for this island is "Abu," which means elephant.
2. The Ancient Egyptian language contains the word "Abu" (elephants) and many other words that include parts of the elephant in the structure, like the word "Behdet," which contains the tusk of the elephant,

among many other examples. So, I say if the language includes symbols and words related to the elephant, the elephant must have existed in the Ancient Egyptian environment.

The pre-dynastic Egyptians had made many products from ivory, such as combs, statuettes, and small labels for pottery jars. Many decorated ivories were found from the pre-dynastic era, like the Hierakonpolis decorated ivories. These ivories were decorated with human figures (in ritual performances and as prisoners), birds, and different kinds of animals. Many knife-handles were also found from the pre-dynastic era, and most of them were decorated with birds and animal figures, like the knife-handle in the Metropolitan Museum (Carnarvon knife-handle), which is decorated with different animals like elephants, lions, deer, and bulls. There is also a line of stork birds in the top part of this handle.

Many ivory combs and small ivory labels were found from the pre-dynastic era. These combs and labels record much information about this era, and we managed to extract some data about the pre-dynastic era from these objects, like the comb of King Djet and the Davis comb.

Djet comb

Davis comb

EGYPT BEFORE THE WRITTEN HISTORY

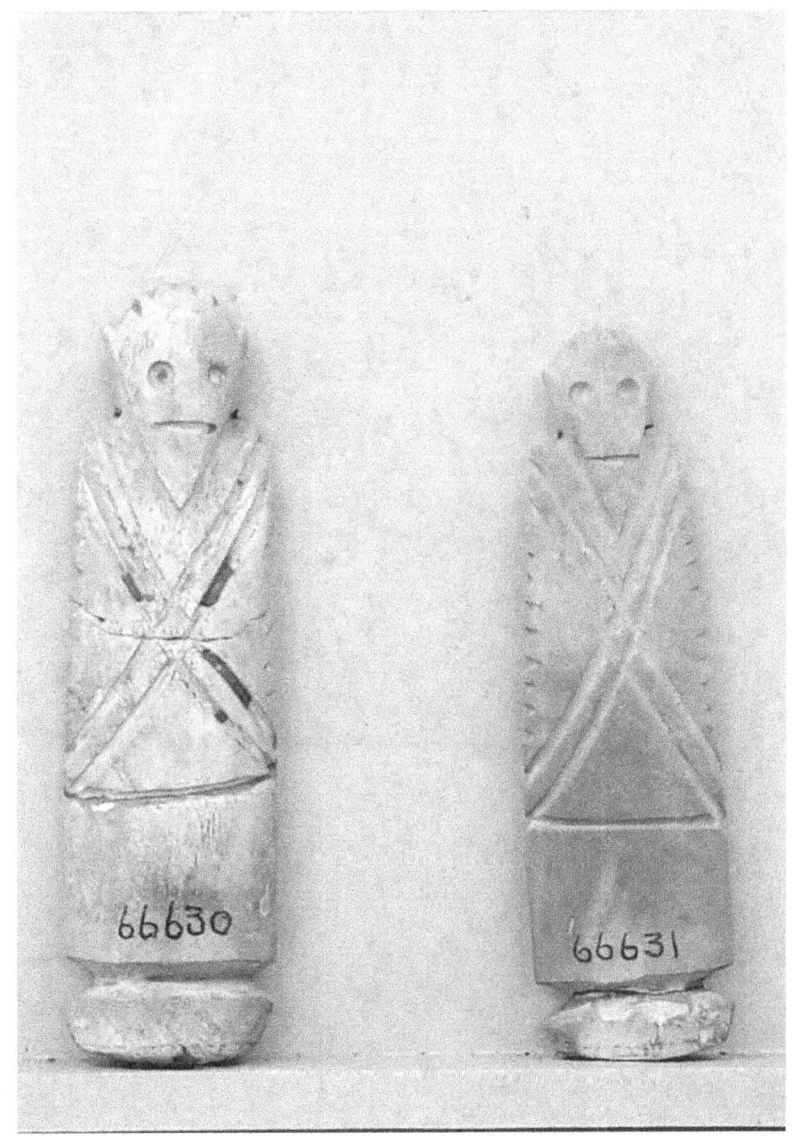

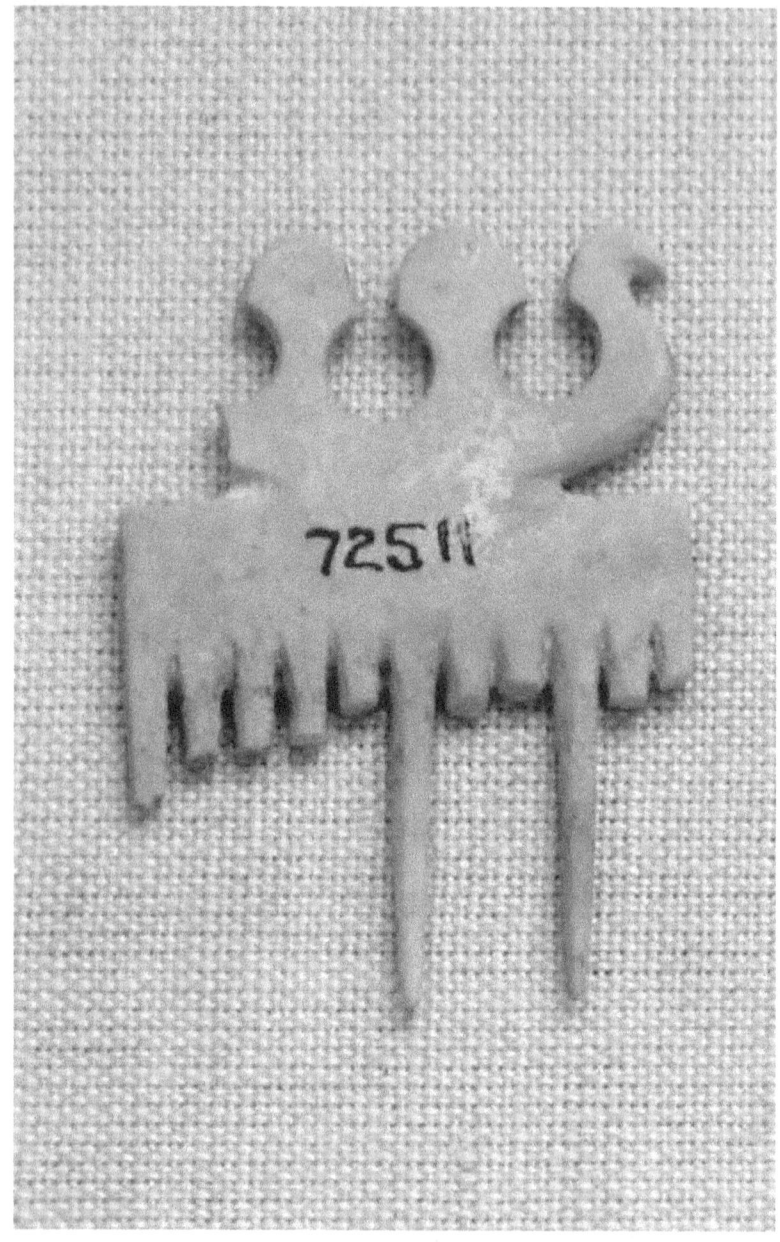

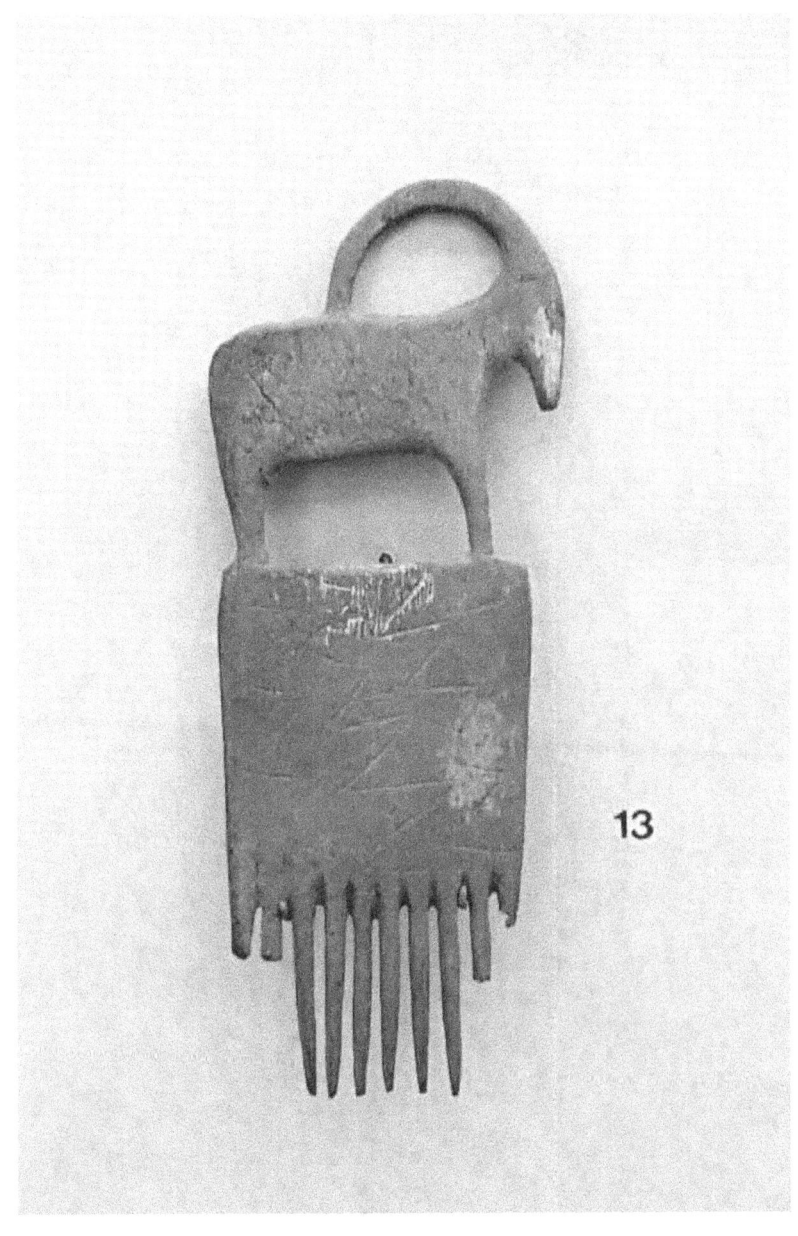

13

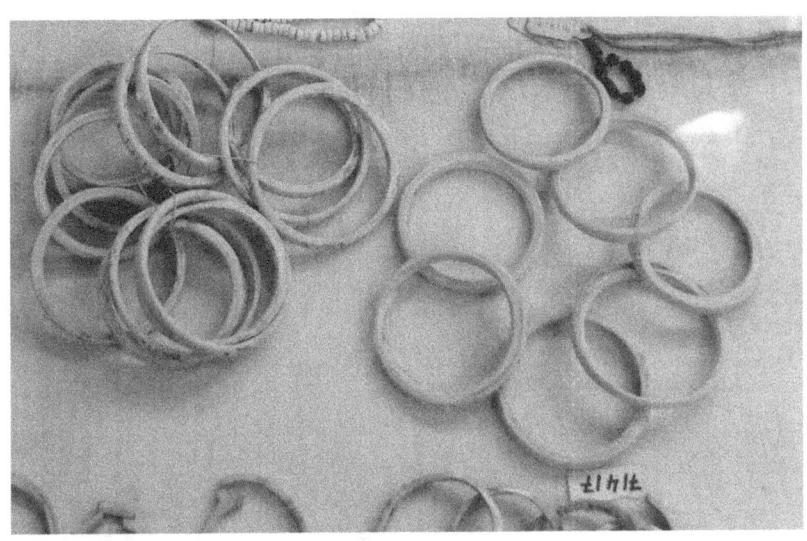

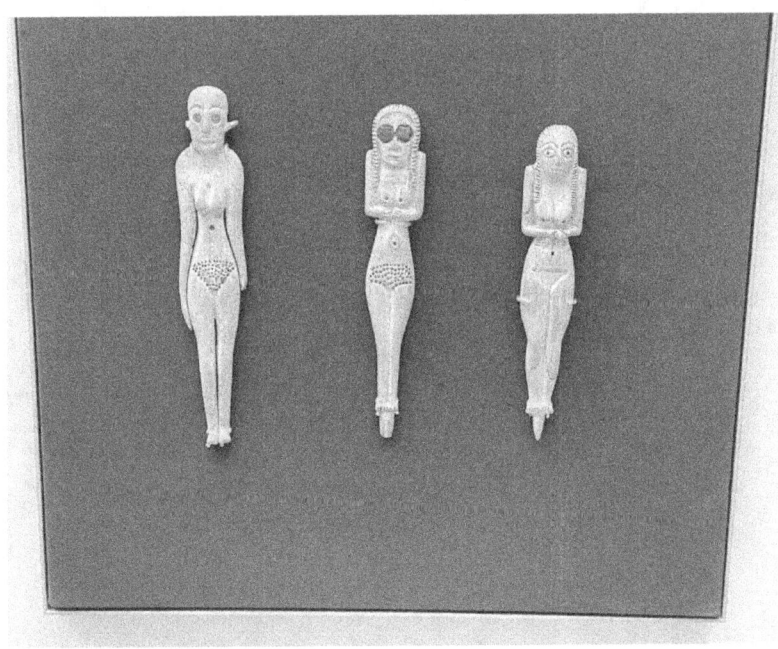

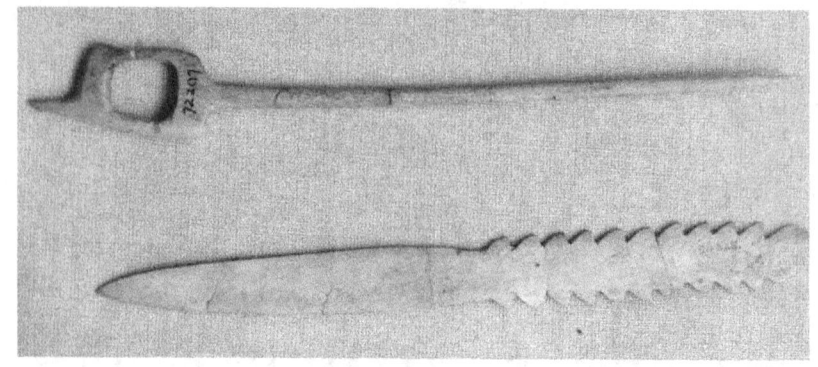

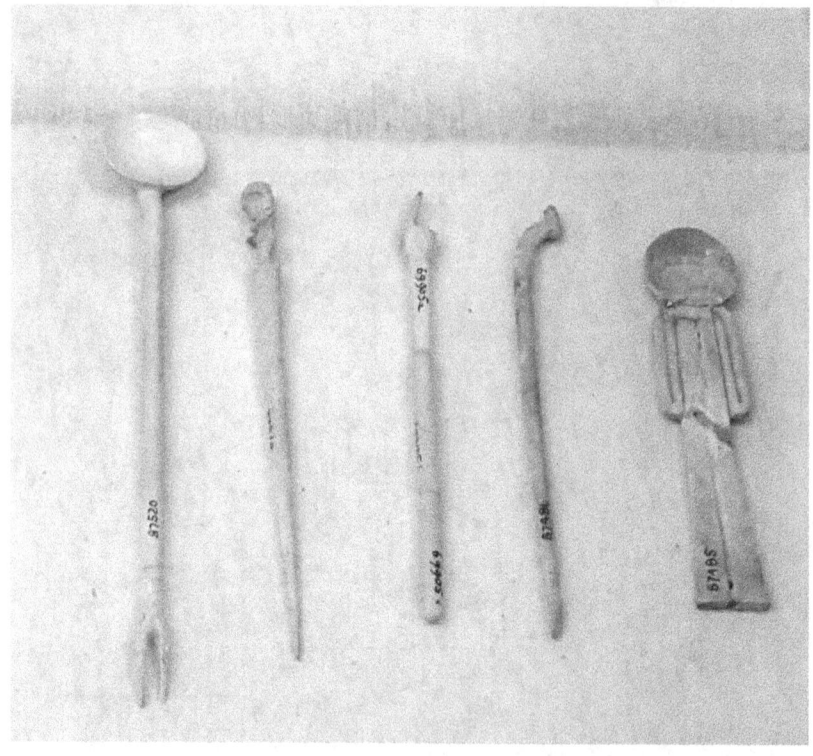

Stone vessels

There are so many stone vessels that were found inside the tombs of the pre-dynastic Egyptians. These vessels were made from different kinds of stones. Some were made of very hard stones like granite and diorite, while others were made of medium-hard stones like alabaster and slate. These vessels represent a huge mystery and open the way for many questions. I will not answer this question here in this chapter; you will find the answer in the following chapter.

Metal tools

Not many metal products were produced by the predynastic Egyptians, and all the metal products that were found from the predynastic Egyptians were made from copper and bronze. Gold was also used during the time of the predynastic Egyptians. Many of the objects were plated with gold leaves, like some of the handles and a few statues. But the most interesting object is a small tube made from lapis lazuli attached to a tube made from gold. Additionally, there is a collection of necklaces and bracelets made from semi-precious stones, and some of the beads are made from gold.

EGYPT BEFORE THE WRITTEN HISTORY

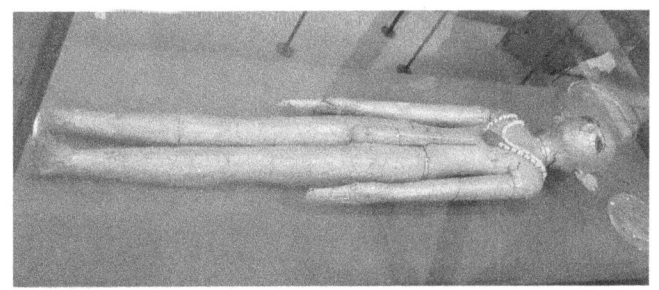

The mystery of the stone vessels from the Pre-Dynastic Era

Within the tombs of the pre-dynastic Egyptians and the Archaic period, numerous stone vessels, jars, and pots were discovered alongside other primitive items such as pottery and ivory products. While the style of the pottery jars and pots can be reasonably attributed to the pre-dynastic Egyptians and the Archaic period, it is not at all acceptable to claim that the stone vessels were crafted by the same people. If Egyptologists who make this assertion were to take just 10 minutes to contemplate it, they would recognize the substantial disparity between the rudimentary pottery jars and the exceptionally high-quality stone vessels.

Those responsible for curating the pre-dynastic section in the Egyptian Museum in Cairo should acknowledge the marked differences between the pottery products and the stone vessels. Why, for instance, were both placed in the same display case? When we explain the gradual evolution of pottery jars from being shaped entirely by hand to the eventual invention of the pottery wheel by the end of Dynasty 2, it becomes clear that attributing the stone vessels to the same era is problematic. These vessels required sophisticated tools for their creation—

tools that were far from primitive, such as flint blades or other sharp stones.

Before delving further into the subject of stone vessels during the Predynastic period, it's important to introduce the concept of mineral hardness. This will help us comprehend the challenges faced by Ancient Egyptian workers as they produced these exquisite vessels. In 1822, Friedrich Mohs, a German geologist and mineralogist, devised the Mohs scale of mineral hardness. This scale illustrates the scratch resistance of various minerals, providing insight into the capacity of harder materials to scratch softer ones.

Mohs Hardness	Mineral Name	Chemical Formula
1	Talc	$Mg_3Si_4O_{10}(OH)_2$
2	Gypsum	$CaSO_4 \cdot 2H_2O$
3	Calcite	$CaCO_3$
4	Fluorite	CaF_2
5	Apatite	$Ca_5(PO_4)_3(OH^-,Cl^-,F^-)$
6	Orthoclase feldspar	$KAlSi_3O_8$
7	Quartz	SiO_2
8	Topaz	$Al_2SiO_4(OH^-,F^-)_2$
9	Corundum	Al_2O_3
10	Diamond	C

There is another challenge beside the mineral hardness, it is the origin of the stone, local origin, and foreign origin.

Local origin

The Ancient Egyptians were very knowledgeable about the different kinds of stones that existed in Egypt. We have many examples of vessels from the pre-dynastic era that were made of different types of stone.

- Diorite
- Rose granite from Aswan: the Ancient Egyptians used many kinds of granite, but the favorite type of granite for them was the rose granite, I think it was because the amount of quartz inside the molecular structure (20% – 60%).
- Alabaster from Hatnub (near El-Minya) and El Amarna.

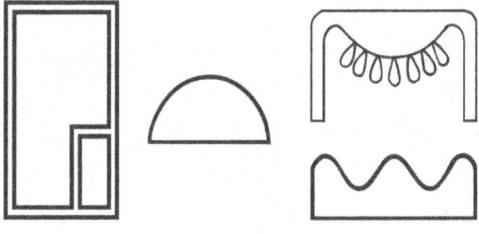

Hatnub

- Granodiorite from Red Sea Governorate
- Basalt stone from Faiyum and Beni Suef
- Slate (Schist stone)

The Schist Disc at Cairo Museum

EGYPT BEFORE THE WRITTEN HISTORY

EGYPT BEFORE THE WRITTEN HISTORY

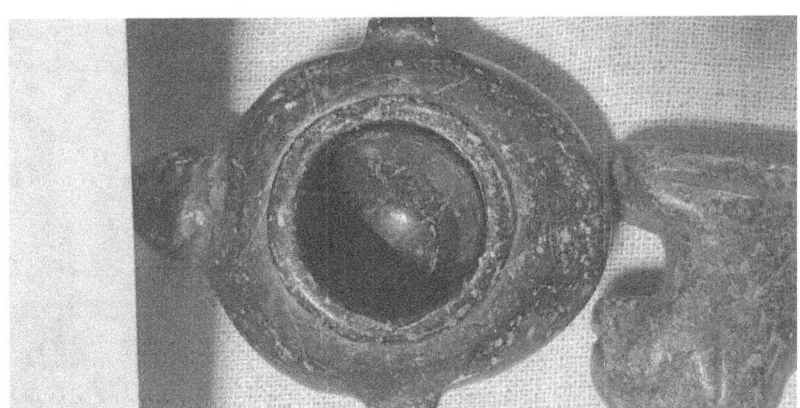

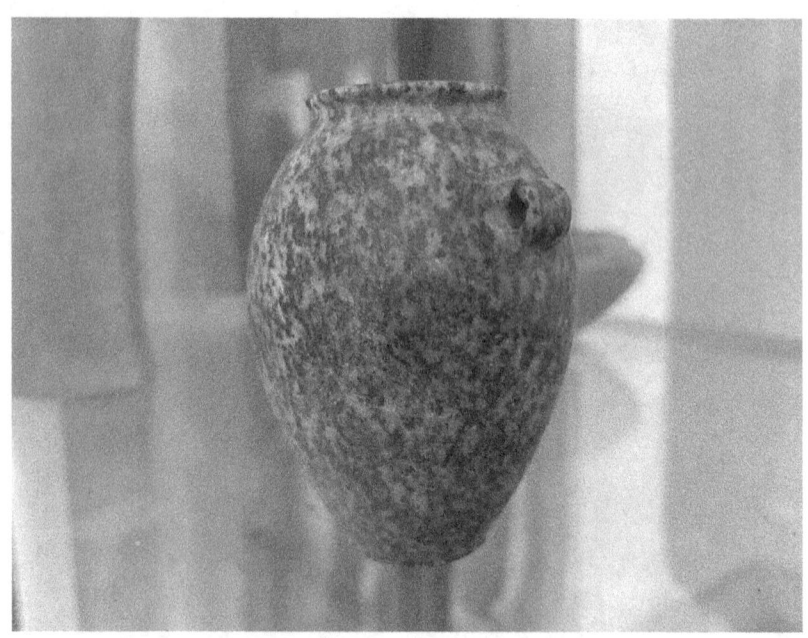

Egypt Before the Written History

Mohamed Ibrahim Elbassiouny

EGYPT BEFORE THE WRITTEN HISTORY

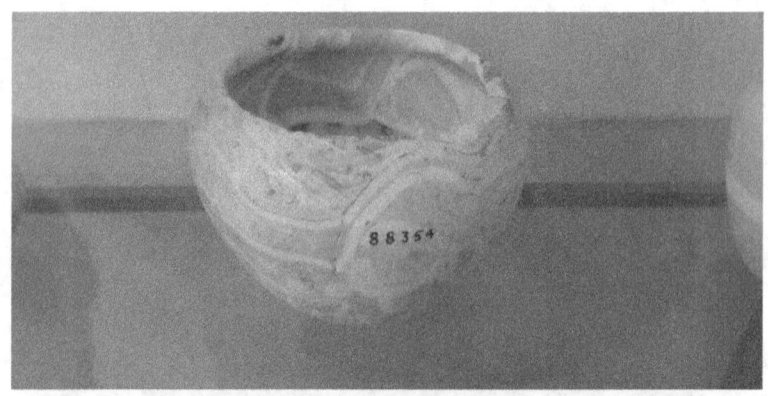

EGYPT BEFORE THE WRITTEN HISTORY

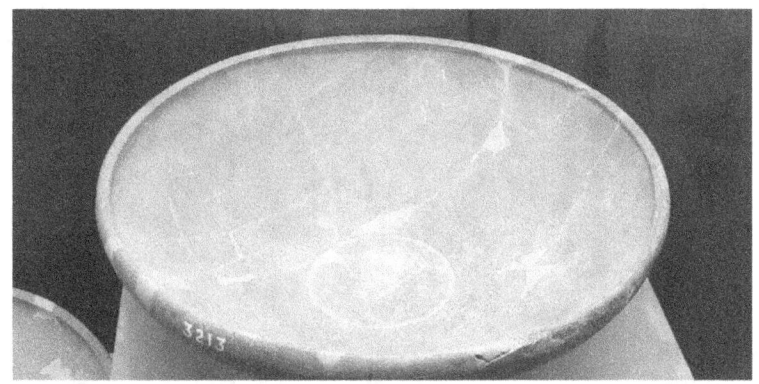

233

EGYPT BEFORE THE WRITTEN HISTORY

EGYPT BEFORE THE WRITTEN HISTORY

Mohamed Ibrahim Elbassiouny

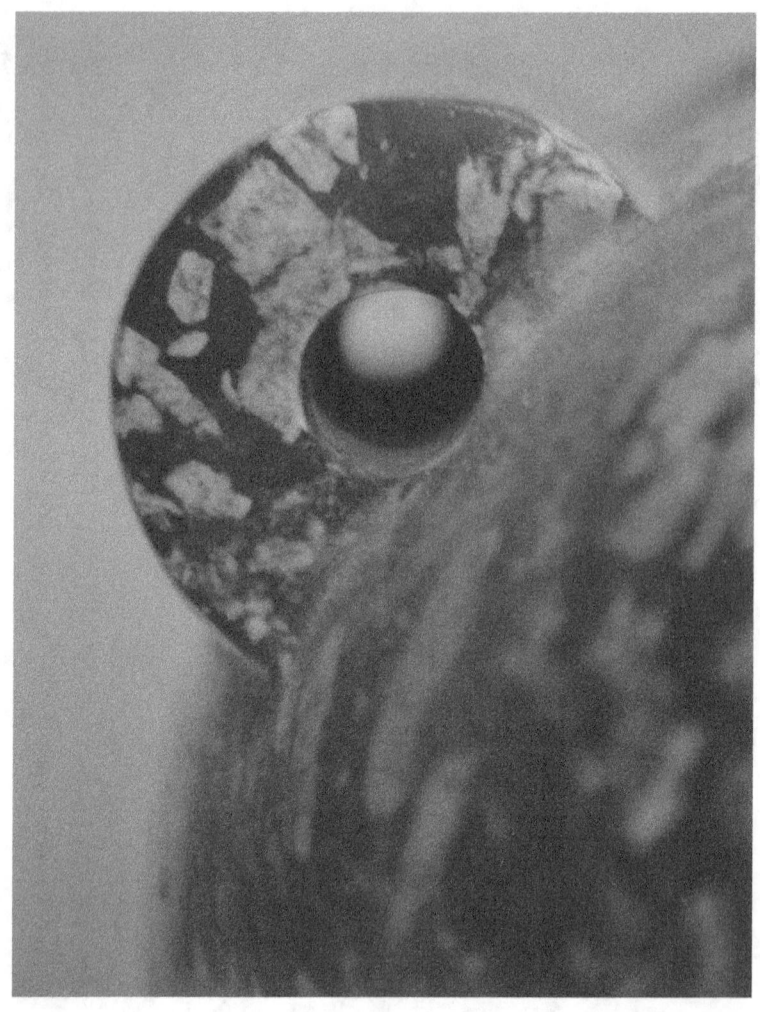

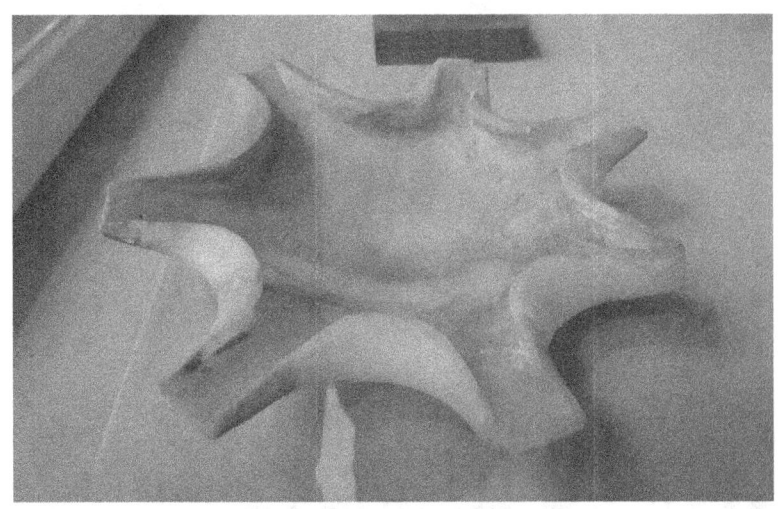

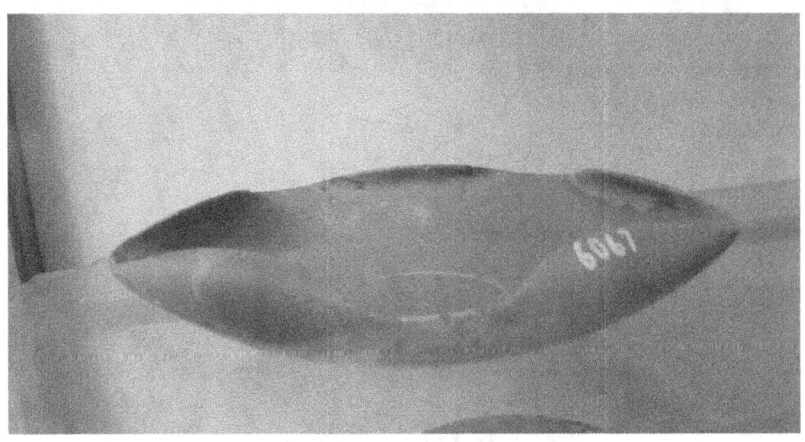

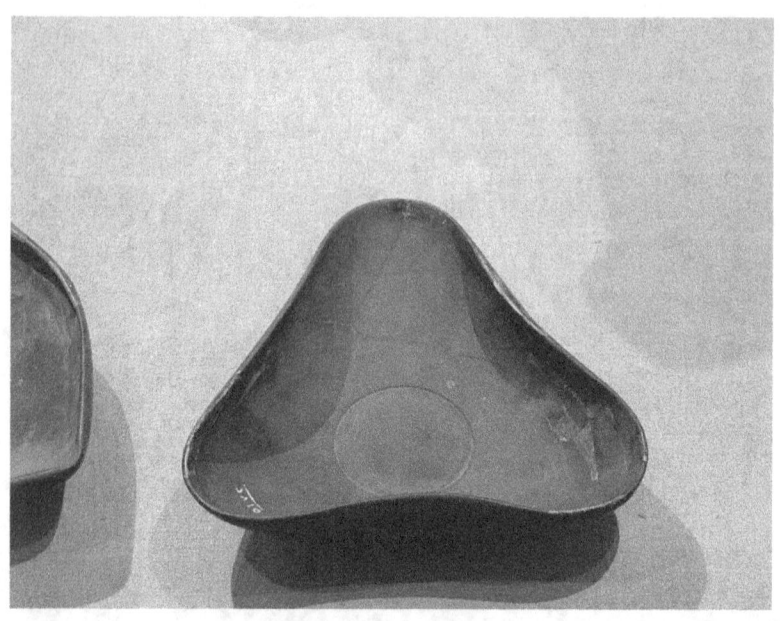

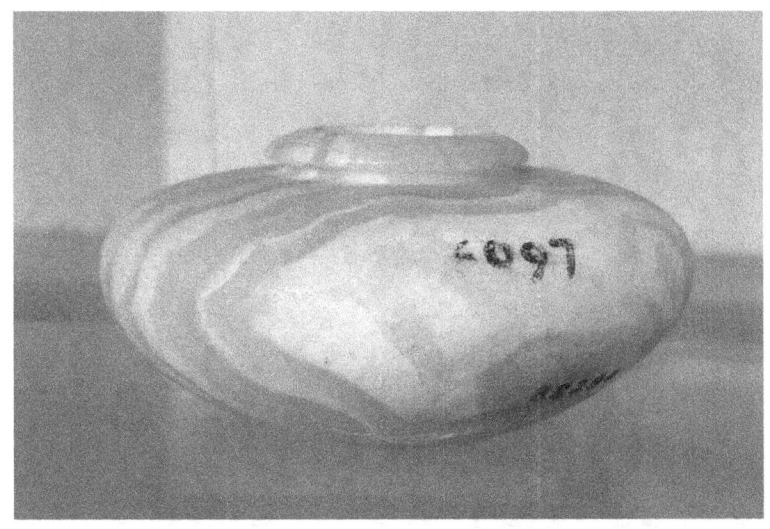

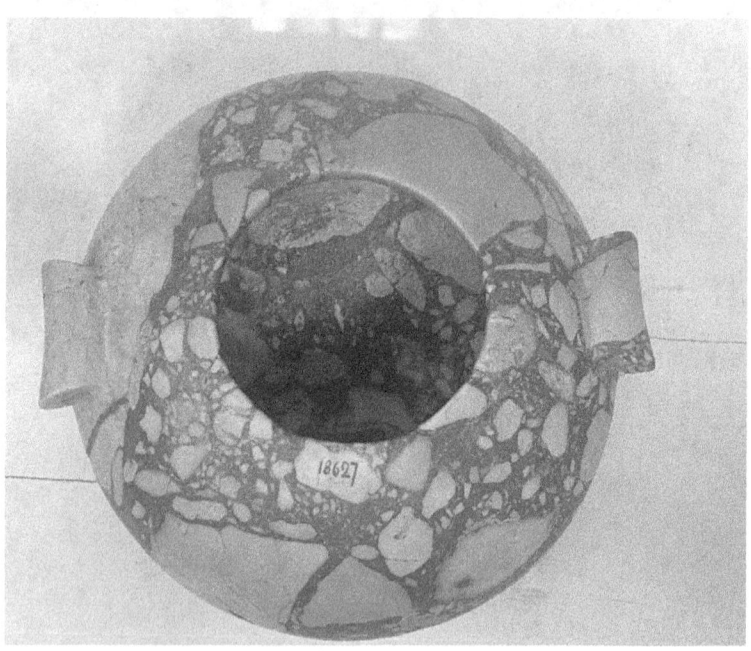

EGYPT BEFORE THE WRITTEN HISTORY

Foreign origin

- Amethyst, I think I can call it purple quartz, Amethyst doesn't exist in Egypt, it exists in many other countries which are not near to Egypt, like Nigeria, Zambia and India. Amethyst is 7 on Mohs scale.
- Lapis Lazuli, because the use of Lapis Lazuli in a very wide scale in Ancient Egypt, most of the people think it is local Egyptian stone, but it is not, it comes from Afghanistan. Lapis Lazuli is 5 on Mohs scale.

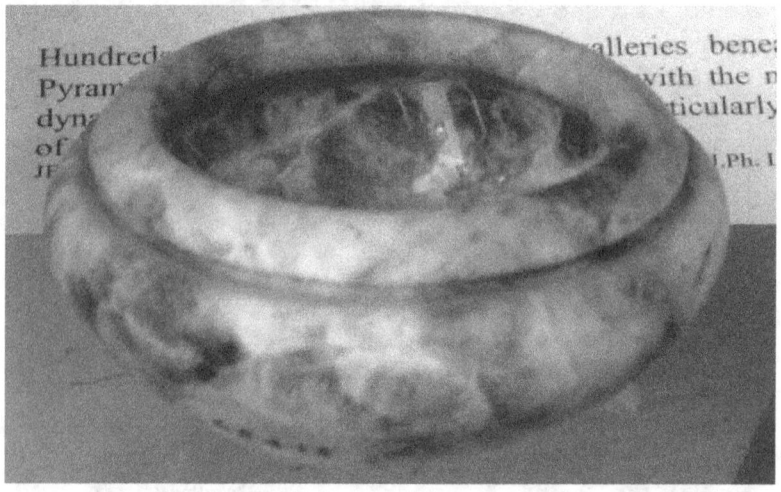

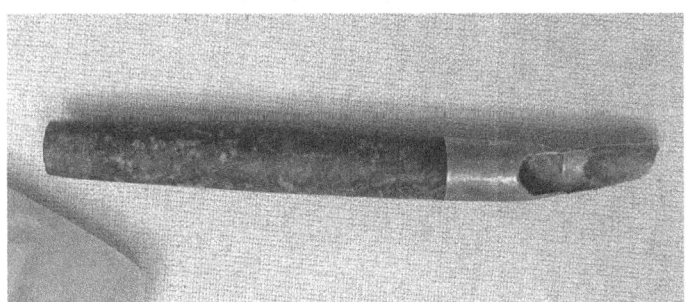

By examining these jars, we will find that making them was an easy job and there is not any indication of development for the manufacture of these jars.

When tourist groups visit one of the Alabaster factories on the West Bank of Luxor, they show a demonstration of how they make Alabaster jars using manual tools. Then they show them a high-quality jar that is heavier and explain to the tourist group that this shiny, heavy jar was made by a machine and it took 10 minutes to be made, while the handmade one takes from 10 to 14 days to be completed.

The interior of these jars is hollow and takes on the curvy shape of the exterior, and it is highly polished.

The very high quality of these jars reflects the existence of high technology and very efficient tools. You can see this clearly when you examine the rim, neck, body, and base of each jar.

There are some jars with very narrow necks and wide bodies, which would create a significant challenge for our modern machines.

If the Predynastic people didn't have the technology to make these jars, then who made them and when?

- These jars were made using high technology.
- These jars were made in an era before the Predynastic Egyptians.

The Sequence of the Tomb Development from the Pre-Dynastic Egyptians to the End of the Dynasties.

One of the widely held pieces of information that you'll frequently encounter in books is the idea that kings constructed pyramids as everlasting, fortified tombs for their bodies.

Pr Dt (per djet) means the eternal house. In the Ancient Egyptian belief, this title is referring to the tomb.

The word coffin/tomb equipment in the Ancient Egyptian language is Qrsw (Qersu), so the eternal house (tomb) must be furnished with the funeral equipment.

I can easily say, "Of course this is wrong information, completely wrong information—logic and science are against this claim, but because this information has been repeated constantly for more than 2000 years, I will explain the development of the funeral structures in Ancient Egypt, including the pyramids."

It has been hypothesized that the early Ancient Egyptians paid attention to the surrounding elements of nature and realized that each element has a cycle that appears and disappears (birth and death) daily, weekly, monthly, and yearly. The Ancient Egyptians understood that because of these cycles, there must be another life after death and the deceased will be alive again to start a new journey, but in the afterlife. When the Ancient Egyptians got this belief, they started to provide the tombs with equipment and food so the deceased could use them during their afterlife journey. Not only this, but they also understood that the body must stay in good condition, so they "invented mummification" and developed their tombs to protect the body from wild animals first and from tomb robbers later.

The story of death and resurrection is the excuse used to explain why the Ancient Egyptians built most of their constructions, especially the pyramids.

A) The tomb in Ancient Egypt was originally a very simple pit in the ground. This pit was an oval or rectangular shape, and it was 1-2 meters deep under the ground. They placed the corpse on its right side (like a fetus inside the womb) surrounded by 3 or 4 pottery vessels and jars.

This kind of pit was not enough to protect the body and the funeral equipment, so they had to dig deeper into the ground, and the bottom of the tomb became 2-4 meters under the ground. They placed some dry plants with some stones above the pit to provide more protection.

This development was not enough; they had to make a serious change to the style of the tomb. They dug a deep shaft 5-12 meters under the ground and built a structure of one floor above this shaft. Inside this structure, there are many rooms for the funeral equipment of the deceased, and they added later what we call funeral furniture. This style of tomb is what we call a Mastaba tomb.

B) The first types of Mastaba tombs were built with mud-bricks, and later they started to add some stone blocks to the structure. These stone blocks were mainly limestone and maybe some other kind of stones. I saw a huge block of rose granite at the Egyptian Museum in Cairo; it has the name of King Peribsen from Dynasty 2. This block seems to be part of a gate or a door jamb.

With the beginning of Dynasty 3, they started to use more limestone in constructions and began to build the style of Mastabas as we know. This style lasted until the end of the Old Kingdom era.

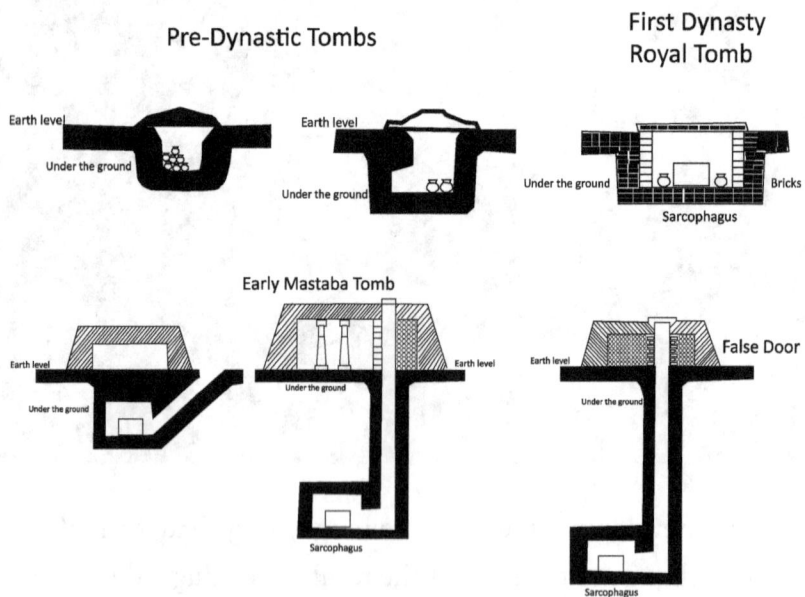

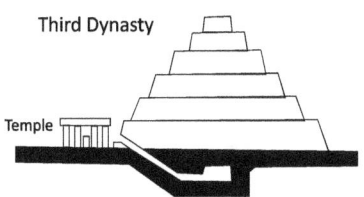 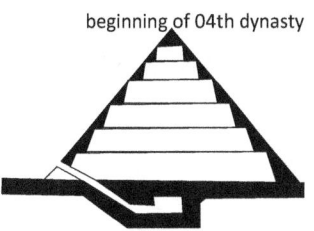

So, from the time of Dynasty 3, we started to see professional work and designs for the Mastaba tombs, and suddenly the Mastaba tombs were developed in a great way.

D) Six Mastabas were built above each other, creating what we call the Step Tomb or the Step Pyramid of Saqqara.

According to the writings inside the Step Pyramid and the surrounding area, this pyramid is attributed to King Netjerikhet (Djoser). With the name Netjerikhet, we saw another name for a non-royal person called Imhotep (ii m hotep).

Imhotep is the mastermind of Dynasty 3, and one of the masterminds of the Egyptian Civilization. Imhotep has many titles, but I believe the three most important titles are:
- The Chancellor of the King
- The High Priest of Iunu (Heliopolis)
- The Supervisor of the Royal Constructions at Upper and Lower Egypt

It is strongly believed that Imhotep is the architect of the Step Pyramid. If we don't think so, it would be a big problem in the sequence of development, as the Step Pyramid was built as a huge step of evolution.

Before the Step Pyramid, there was the Mastaba tomb style which consisted of one Mastaba. They didn't build Mastaba tombs with 2 or 3 mastabas above each other. However, the Step Pyramid had 6 Mastabas stacked above each other. There is also an interesting granite box lying at the base of the shaft under the pyramid (28 meters). This box, or as they call it, "the vault," consists of 32 big pieces of rose Aswanian granite.

On the southern side of the pyramid, there is a deep shaft under the ground called the southern tomb. There is another "vault" consisting of 32 large pieces of rose Aswanian granite at a depth of 28 meters under the ground. I can say it is a copy of the shaft under the pyramid. The Step Pyramid was considered a stairway that leads to the sky (heaven).

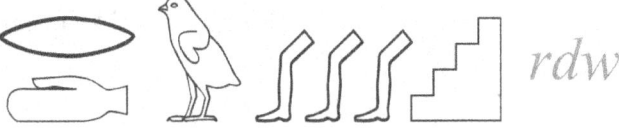 *rdw*

After the Step Pyramid of Djoser, King SekhemKhet ordered the construction of a step pyramid for himself, a pyramid of 7 mastabas stacked on top of each other, but it wasn't finished. The interesting thing is that the name Imhotep was found written on the enclosure wall of this pyramid.

The pyramid of SekhemKhet is called the Buried Pyramid. I believe it was built to be similar to Djoser's Step Pyramid or slightly bigger.

The construction of pyramids became very popular during Dynasty 3. There are 2 pyramids at Zawyet El Aryan that are attributed to Dynasty 3.

The 2 pyramids were discovered by Alexander Barasanti, and a few years later George Reisner conducted some digging and research in the surrounding area.

- The Unfinished Pyramid (the northern pyramid)

It is attributed to King Nebka (Neb-Ka), maybe he is the first king of Dynasty 3 who is also known as Sanakht.

There is an opinion that suggests this pyramid was built by King Baka (Ba-Ka) or Bikheris according to Manetho's king list. This king might be the son of King Djedefre of Dynasty 4, and they say that the unfinished pyramid of Zawyet El Aryan is very similar to the unfinished pyramid at Abu Rawash.

- The Layer Pyramid

It is attributed to King Khaba (Kha-Ba), who is also known as Neb-Ka-Ra, so maybe he is the one who built the Unfinished pyramid in Zawyet El Aryan, and this name Nebka is part of his name Nebkara.

This pyramid is very close to the Buried Pyramid of King Sekhemkhet, and it was designed to be a step pyramid.

It was called the Layer Pyramid because there are 14 layers of mud bricks surrounding the first Mastaba of this pyramid. One of the main features of the pyramids of Dynasty 3 is underground designs, or the tunnels under the pyramid, like the network of tunnels under Djoser's Step Pyramid.

E) King Huni, the last king of Dynasty 3, decided to build a pyramid at Meidum. It is not clear why he didn't build the pyramid at Sakkara like his ancestors. According to famous explanations by most Egyptologists, this pyramid was the middle stage between the step pyramid shape and the true pyramid shape. The Meidum pyramid was designed as a step pyramid first, and they were planning to cover the sides of the mastabas with limestone casing stones to create what we call a true pyramid.

The pyramids of Dynasty 3 have the entrance of the descending tunnel at the base level on the northern side of the pyramid. The descending passage was cut into the bedrock itself. King Huni didn't complete the pyramid, and King Sneferu is the one who completed this pyramid.

The famous reason for having unfinished pyramids or other unfinished structures is often attributed to the death of the king before completing the job. However, I don't fully agree with this opinion. There are some pyramids that were built in various locations in Egypt and were attributed to King Sneferu, but these pyramids do not reflect the same high quality, and they are quite small. Examples include the pyramids of Elephantine, Seila, Sinki, Kula, and Edfu.

F) After Dynasty 3, they continued building pyramids on a wide scale. King Sneferu built 2 pyramids at Dahshur. He first built the Bent Pyramid and then he built the Red Pyramid.

King Sneferu, as we know, is the founder of Dynasty 4, and he and his successors are considered the Great Pyramid builders.

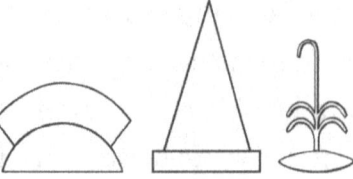

The Ancient Egyptian name for the **Bent** pyramid is The Southern Shining Pyramid.

The Ancient Egyptian name for the **Red** pyramid is (The Shining Pyramid).

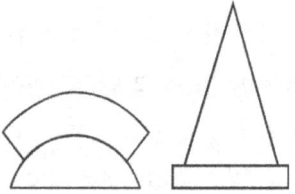

There is a very famous story about the Dahshur pyramids that says that the engineers who designed the Bent Pyramid made a "big" mistake with the wide angle of 54°27'44". They found that this wide angle would cause significant problems for the pyramid and could potentially lead to its collapse. To avoid this, they had to change the angle at a height of 47.04 meters. The new angle became 43°22', and the height after the bend is 57.67 meters. It appears that the Bent Pyramid project was considered a significant failure, leading the king to decide to build another pyramid just 2 km north of the Bent pyramid. This pyramid is known as the Red Pyramid and is referred to by Egyptologists as the first TRUE pyramid. The sloping angle of this pyramid is the same as the sloping angle of the Bent pyramid, 43°22' after the bend.

The three pyramids – Meidum, the Bent, and the Red pyramid – have the entrance of the descending tunnel on the higher level of the northern side of the pyramid. The descending passage was cut into the body of the pyramid itself. In the Meidum pyramid and the Bent pyramid, the descending passage was cut into the body of the pyramid, going under the base of the pyramid and then slightly above the base.

The ceilings of the rooms in the three pyramids are designed like step pyramids, or one could say the ceilings are designed as corbel vault ceilings.

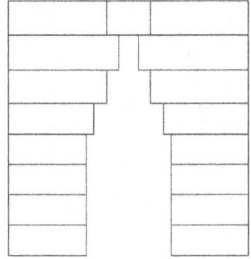

I want you to understand that considering the pyramid as an individual structure is not correct. The pyramid is part of what we call The Pyramid Complex, and of course, the pyramid is the main structure in this complex. Other elements of the complex were also developed, not just the pyramids. So, when we talk about the pyramid complex, we must understand that it underwent different designs until it almost became one design during the time of Dynasty 5.

One of the main components of the pyramid complex is what we call The Southern Tomb (similar to the one in the complex of Djoser's Step Pyramid). We are not sure about the function of this tomb. It might have been used for the burial of the king's canopic jars or as a symbolic function for the king's Ka. This southern tomb was developed and took the shape of a small pyramid (similar to the pyramid at the south of the Bent pyramid).

The pyramid complex contains three important components:

1. The so-called Funerary Temple (mortuary temple)

In the pyramid complexes of Dynasty 3, we don't have this funeral temple clearly. We do have the foundation of a structure (possibly a temple) on the north side of Djoser's Step Pyramid. Starting from Dynasty 4, this temple was designed to be on the eastern side of the pyramid. The famous opinion about this pyramid is that it's the place where the final funeral ceremonies for the deceased king were performed before placing the mummy inside (or under) the pyramid.

2. The so-called Valley Temple

This temple is called the valley temple because it's always built close to the Nile Valley. We are not sure about the function of this temple. Some opinions suggest it was the gate for the funeral procession to enter the pyramid complex, and it served as the last station for the public and commoners (who couldn't proceed further into the pyramid complex).

3. The Causeway that links the funeral temple and the valley temple

This is a direct road link between the funeral temple and the valley temple. The causeway is a substantial construction – a kind of "tunnel above the ground." It features large blocks creating the floor, two walls (sides) made of big blocks that create a passage from the valley temple to the funeral temple. Finally, the causeway is covered with wide slabs decorated from inside with star carvings. A great example of the causeway can be seen in Unas' pyramid complex.

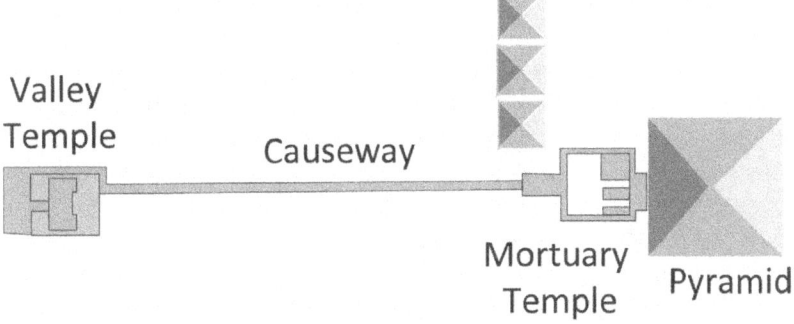

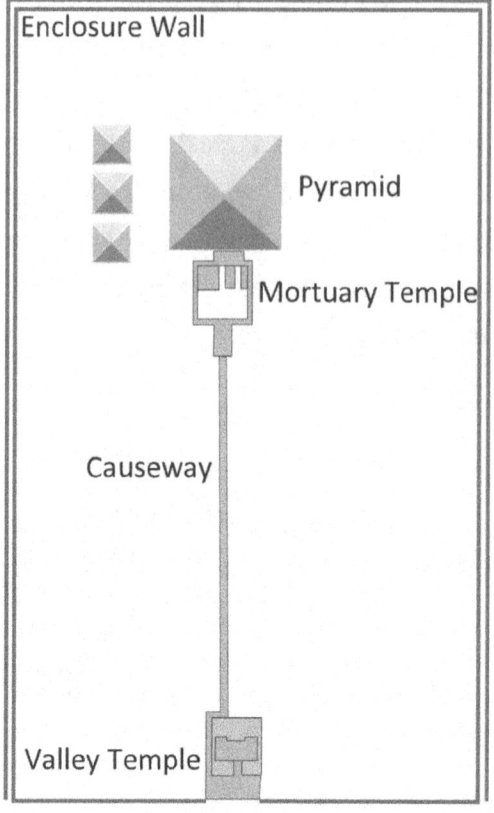

After King Sneferu and his significant contributions to pyramid construction, the Red Pyramid gained fame as the first true pyramid and an iconic structure. King Khufu, however, achieved something remarkable – the construction of the Great Pyramid, often synonymous with the word "pyramid." The angle of the Great Pyramid is 51°50'40", with a square base measuring approximately 230.34 meters on each side. The height of the Great Pyramid is 138.8 meters, which increases to 146.7 meters if the top is completed.

King Khufu chose a new location for his pyramid – Giza Plateau – not far from Dahshur and Sakkara. Comprising nearly 2.3 million limestone blocks, the Great Pyramid also contains 40-50 granite blocks in the upper chamber, some weighing 100 tons. The average weight of the blocks is 2.5 tons, making the total weight of the Great Pyramid around 5.5 million tons. The pyramid's sides are aligned with the four cardinal directions, with the north side facing true north, not magnetic north.

The Great Pyramid was covered with a fine layer of limestone, commonly believed to have been sourced from the Tura quarry on the east side of the Nile. I have a different perspective and suggest that the high-quality limestone (pure Calcium Carbonate) could be from the limestone quarry at Abu Rawash.

The Great Pyramid includes 3 chambers (this what we know so fare):
- The Subterranean Chamber
- The so-called Queen's Chamber
- The so-called King's chamber

The Great Pyramid has 5 pits known as boat pits. Among these, 2 pits on the south side of the pyramid contained dismantled boats. The other 3 pits on the pyramid's eastern side are empty, although it's believed they were designed to resemble boat shapes. Adjacent to the eastern side of the pyramid, you can find 3 small pyramids known as the Queens' pyramids.

Following the Great Pyramid and King Khufu's era, one of his sons, Djedefre, ascended to the throne of Egypt. He chose to construct his pyramid, but yet again, an unusual scenario unfolded. He changed the location selected by his father and opted for an area known as Abu Rawash, nearly 8 km north of Giza Plateau. This pyramid remains unfinished. If you visit this pyramid (which requires permission), you will encounter the subterranean design, devoid of any upper structure. There is also a boat pit adjacent to the pyramid, designed to resemble a boat.

After Djedefre's rule, King Khafra took the reins of Egypt. Returning to Giza Plateau, Khafra undertook another significant project in the region. He erected the second pyramid, commonly referred to as the Pyramid of Khafra.

This pyramid is slightly shorter and smaller than the Great Pyramid. Its height is 136.4 meters, and it has a square base with sides measuring 215.25 meters in length. The slope angle is 53°10'. The so-called burial chamber of this pyramid is not elevated within the pyramid; instead, it is almost at ground level.

At the summit of the second pyramid, we can still observe a portion of the limestone casing stones affixed to the pyramid. On the base of the pyramid, we can spot scattered blocks of rose granite. This leads me to believe that the casing stones of this pyramid were constructed using two different materials: limestone and granite. The lower half was adorned with rose granite, while the upper half was adorned with fine limestone.

Following the passing of King Khafra, King Menkaura ascended the throne of Egypt. He continued construction on the Giza Plateau, creating the third pyramid at Giza Plateau, known as the Pyramid of Menkaure. This pyramid is the smallest among the three, but I must say it boasts a delicate design. Adjacent to the eastern side of the pyramid, you'll find three small pyramids known as queens' pyramids, a setup similar to that of the Great Pyramid.

King Menkaura passed away, and his son Shepseskaf took the throne. Strangely, King Shepseskaf not only abandoned the Giza Plateau but also ceased pyramid construction. For reasons unknown, he chose to construct a mastaba tomb at Sakkara, to the south of Sakkara. This mastaba tomb is composed of two levels (two mastabs).

Locally known as Mastabat al-Fir'aun, the mastaba's height reaches 18 meters, and its base is rectangular, measuring 99.6 meters by 74.4 meters. Crafted from red sandstone, the lower portion of the mastaba was encased in rose granite, while the upper sections were adorned with fine limestone.

Upon King Shepseskaf's passing, King Userkaf took the reins of Egypt's rule. As the founder of Dynasty 5, he built his pyramid in central Sakkara. Fashioned from limestone blocks, the pyramid boasts a square base, with each side measuring 73.5 meters. Its height stands at 49 meters, and the slope angle measures 53°07'48".

King Sahure, the second monarch of Dynasty 5, followed in the unusual footsteps of some of his predecessors. He altered the chosen location of his pyramid, moving to Abusir, approximately 3 kilometers north of Sakkara, to construct his pyramid.

The pyramid of King Sahure, built from limestone blocks, features a square base with each side measuring 78.75 meters. Its height reaches 47 meters, and the slope angle is 50°11'40".

Undeterred, King Neferirkare continued building at Abusir, situating his pyramid close to the pyramid of Sahure. This pyramid, constructed from limestone blocks, showcases a square base with each side measuring 72 meters. Its height is 52 meters, and the slope angle measures 54°30'.

King Neferefre embarked on constructing an unfinished pyramid at Abusir. He managed to construct only the first layer or mastaba, which is a mere 7 meters in height, and the construction was never finalized.

King Niuserre also chose Abusir for his pyramid's location. His pyramid, made from limestone blocks, presents a base with sides measuring 78.9 meters each. Its height is 51.68 meters, and the slope angle measures 51°50'35". Unfortunately, pyramids at Abusir are not accessible to the public.

Adjacent to Abusir is an area known as Abou Ghorab, where some rulers of Dynasty 5 built sun temples.

King Menkauhor departed from the favored family site and constructed his pyramid north of Sakkara, near the pyramid of Teti. Regrettably, this pyramid remains unfinished and is commonly referred to as the Headless Pyramid or Lepsius XXIX. Unfortunately, this pyramid is not open to the public.

Once again, for reasons unknown, the later rulers of Dynasty 5 refrained from constructing their pyramids at Abusir, unlike their predecessors. King Djedkare Isesi, instead, built his pyramid to the south of Sakkara. This pyramid is constructed from limestone blocks.

It has a base square of 78.75 meters on each side, the height of the pyramid is 52.5 meters, and the slope angle is 52°. This pyramid is not open for public visits.

King Unas, the last ruler of Dynasty 5, also didn't build his pyramid at Abusir. He chose to build it at Sakkara, to the south of the Step Pyramid.

Unas' pyramid is constructed from limestone blocks.

It has a base square of 57.75 meters on each side, the height of the pyramid is 43 meters, and the slope angle is 56°18'35".

An addition was made to the pyramid of Unas. On the walls of the "burial" chamber, there are inscriptions. This marks the first instance of writings inside a pyramid. While there were some writings under Djoser's Step Pyramid, they were located in the tunnel system beneath the pyramid and not inside the pyramid itself, nor on the chamber walls.

Enormous text covers the walls of the two chambers within Unas' pyramid. Egyptologists refer to this text as The Pyramid Text. Originally thought of as religious or funerary texts, these texts later evolved into what is now known as the Book of the Dead. Unas' pyramid is open for public visits every day from 08 AM to 12:00 noon.

After the passing of King Unas, Dynasty 5 came to an end, and King Teti inaugurated Dynasty 6.

King Teti constructed his pyramid at Sakkara. The pyramid is crafted from limestone but is in poor condition, having lost its casing stones.

Its height is 52.5 meters, the base is a square measuring 78.75 meters on each side, and the slope angle is 53°07'48".

This pyramid, the second to bear Pyramid Text inscriptions in its chambers, is open for public visits from 08 AM to 04 PM.

King Pepi built his pyramid in Sakkara as well, following the footsteps of his predecessor King Teti. His pyramid is named Men-Nefer, which, as mentioned earlier, is the origin of the name Ancient Memphis.

Crafted from limestone, the pyramid is in a very deteriorated state and has lost its casing stones.

The intended height was 52.5 meters, but the current height is 12 meters. Its base is a square measuring 78.75 meters on each side, and the slope angle is 53°07'48". This pyramid is not accessible to the public.

King Merenre constructed his pyramid in Sakkara as well, but sadly, the pyramid is in a severely dilapidated condition. The intended height was 52.6 meters, the base is a square measuring 78.6 meters on each side, and the slope angle is 52°. This pyramid is not open to the public.

King Pep II, the last ruler of Dynasty 6, followed the pattern of his predecessors and built a similar pyramid in Sakkara. However, this pyramid is also not open for public visits.

As Dynasty 6 came to a close, the First Intermediate Period began, and the curve of civilization declined. The rulers of this era, marked by weakness, attempted to build pyramids—like Qakare Ibi, Khui, and Merikare—but these structures were of poor quality or remained unfinished.

After the First Intermediate Period, the Middle Kingdom began, and the rulers of Dynasty 12 continued to build pyramids. These rulers utilized a very NEW technique and material for building pyramids: they used mud brick!

King Amenemhat I constructed his pyramid in a new area further south of Sakkara and Dahshur, known as El Lisht.

The core of the pyramid was constructed from rough limestone blocks and then covered with mud bricks and sand.

The base is a square measuring 84 meters, the height is 59 meters, and the slope angle is 54°27'44". This pyramid is not open for public visits.

King Senusret I erected his pyramid in the same location as his father, King Amenemhat I. He also built his pyramid at El Lisht.

The builders of this pyramid used a very unique technique that had not been employed before. They constructed four walls along the base lines, forming a massive room over the base. From the center of this room, they extended four walls towards the four corners, creating a shape resembling an "X". Additionally, they added another four walls extending towards the centers of the sides of the base, forming a shape similar to a "+" sign. These eight walls are akin to eight diameters. Subsequently, they constructed eight more walls, each originating from the center of a diameter and extending to the center of the halfway point of the side. This approach resulted in the creation of sixteen enclosed spaces, or rooms. These spaces were filled with stones and debris, and the casing stone, crafted from white fine limestone, was placed over them.

The original height of this pyramid is 61.25 meters, the base is a square measuring 105.2 meters, and the slope angle is 49°23'55".

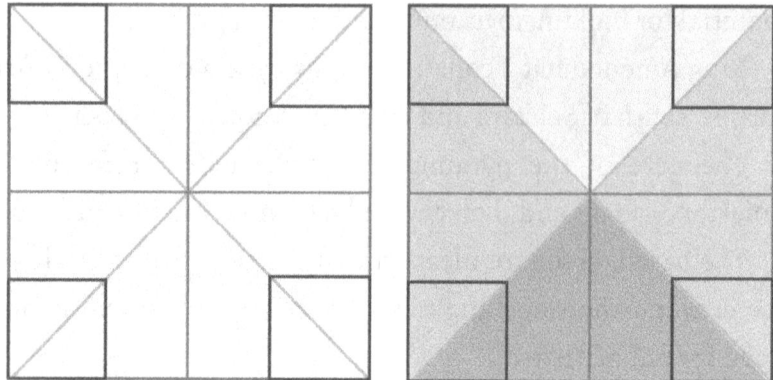

Part of the ramp that may have been used for the construction still exists.

King Amenemhat II followed the pattern of change that many of his predecessors had exhibited; he altered the "burial" location of those who came before him.

He chose to construct his pyramid at Dahshur, the favored site of King Sneferu.

His pyramid is known as the White Pyramid, though most of its stones have been taken away, leaving only the white limestone core. This pyramid is not accessible for public visits.

King Senusret II, on the other hand, disagreed with this shift and did not build his pyramid at Dahshur or El Lisht. Instead, he selected a different location further south, building his pyramid at Lahun, in the Faiyum Oasis south of Cairo.

Similar to his grandfather, King Senusret II employed a distinct technique or material: he utilized mudbricks to construct the entire pyramid, which were then covered with yellow limestone.

It's worth noting that this pyramid had its entrance on the southern side, a departure from the usual northern orientation.

The pyramid's base is a square measuring 107 meters, its height is 48.65 meters, and the slope angle is 42°35'.

This pyramid is open to the public from 08 AM to 04 PM.

Senusret III, the son of Senusret II, returned to Dahshur and erected his pyramid there. Like his father, he opted for a mudbrick pyramid. However, the same fate befell this pyramid; it lost its limestone casing stone and the mudbricks deteriorated due to exposure to air and rain, leaving it in a poor condition.

The pyramid's base is a square measuring 105 meters, its height is 78 meters, and the slope angle is 56°18'35".

King Amenemhat III followed in the footsteps of his ancestor, King Sneferu, by constructing two pyramids. He built the first at Dahshur, similar to his father Senusret III. Additionally, he erected a pyramid at Hawara, in the Faiyum Oasis south of Cairo, mirroring his great grandfather Senusret II.

The pyramid at Dahshur is known as the Black Pyramid, built from mudbricks and adorned with limestone. The base measures 105 meters square, the height is 75 meters, and the slope angle is 55°.

This pyramid lost its casing stone entirely, and its mudbrick core has deteriorated to resemble melted ice cream. It is not open for public visits.

The second pyramid at Hawara, also built from mudbricks and covered with limestone, experienced the same fate: loss of casing stone and exposure to the elements. Again, its entrance was on the southern side, not the northern.

The Greek historian and geographer Strabo mentioned a grand structure built near this pyramid, referred to as the Labyrinth (the Egyptian Labyrinth). Herodotus also wrote about this same building in his accounts of Egypt.

The pyramid's base is a square measuring 105 meters, its height was originally 58 meters (but is currently 20 meters), and the slope angle is 48°45'.

This pyramid is accessible to the public from 08 AM to 04 PM.

Following King Amenemhat III, the Middle Kingdom came to an end, and pyramid construction ceased. While some smaller pyramids may have been built until the time of King Ahomse I, these are not included in the count. From the start of the New Kingdom until the end of Egyptian civilization, Egypt's rulers constructed massive and deep tombs beneath the ground, such as the tombs in the Valley of the Kings on the west bank of Luxor.

I have just shared with you the well-known narrative regarding the evolution of Ancient Egyptian tombs, specifically focusing on the development of pyramids. Now, I will offer my own insights on this narrative. I must emphasize that comprehending and accepting this story without any doubts is relatively easy. During my time as a student, and throughout my nearly two decades in this field, this story has been both intriguing and logically sound. However, my extensive experience includes countless visits to these sites, along with discussions with numerous experts from various disciplines such as engineering, science, geology, and craftsmanship.

Indeed, the pre-dynastic Egyptians buried their deceased in simple underground pits, a practice that evolved gradually up to the First Dynasty with the construction of Mastaba tombs in Abydos and Sakkara. Tomb number 3038 in northern Sakkara, associated with a high-ranking official named Nebitka from Dynasty 1, King Den, and King Anedjib, exemplifies this development. Some scholars contend that this particular mastaba might even belong to King Anedjib himself.

Originally a stone mound, this mastaba featured sides shaped as small steps on three sides (north, south, and west). It was subsequently covered with mudbricks to create eight steps. The dimensions included a base of 22.7 meters by 10.6 meters and a height of 2.3 meters. Subsequent mastaba tombs had a single level.

However, a question emerges from this progression. The Step Pyramid at Sakkara is comprised of six mastabas, while the prior tomb was a single level. What happened to the mastaba tombs of two, three, four, and five levels? This inconsistency raises further queries. How did a mastaba with eight steps arise during Dynasty 1, while a pyramid with only six steps emerged in Dynasty 3? How can mastaba tombs built in between feature only one level?

Something else is very strange about this story. The story of the development of early tombs explains that the underground design initially straightforward and gradually grew deeper and larger until Dynasty 3. The discovery of two tombs attributed to Dynasty 2 at the southern side of Djoser's Step Pyramid and near Unas' Pyramid adds complexity to this narrative. The first tomb belongs to King Hotepsekhemwy or King Nebra, with the tomb encompassing a vast underground network of around 4000 square meters at a depth of 7 meters. The second tomb, attributed to King Nynetjer, extends 25 meters underground, measuring 94 by 106 meters and containing 56 flint knives and 44 razors. Remember how I was just explaining to you the story of the development of the tomb and how they made the pit deeper into the bedrock. Now it is time for the big question, how they made such amazing underground networks (labyrinthic style), and what kind of tools can achieve this perfect work?

As I mentioned above, the galleries of the tomb of Hotepsekhemwy are oriented perfectly to the cardinal directions. I'm talking about a considerable distance beneath the ground, with numerous "rooms" on both sides of the main entrance. What are the odds of achieving such impeccable alignment? Before I address this question, let's briefly consider the conditions and challenges of this undertaking:

Tools: The tools available were primitive, such as stone pounders or perhaps copper chisels.

Light: How did workers illuminate their way underneath? Candles or oil flames? Keep in mind, we're discussing precise alignment.

Ventilation: These workers were excavating limestone bedrock, rich in Calcium carbonate (CaCO3). This substance creates a powder akin to gypsum Calcium sulfate, which can lead to respiratory issues when inhaled. Furthermore, if candles or oil flames were used for light, oxygen consumption would be swift. Hence, the work environment wasn't conducive.

Given these factors, I'd venture that the likelihood of achieving such flawless alignment is less than 20%. In my perspective, they might have employed a mechanical system, power tools, or even some form of radar to guide workers accurately.

Before I conclude this topic about burials in Ancient Egypt, I want to quickly address a common belief in Egyptology. It posits that due to the daily movement of the sun, the Ancient Egyptians associated east with life, symbolized by sunrise, and west with death or disappearance due to sunset. However, this notion is erroneous. Evidence contradicts it, as we find tombs in Maadi, Omari, Helwan, and other sites from the predynastic and early dynastic periods, including the prominent Bani Hassan site

tombs at El Minya from the Middle Kingdom time. The Ancient Egyptians built houses and tombs in both banks of Nile river, the west bank and the east bank.

Understanding the construction of Djoser's Step Pyramid isn't straightforward. The concept of stacking six mastabas atop each other, gradually diminishing towards the top to create a step pyramid, becomes somewhat acceptable, especially given the genius of Imhotep, Djoser's chancellor. However, when delving into the underground design, numerous questions arise:

Huge Shaft: Why was there a need for a colossal 28-meter-deep shaft under the pyramid? This shaft defies the pyramid's stability, posing significant risk of collapse due to the initial mastaba's base center being supported by "wooden logs"! Unless an unknown technique was employed, this remains a mystery.

Granite Box: The placement of a massive granite box precisely within this shaft raises eyebrows. Comprising 32 large pieces of rose granite, the box has a small opening closed by a rounded granite block resembling a pestle. Strangely, another shaft similar to this one lies across the so-called open court at the pyramid's southern side.

Additional intriguing information about the Step Pyramid, unbeknownst to many scholars, is the strong belief that the open court's ground was once entirely covered in Alabaster blocks. Despite numerous Alabaster blocks being quarried from the site, the curious twist is that they were dubbed "Sakkara Alabaster." Alabaster is indigenous to Hatnub, located more than 200 km south of Sakkara. The question remains unasked by many scholars: How can it be asserted that Dynasty 3 saw the utilization of stones, particularly limestone, showcasing remarkable expertise in handling not only limestone but also other stone types like granite and alabaster?

The concept of a substantial shaft under the pyramid's base was replicated post Djoser's Step Pyramid. Two renowned examples stand out:

Unfinished Pyramid at Zawyet El Aryan

Unfinished Pyramid at Abou Rawash

Although I've yet to visit the "unfinished" pyramid at Zawyet El Aryan, I have explored the one at Abou Rawash. Observing the sky-piercing shaft, you're bound to ask a logical question: How did they support the pyramid's base? A possible response might mention the use of cedar wood logs.

The Step Pyramid in Sakkara seems to incorporate cedar wood support for its ceiling, yet I doubt this as an original design element. It appears more like a dynastic restoration. This impression becomes clearer when you observe the size of the shaft in the Abou Rawash and Zawyet El Aryan pyramids.

The Medium Pyramid also strikes me as an enigmatic structure that doesn't seem to fit the chain of mastaba pyramids. It doesn't appear that the pyramid was initially designed as a step pyramid, destined to be transformed into a true pyramid. Instead, the casing stones were added above the mastaba-style sides, retaining the mastaba aesthetic.

The surroundings of the Medium Pyramid are also captivating. Mastaba number 17 encompasses an immense rose granite box beneath it. This box features a minute tunnel leading to the so-called burial room, devoid of carvings. The box itself is unadorned. Regarded as one of the earliest examples of granite boxes in Dynasty 4, its owner remains unidentified. I speculate it belonged to a high-ranking official or perhaps a royal relative, potentially dating back to a prior era and repurposed during Dynasty 4.

The Bent Pyramid holds significant importance for me, both as a tour guide and a researcher. My journey of questioning Egyptology narratives commenced when I encountered the claim that this pyramid was a "mistake." Should I embrace this inaccurate tale, numerous unanswered queries arise:

1. Continued Construction: Why did they persist in completing the pyramid if they realized a base angle error? Why not dismantle the flawed part and begin anew? Some might argue practicality, but I contend that they were crafting an eternal afterlife abode – a tomb for the king – and perfection was paramount.

2. Comprehensive Finishing: Not only did they conclude construction, but they also meticulously completed the exterior, encompassing the casing stones – renowned as some of the finest among all pyramids.

3. Causeway and Valley Temple: What drove the decision to finalize the causeway and Valley temple? Their completion adds another layer of intrigue to the pyramid's complex.

4. The Red Pyramid: If they erred in the Bent Pyramid's angle, why build another pyramid nearby – roughly 3 km north? The construction of the Red pyramid demanded fresh limestone blocks, sourced from a distance rather than a local quarry.

5. Missing Burial Signs: Curiously, no burial indications have been unearthed within these two pyramids. Their

absence raises intriguing questions about the true purpose and design.

The base angle, contrary to what has been explained, isn't an insurmountable predicament. Here, a comparison between the Bent Pyramid and the 2nd Pyramid at the Giza Plateau – attributed to King Khafra – sheds light on this matter.

	Bent Pyramid	**Khafra Pyramid**
Base	188 X 188	215 X 215
Hight	105	143.5
Base angle	54°27'	53°10'

As you can see, the "Khafra" Pyramid is bigger than the Bent Pyramid and the angle is very similiar, the difference is 01°17' only, so if this angle was considered a mistake in the project of the Bent Pyramid, it would be a BIG mistake in the project of Khafra Pyramid.

If you one day visit the Bent Pyramid and have the chance to walk around it, you may find small pieces of quarts or alabaster scattered on the ground, especially after rain (you will see it sparkling from a distance). The fact is, these pieces are white mica, and we keep finding hundreds of pieces of mica for more than 20 years, the size of the pieces starts from the thumb size to the size of a hand.

I was told from a geophysicist that mica is used as an insulator material, so I think that the whole pyramid was covered with a layer of mica above the casing stone.

The Great Pyramid

The Great Pyramid is considered the second true pyramid built; the first true pyramid was the Great pyramid, which is very strange because the second example would be better than the first example, but what happened is that the Great Pyramid is the best pyramid among all the pyramids, and I can say it is the best structure not only from the Ancient Egyptian Civilization but also from all the mankind civilizations.

The blocks of limestone used to build the Great Pyramid are of the highest quality among all the other pyramids. We are talking about approximately 2,300,000 blocks of stones, and if we add the missing blocks of the casing stone, the number will be around 3,000,000 blocks. The average weight of the blocks is 2.5 tons, so we are dealing with substantial stones, and each block would take considerable time to complete. Thus, if we perform a simple logical calculation, it becomes clear that the stories about using primitive techniques to build the Great Pyramid are not true.

If the Ancient Egyptian workers managed to cut, transfer, and shape 100 stones daily, they would need almost (3,000,000 / 100 / 365) = 82 years to just prepare the blocks. Considering that 100 blocks are an excessive amount of work for one day, if we double the number to 200 blocks, they would still need almost 41 years. Most scholars assume that King Khufu ruled Egypt for 23 years, so even if they managed to cut, transfer, shape, and build 200 stones every day, 41 years would be required, and Khufu ruled for only 23 years, which is insufficient time. Additionally, there are huge blocks weighing 5, 10, 20, 50, and

100 tons, which would undoubtedly need more time than the 2.5-ton blocks.

The granite blocks used to build the so-called king's chamber are made from rose granite from Aswan. I must mention that there was a major quarry behind the southern side of the Great Pyramid and to the eastern side of the second pyramid. The casing stone is from pure calcium carbonate. While the famous story suggests that the Ancient Egyptians brought this high-quality limestone from the Tura quarry south of Cairo on the east side of the Nile, I believe this is incorrect. In my opinion, the Ancient Egyptians obtained this high-quality limestone from the limestone quarry at Abou Rawash.

Some scholars, like Joseph Davidovits, have adopted the idea that the blocks of the pyramids in general, and especially the blocks of the Great Pyramid, are made of geopolymer stone. He claims that he analyzed a sample from the casing stone and found that the casing stones do not match Tura's fine limestone, so the casing stones are also geopolymer stones. Tura is not the only place in Egypt to obtain fine limestone, and as I mentioned above, I strongly believe that the casing stone or this layer of fine limestone was brought from the limestone quarry of Abou Rawash, where this high quality of pure calcium carbonate can be found.

Davidovits claims that the blocks of the Great Pyramid were not cut from the quarry; they were cast in molds. He stated that he obtained a small piece from the blocks of the pyramid and found human hair inside the fabric of this stone. I think he got a sample from the mortar, which was used to fill the gaps between the blocks. In my opinion, this mortar was added by the dynasties as a kind of restoration work to the pyramids and other sites. We know that many Ancient Egyptian sites were restored by the dynasties, like the Sphinx and others, but we used to think it happened during and after the New Kingdom. I can tell you that it occurred during the Old Kingdom as well, and this type of concrete was added to the pyramid. There is no chance to claim it is part of the original design, because this concrete layer was made to fill the gaps between the blocks. These gaps did not exist when the pyramid was built and finished in a PERFECT way; they appeared later.

I want to explain another essential note about this subject: the Geopolymer stone. If you take a careful walk around the Great Pyramid and inspect the blocks, you will realize that the blocks do not all show the same texture. That's because limestone is not uniform; they built the Great Pyramid using blocks of limestone of different types.

1. Regular white and beige limestone

This is the most common limestone in Egypt, and it is located at Giza Plateau, Sakkara, Meidum, 06 of October city, Tura and Mokattam. I want to add Abu Rawash to this list. Beige limestone is the major type of limestones used to build the Ancient constructions.

2. Regular red limestone

The color of the red limestone is because of the Hematite which is in the fabric of the stone. This is the reason we call the northern pyramid at Dahshur, the Red Pyramid. This type contains low number of fossils and seashell.

3. Fossiliferous Limestone

This type can be seen in Giza Plateau specially at the eastern side of the Great Pyramid, we call in Arabic language, Qurashy stone (Qurosh = pennies), because this stone contains high number of fossils and seashell.

4. Fine limestone

This is regular limestone but with very low number of fossils and seashell.

5. Pure limestone

This is a pure calcium carbonite, and it doesn't contain any fossils nor seashell.

So, there is no chance to claim that the Great Pyramid was built from artificial limestone.

I want to say that, I'm against the theory of poured stones (geopolymer stones), the Ancient Egyptians made all their stone products from real stone, and I believe it is very obvious to see the difference between the texture of the natural stone and the texture of the artificial stone.

The most important thing we need to understand that the Ancient Egyptians used natural stones from the Egyptian environment, so we located all the quarries of these stones such as:

- Limestone from Cairo, Giza and Sakkara
- Rose granite from Aswan
- Basalt from Beni Suef and Faium
- Alabaster from El Minya
- Sandstone from Edfu and Aswan
- Quartzite from the east of Cairo

When I talk about the Great Pyramid, I love to talk about the so-called king's chamber, this chamber was fully built with blocks from rose granite, some of these blocks are more than 50 tons and there is a block could be 100 tones, above the ceiling there are 5 blocks and there is a space between each 2 blocks creating 5 spaces above the ceiling, these 5 rooms are called Relieving Chambers. I don't think these 5 rooms are Relieving Chambers because if this is the case, why we don't find these Relieving Chambers above the ceiling of the so-called queen's chamber? It exists in a lower level then the upper chamber, so its ceiling is carrying more weight, also the chambers under the 2nd pyramid, the Red Pyramid and the Bent Pyramid.

The Second Pyramid

The Second Pyramid, "Khafar Pyramid," was built next to the Great Pyramid to the southwest we will see the 2nd pyramid in Giza Plateau, if we extend the square diameter of the base of the Great Pyramid it will be the same square diameter of the 2nd pyramid.

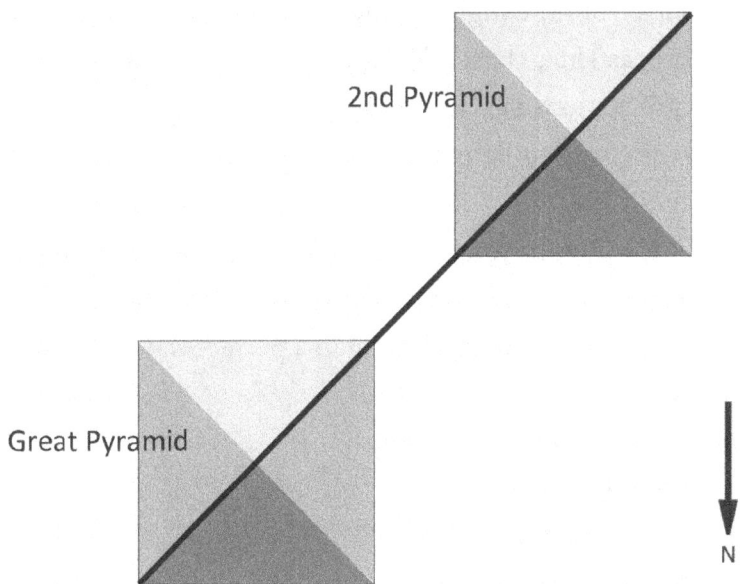

In my opinion, if we give this project (building the 02nd pyramid) to 1000 construction companies, they will not choose the current location of the 02 pyramid. The ground at this location is high at the west side and low at the east side.

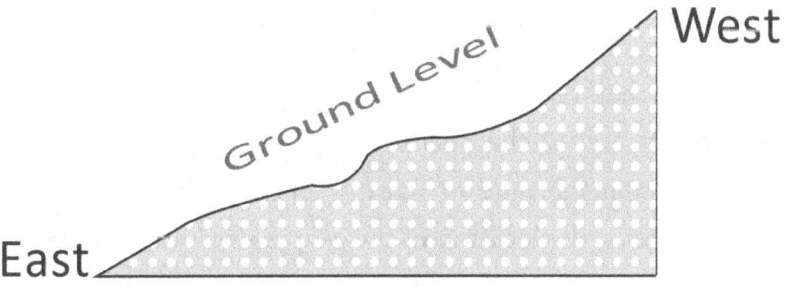

I want to say that, this is the worst location to place the pyramid, because they builders had to flatten the base first before they start to build the pyramid, the hard part of this story is not just leveling the ground, it is the way how they cut the stones from the high ground from the westside and place it at the eastside, these blocks are huge and many of these blocks are 20-30 tones, these blocks were cut in a very careful and precise way to be placed without ill proportioned in the eastside.

After visiting the Ancient Egyptian sites hundreds of times, I understood that there are 4 rules must exist in each site to get the site working and functioning in a perfect way.

1. The Location
2. The Design
3. The Material
4. The Alignment

If any of these elements is missing or changed the function of the site will be inactive, and unfortunately most of the Ancient Egyptian sites are not keeping these 4 elements.

Isis temple was on Philae island but it was moved few hundred meters to Agilika island, Abu Simbel temple was moved to higher level, Kalabsha temple was moved to another location, many of the sites lost important elements from its design, Karnak temple lost many obelisks and statues, Luxor temple lost one of the obelisks at the front gate and some statues from inside, and so many other examples.

My point is, the location of the 2nd pyramid was not chosen randomly, or not because the builders loved to do hard work, this location was chosen because it is the perfect spot to place the base of the 2nd pyramid, and no matter how difficult were the challenges to cut the blocks from the westside and put it at the eastside, this was a very difficult job because it was easier to smash the stone from the westside to lower down the ground level, but they needed this blocks so they can put it on the eastside, so they had to be very careful while cutting and transferring these blocks. We must know the Ancient Egyptian builder was following a very restricted role, the **material** they use must be from the same location or from the same spot, so they had to balance the eastern side of the 2nd pyramid using limestone from the same location.

The pyramid still keep part of the casing stone at the top level of the pyramid, this remaining casing stone is made of limestone, but we can see scattered blocks of granite at the base of the pyramid and we can see some of these blocks are taking the shape of casing stone too, so we understand that the lower part of the 2nd pyramid was cased by granite, rose granite from Aswan, and the upper part was cased by fine limestone, I think it was 50:50.

There are 2 entrances to this pyramid from the northside leads to the same chamber under the pyramid, I have a question here about the celling of this chamber, they say that there are 5 chamber above the so-called king chamber in the Great Pyramid to reduce the heavy pressure above the celling, this room is in a high level inside the Great Pyramid, the chamber of the 2nd pyramid is under the pyramid so there are millions of tones above it, but there are no releasing chamber above the celling!!??

The Great Pyramid complex includes 3 small pyramids at the eastern side, it was mistakenly called the queens' pyramids, the 2nd pyramid complex doesn't include any queens' pyramids.

The 3rd Pyramid at Giza Plateau

The 3rd pyramid at Giza Plateau is attributed to king Menkaura, one of the kings of the 4th Dynasty.

This pyramid is not huge like the other 2 pyramids but it was built from a good quality of limestone, this pyramid was cased entirely with rose granite, although most of the academics believe it was unfinished pyramid and the casing stone was never completed, but I believe the opposite, the pyramid was completed and the casing stone was built to the top of the pyramid.

The granite casing stones of the 2nd pyramid, were smoothed and the angle of it was the same angle of the pyramid, but the casing stones of the 3rd pyramid are rough from the front side and not flat surface.

At the eastern side of the 3rd pyramid there is a huge building (the so-called funeral temple), when you visit this temple you will immediately recognize the huge size of the limestone blocks were used to build this structure. Inside this build there is a corridor which is cased with blocks from grano-diorite, these grano-diorite blocks are smoothed from the front part, they are rough like the granite casing stones of the pyramid.

The complex of the 3rd pyramid includes 3 small pyramids like the case of the Great Pyramid, but it is not located at the eastern side, it is located at the southern side of the 3rd pyramid.

The Great Pyramid was built from limestone and cased with fine limestone, the 2nd pyramid was built from limestone and cased with limestone from the middle part to the top and with rose granite casing stone from the bottom level to the middle, the 3rd pyramid was built from limestone and cases entirely with rose granite. So, the Great Pyramid would reflect white color and the 3rd pyramid would reflect red color and the 2nd pyramid would reflect both white and red color. I understand that the second pyramid is playing as a middle point between the Great Pyramid and the 3rd pyramid.

The Sphinx

When you get inside Giza Plateau from the east side (from the village Nazlet El Samman), you will see first the Sphinx, it is located in front of the 3 pyramids, specially in front the 2nd pyramid, the Sphinx was carved from the bedrock itself, the area around the Sphinx was designed to be like an open court surrounding the Sphinx.

So many scholars and historians didn't know who built or who made the Sphinx, but in the recent time they believe that king Khafra who made the Sphinx.

We don't have very strong evidences to support the opinion that the Sphinx was made by king Khafra, that's why some scholars attributed the Sphinx to king Khufu, and some of them attributed the Sphinx to Khufu's son, king Djedefre.

No names were found for the king who built the Sphinx, the only name is written very close to the Sphinx is the name of Tuthmosis IV, the name is written on rose granite stele (stela), this stele was made by king Tutmosis IV and it was placed between the paws of the Sphinx to commemorate the story between the Tuthmosis and the Sphinx, and commemorate the promise of the Sphinx to make Tuthmosis IV the king of Egypt.

The Sphinx was not made from a block which was brought from a nearby quarry or a faraway quarry, no, the Sphinx statue is carved into the bedrock as I mentioned above, this bedrock in Giza Plateau and in this area is limestone. This Sphinx is the biggest Sphinx in Egypt and of course the whole world, that's why it is being called the Great Sphinx, it is 73 m long and the height is 20 m.

If you pay attention when you look at the Sphinx you will realize 2 things;

1. The size of the head in compare with the size of the body is ill proportioned.
2. The quality of the head is much better than the quality of the body, the body is eroded more than the head. If I use simple logic I will say, the head must be eroded more than the body because the body was buried under sand for hundreds of years so sand would protected the body from weathering, but the head was exposed to wind and rain and sandstorms most of the time so it would be effected more than the body.

So, I agree with the opinion which says that the head was RE-CARVED.

This will lead use to talk about 2 possibilities;
1. The head was made as a head of a king and was re-carved to be the head for another king.
2. The head was not made as a king a head and it was re-carved to be the head for a king.

I feel that the 2nd possibility is the correct one, and I can say the Sphinx was originally made as a complete lion, or complete lioness, I believe the Sphinx was representing nTr Tefnut. Tefnut was represented in some drawings and carvings as recumbent lioness side by side to her brother Shu as a recumbent lion. There is a statue for a Sphinx as a complete lion at the Egyptian Museum at Cairo, this statue is next to the statuette of King Khufu, I use this as evidence that the idea of the Sphinx with full lioness shape existed before or during the 4th dynast.

There is another considerable opinion about the original identity of the Sphinx, Dr. Manu Seyfzadeh in his book (Under the Sphinx) suggested the Sphinx was originally a lioness but she is an old Egyptian nTr called Mehit.

According to Dr. Robert Schoch, the Sphinx was already carved during 9,700 BC at the end of the last ice age, he explained his theory in his book Forgotten Civilization in a very clear scientific way.

The sever erosions on the body of the Sphinx and the fissures on the surrounding limestone enclosure around the Sphinx, cannot happen during the time of the dynasties, the Egyptian weather is almost dry weather and it doesn't rain much in Egypt, that was the case also during the dynasties time, so get these sever deep erosions we must have lots of rain and running water. Dr. Schoch suggested that this might happen because of the climate change during the time of the last ice age, and I can add to this theory and say maybe it happened in earlier time with similar climate like the climate at 9,700 BC.

I found similar erosions and fissures in Giza Plateau; at the west side of Giza Plateau you can see the effect of running water towards the west. Also, I can say that the Great Pyramid itself was affected with the same climate at 9,700 BC. Yes, the pyramid was there during that time.

When you walk next to the Great Pyramid from the eastern side close to the northern corner, you will see sever vertical erosions on the blocks of the lower level of Great Pyramid, and it is not on the casing stone layer, it is on the 3rd layer behind the casing stone. I see it very similar to the erosions and fissures at the Sphinx, so I can say that the Great Pyramid and the Sphinx were built before 9,700 BC.

Someone might say that these erosions and fissures are on the bedrock layers of the base of the Great Pyramid, so yes it happened at 9700 BC but before the Great Pyramid was built, and then they built the pyramid on top of it. This claim is not true because there are what they call it symbolic Boat Pits at the eastern side of the Great Pyramid, the sides of these pits show the same erosions and fissures, so these pits were already there before 9700 BC.

In front of the Sphinx there are 2 temples:

The temple on the right side of the Sphinx (south) is called the Valley temple and it is considered as one of the elements of the complex of the 2nd pyramid (it is open for the public visit. The walls of this temple were designed like a big sandwich, they built the wall from huge blocks of limestone, some of these blocks are exceeding 30 tons, the builders add a layer of huge rose granite blocks as a casing stone above the limestone blocks from the external part of the temple, and add another rose granite layer to the internal part of the temple.

The sizes and the designs of the limestone blocks are almost the same, but the sizes and designs of the rose granite blocks are not the same, specially from the interior, there is a very special rose granite block is part of the interior design, it is not big size but it has 8 sides and surrounded with 6 blocks, this design is very strange and I don't know exactly what is the reason to do it, because it needs great abilities and advanced tools to do it (advanced saw table), we can find another stone like this (8 sided stone) when we walk at the eastern side of the Great Pyramid, it is one of the stones put above the ground to create the 'limestone platform' around the pyramid, there are other 8sided blocks inside Egypt and in other locations outside Egypt like Peru. From the north-west corner of this temple there is a passage leads to the other temple close to the Khafra pyramid, this passage is called "the causeway".

The second temple:

This temple is located exactly in front of the Sphinx, but the entrance of this temple is from the eastern side, there is no door or passage in the temple leads to the Sphinx.

It is strongly believed that the limestone blocks which were used to build this temple were cut from the area around the Sphinx itself, again the Ancient builder used an advanced technology to cut these blocks precisely so he can put it together to build the so-called valley temple

The limestone blocks are reflecting the same erosions as the Great Sphinx, because of these erosions, some scholars adopted a very strange opinion, this opinion suggesting that these blocks were cut with these erosions already existed on it.

I visited this temple from inside in 2019 and I realized that the valley temple and the Sphinx temple are reflecting the same style and technique, so I think both temples were designed as one temple.

In order to place the granite blocks above the limestone wall, the builder slightly carved the surface of the limestone to fit the backsides of the granite blocks, these designs have the same erosions, so it is very clear that the erosions happened after the stone was constructed, not before.

If you still agree that the builders of the pyramids of Dahshur and Giza Plateau are the rulers of Dynasty 4, then I must say that the end of Dynasty 4 witnessed a great decline and it seems that they lost their "ADVANCED" knowledge suddenly.

The last ruler of Dynasty 4, king Shepseskaf made a dramatic change in the construction techniques of Dynasty 4, he didn't build a pyramid, he built a mastaba tomb, and he built this mastaba tomb at Sakkara close to Dahshur, he did not build this mastaba at Giza Plateau. This mastaba is famous with the name Mastabat al-Fir'aun.

I always asked myself this question, how come the grandson of the rulers of Dynasty 4, the builders of these Great Pyramids at Dahshur, Giza and Abu Rawash, didn't build a pyramid? And he built a mastaba tomb.

This mastaba tomb consists of 2 layers only, not 6 mastabas like the Step pyramid at Sakkara or more than 6 mastabs, as if the builders of the Step pyramid had better technologies than the builders of this mastaba.

The first pyramid was built after Dynasty 4 is the pyramid of Userkaf, king Userkaf is the first king of Dynasty 5. The local name for this pyramid is Al Mekharbish (heap of stones), it was called by this name due to the rough shape and condition of the external layer of the pyramid.

The pyramid was built from small blocks of limestone which are arranged perfectly together, and it was cased with fine limestone, the pyramid is reflecting very poor quality of construction and primitive techniques, so after the pyramid lost its casing stone it was crumbled, and it is in a very bad condition nowadays.

So, there is no way to believe that Mastabat al-Fir'aun and Al Mekharbish pyramid were built by the same groups of workers who built Giza pyramids, and if someone will say, they are not the same groups, so, the question will be, what happened to the workers who built Giza pyramids and what happened to their knowledge? Did they suddenly disappear? Or they are not the true builders of Giza pyramids?

The later rulers of Dynasty 5 built their pyramids at Abusir and not at Sakkara like the founder of the Dynasty.

In my opinion the name Abusir is derived from the Ancient Egyptian 2 words, bw wsir (the place of Osiris), I think it was pronounced as Busir and the Arabs add letter A to the word Busir to become Abusir.

There are three major pyramids at Abusir;
1. Pyramid of Sahure
2. Pyramid of Neferirkare Kakai
3. Pyramid of Niuserre

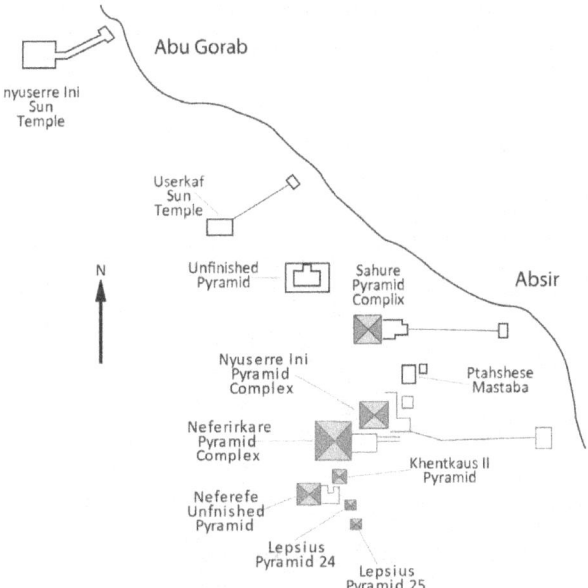

The techniques and constructions of these pyramids don't reflect advanced technologies or the use of power tools, the pyramid of Sahure is very close to the pyramid of Userkaf, the other 2 pyramids at Abusir (pyramid of Neferirkare Kakai and pyramid of Niuserre) were built as step pyramids first and then got the shape of true pyramid after the pyramids were cased with the casing stone.

If you move few hundred meters north of Abusir, you will reach a site called Abu Gorab, in this site there is what is called by Egyptologists "sun temple", the sun temple is a very unique structure which was built only during the time of Dynasty 5 (or attributed to Dynasty 5), according to most of the Egyptologists, it is connected to the sun, or as they claim, it is connected to the sun cult.

The sun temple design is very simple to explain but it is very difficult to figure out how it was made, it consists of 2 major parts

- The base
- The obelisk

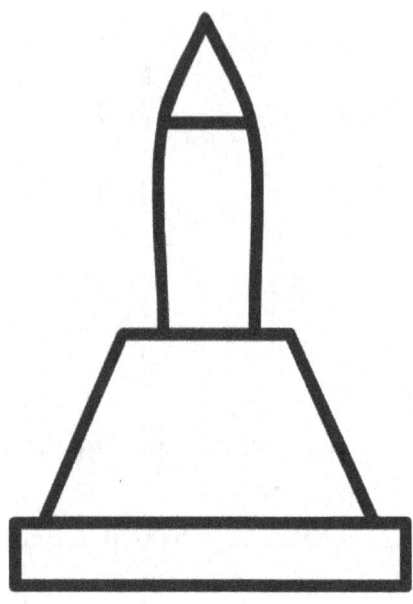

Sun Temple

The base which looks like a pyramid, it is bigger than the size of the small pyramids of the Great Pyramid at Giza. The base is made of limestone and it is oriented to the 4 cardinal directions.

The obelisk which was placed above the base is completely destroyed, and according to the scattered granite chunks in the area, I assume it was made out of rose granite.

According to a carving was found on one of these granite blocks, the size of this obelisk will be enormous, I think the weight would be around 1000 tons or even more.

The pyramids of Dynasty 6 are not reflecting any advanced technologies, and it is not close to the quality of the pyramids attributed to Dynasty 4, all of these pyramids are not big pyramids and the quality of the stone is not very high, also all of these pyramids lost the casing stone and not in a good shape or good condition.

Egypt had lost its power by the end of the Old Kingdom, but this power was restored by the beginning of the Middle Kingdom, they enhanced and developed so many of the aspects of life in Ancient Egypt, including art, statuary and constructions and I expected that the pyramid construction would be part of this development, but no, the pyramids of dynast 12 don't reflect again any high technologies like the pyramids attributed to Dynasty 4.

I want to say if we don't include the pyramids of Dynasty 4 to the graph of pyramid's development it will be correct.

So when I talk about the development of the pyramids I must mention Dynasty 1, Dynasty 2, Dynasty 3, Dynasty 5, Dynasty 6, Dynasty 12

This sequence will make more sense, but if I add Dynasty 4 to this sequence, the whole story will not make any sense.

The Lost Technologies and Advanced Knowledge

The strange cut marks on many statues and many blocks

After almost 20 years as a tour guide visiting the Ancient sites all the time, I can tell you that I found so many strange cut marks on hundreds of ancient blocks and stones, and on many statues exhibited at the Egyptian museum in Cairo.

My first cut marks to observe were at Giza Plateau, the eastern side of the Great Pyramid, when you walk around the area which is covered with blocks of basalt stone (so-called the mortuary temple) you will realize that there are so many cut marks on these basalt blocks, when you get closer to have a good look you will clearly see that it is a mark of a power tool, no way to be a mark of a chisel or a manual saw.

The cut mark is long, and it is a continues mark and the striations show that the saw blade used to wrap in some levels, we are very lucky to have these mistakes happen so we can understand more about the type of blades they were using to cut these blocks, I don't need to remind you that basalt stone is a volcanic stone, so it is classified as one of the hard stones, the solidness of basalt according to MOHS scale is 5-6, so it is hard stone and it requires a proper tool to cut it, especially with the high quality we see in the Ancient Egyptian sites.

It was suggested that cut marks like these were made by a manual saw!

Of course, the Ancient Egyptians used a manual saw, but we have a small problem here, there is not any iron tools were found from the entire Old Kingdom!!

EGYPT BEFORE THE WRITTEN HISTORY

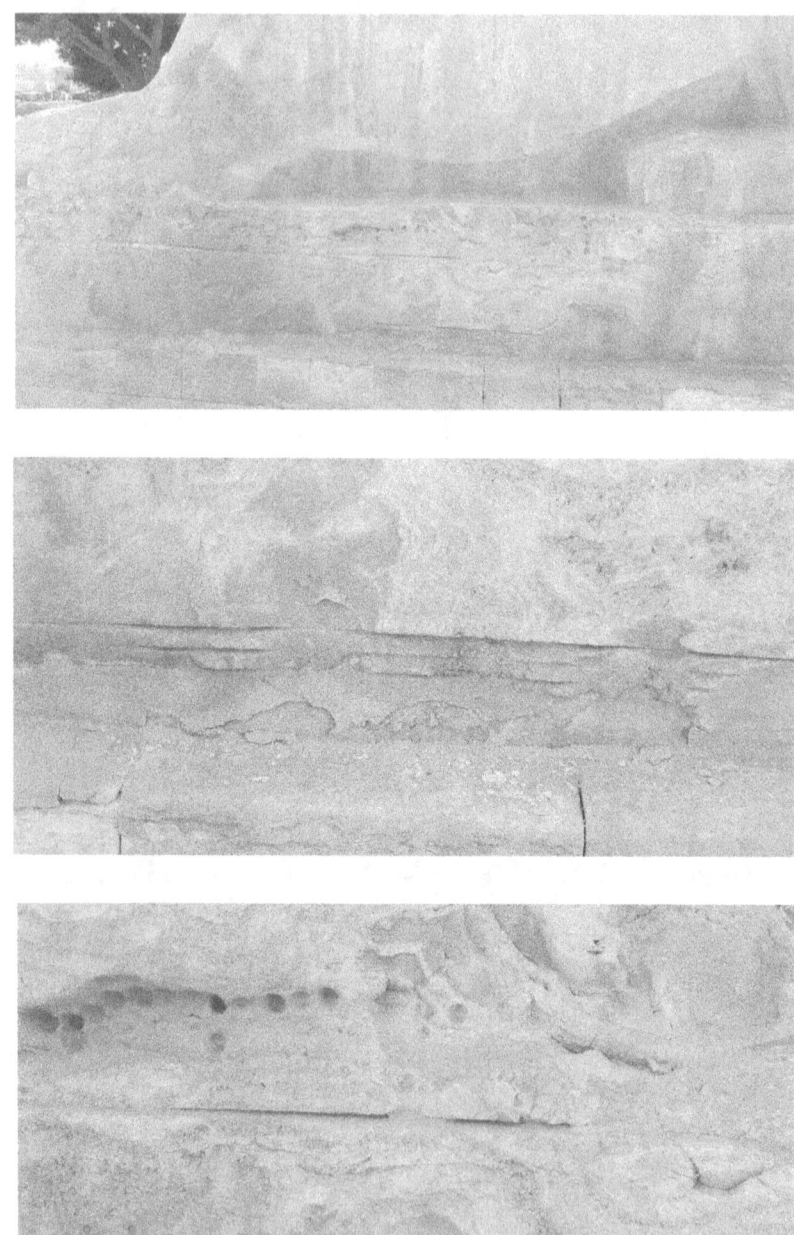

Egypt Before the Written History

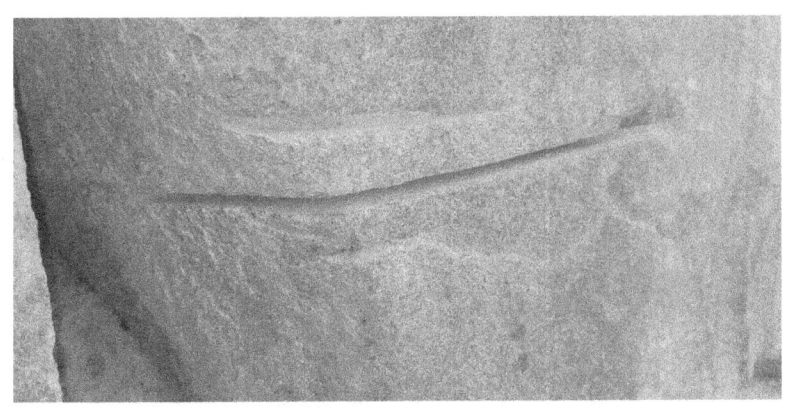

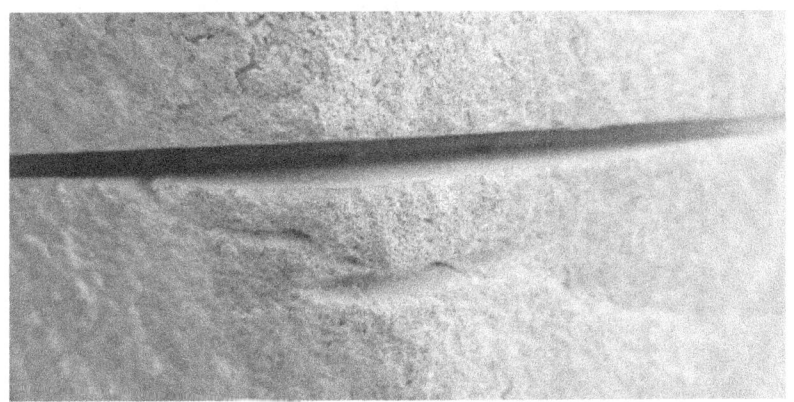

In this case, there is another suggestion was made by the academics, they say that the Ancient Egyptians used a rope filled with gems (hard stones)!?

They are talking about a rope filled with small pieces of hard and sharp stones, to understand the shape of this tool, imagine a sandwich, the rope is the bread and the sharp stones are the beef.

I can easily say that there is not a single demonstration to such claim, and again, we didn't find such tool except a primitive sickle to cut clover and wheat.

This suggestion is not accepted at all, and even if we agree that it was one of the ways to cut these blocks, you are going to find completely different cut marks, according to the cut mark we can understand the type of the tool and also the speed of this tool and the blade.

There are many cut marks in this area, but I like to talk about a strange cut mark there, it is triangular cut mark, as if it was cut with a tool with 3 blades, sometimes I see these 3 cuts in a horizontal position and sometimes in a vertical position. I saw this triple cut in 3 different places, 2 places are inside Egypt and one place is outside Egypt;

1. Triple cut on one of the basalt blocks at the so-called mortuary temple of the Great Pyramid.
2. Triple cut on the 2nd biggest sphinx in Egypt, the alabaster sphinx at Memphis museum.
3. Triple cut on a rose granite block at Baalbek in Lebanon, Temple of Bacchus.

I visited Lebanon in 2015, I went there with one of my groups to do a trip to Lebanon, this trip included a visit to this famous and huge site, Baalbek. When I first entered the temple I was impressed with the design and the size of the blocks, I saw some limestone blocks are more than 1000 tones, honestly, I didn't expect to be impressed by any site outside Egypt, while exploring every block in the temple I found this rose granite piece with the triple cut on it, and later I found another one, so maybe because of this piece I can attribute this temple to the Ancient Egyptian civilization.

At Karnak temple before you reach the so-called holy of holies (Philip Arrhidaeus holy of holies) at the sixth pylon, you can see a long vertical cut on the rose granite stone, not only this vertical cut but also a horizontal cut too.

If you have the chance to visit the east side of the pyramid of Teti at Sakkara you will see an alabaster block with a very strange cut on it, the cut mark is not straight cut, it is slightly takes the shape of a circle, huge circle, and again if we look closely to the cut mark you will see the effect of the blade when it was vibrating (blade warping).

On the lid of one of the granite boxes at the Egyptian Museum at Cairo we can see the result of blade warping, we can see the striations still exist above the surface of this lid.

In another site to the north of Giza Plateau called Abu Rawash there is a very strange piece of rose granite, but you must know that the visit of this site is available only through a private visit, next to the pyramid from the east side, there is a slab from rose granite, the slab itself is not flat, the surface is slightly curvy, on top of this slab there is a horizontal cut, and again I believe it happened because of the blade warp.

Because I mentioned this slab next to Abu Rawash pyramid and how it has this angle, as if this slab was part of a huge circular design, I must mention another similar slab at Karnak temple, this small slab is located in the area I call it Karnak junkyard, it is the area to the south of the main temple at Karnak, it has thousands of broken pieces of stone which one day were part of walls, statues and obelisks.

These strange cut marks are not only above stone blocks at the sites, no, you can see some cut marks above some statues too.

At the Egyptian Museum in Cairo when you go to the Old Kingdom section to the room of Dynasty 4, you will see the famous statue of King Khafra, when you face this diorite statue to the left side there is another diorite statue (attributed to Khafra) but smaller in size, under the right thigh you will see that there are some cuts slightly deeper than the level of the line forming the edge of the thigh, also from the front side if you look to the space between the 2 calf muscles, you will see a short vertical cut mark. I always explain these cut marks on this statue as a MISTAKE, yes the blade supposed not to go deeper and create this mistake (cut mark), and because of such mistakes I understand that there was a kind of mechanism to control the advanced tool, but sometimes the humane element can cause some mistakes.

There are other examples of using superior tools, but this time I don't call it mistakes, these cuts are shaping the outlines of statue or some parts of it.

In the stone junkyard of Karnak temple there are remains of a huge alabaster statue, one of the big pieces there is the feet (right feet), we can see that the tool was used to create the outlines of each toe is an advanced tool, not a hammer and a chisel. We can see the continues straight sharp cut which is not easy at all to make it on this type of stone (alabaster) unless you have such advanced tool.

There are so many examples for these cut marks and I need a sperate book to talk about it, so before finishing this chapter I must talk about another strange cut or core drill holes, which can be seen in many sites.

While exploring many ancient sites in Egypt, especially when you cross through the gate of the structure you are going to see perfectly rounded holes in the stone block, the size of these holes is not the same in every case and also the depth is not same, I didn't have the chance to measure it, but I can tell you that the diameter of some of these holes is cm, cm and cm and the depth of some of these holes is cm, cm and cm.

All the example I saw for these holes were made into granite stone, and most of it were made in the location of the upper part of the door lintels (header), the second location for these holes is the door jambs.

When you look carefully inside these holes you will easily recognize spiral lines carved into the sides of the hole, these lines or striations were explained to be the effect of the revolving blade which was used to make this hole, again when you look to these holes you will easily realize the precise cut and the direction of the cut going deep into the stone is perfectly straight.

After seeing many of these holes you will immediately understand the tool was used to make these holes is a core drill, not a manual core drill, but a mechanical advanced core drill.

So, I can say that the Ancient Egyptians had use tubular drills to make holes into door lintels and jambs to fit the hinges and locks of the doors.

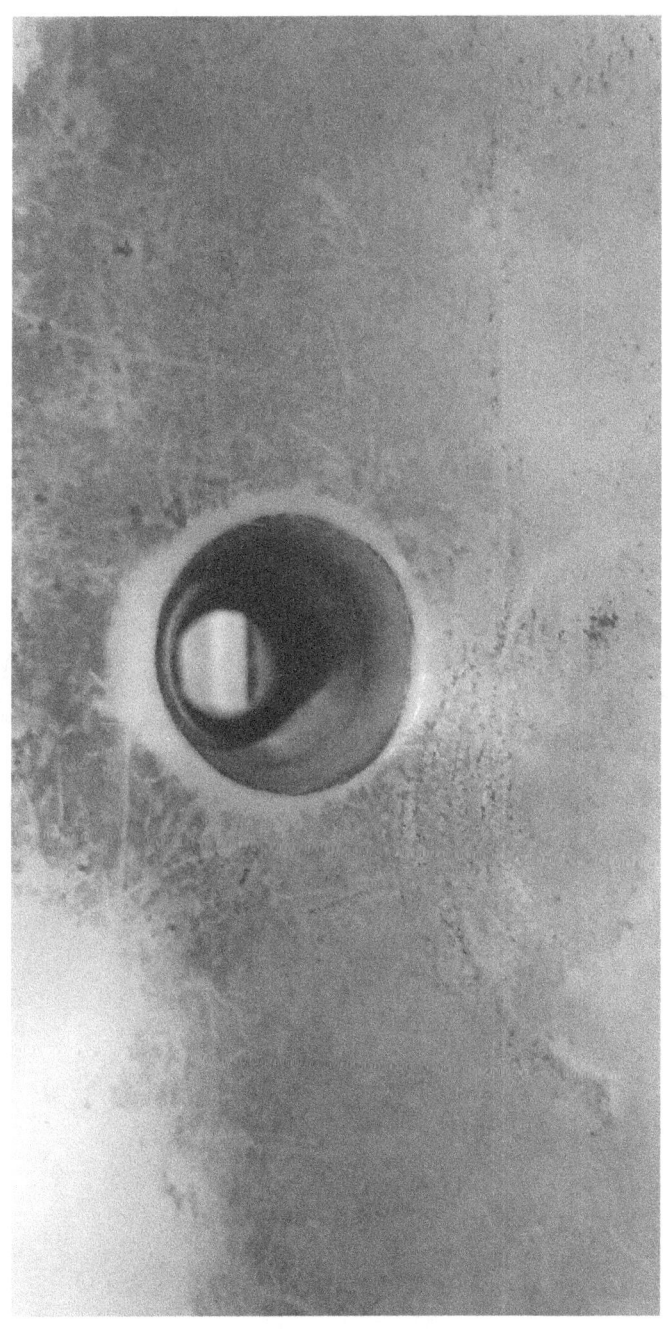

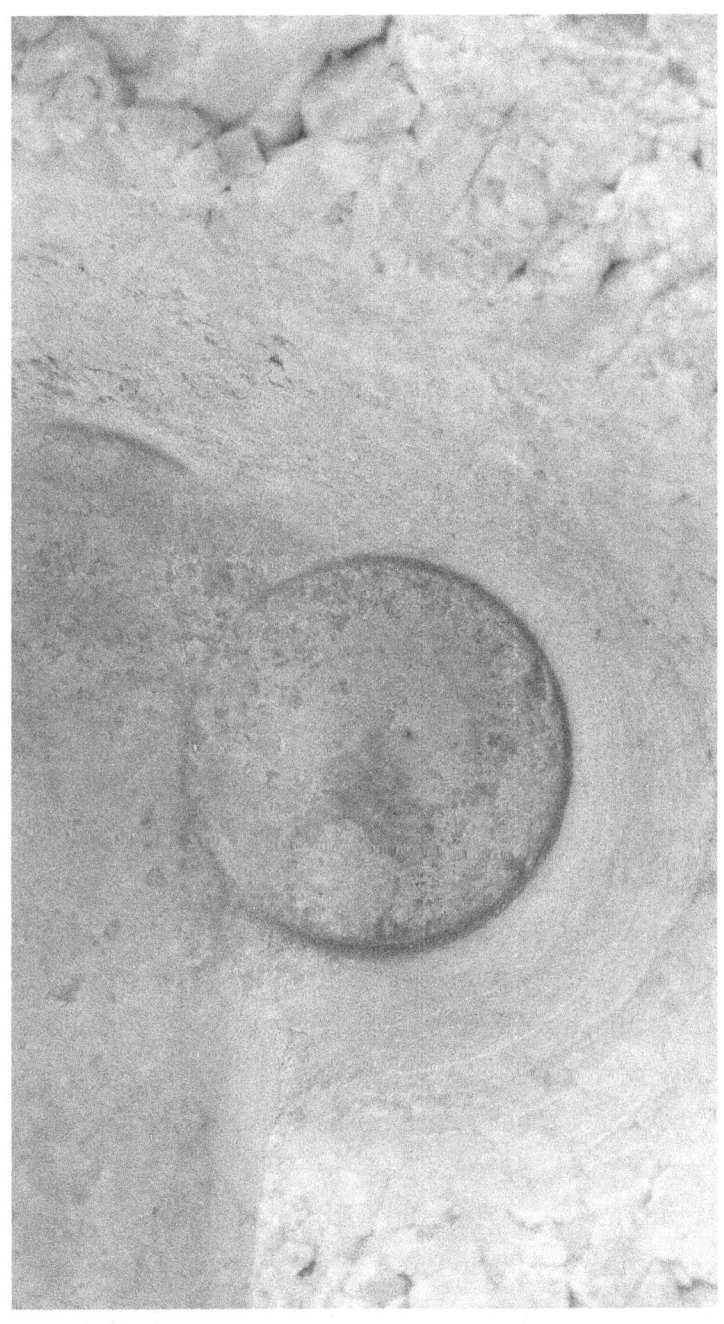

I understood from many engineers who joined many of my tours that the striations inside the ancient holes are not close to each other, and the striations inside the modern holes are close to each other, the ancient tool was more efficient than the modern tool because it cuts deeper and maybe it didn't need to spin so fast like our modern drills.

Sir Flinders Petrie paid attention to these holes, and he found several cores from alabaster and granite, he collected many of these cores and it is located now in Petrie Museum in London.

Both Flinders Petrie and Alfred Lucas paid attention to this technique, and they tried to answer this important question, how the Ancient Egyptian managed to drill granite and other hard stones 5000 years ago?

Lucas stated that neither copper nor bronze tools can cut hard stones (like granite, quartzite, basalt and diorite), but he said, if they use an abrasive powder it can do the job.

Petrie said, to make this hole into granite you will need a jeweled tubular drill.

Lucas didn't accept the idea that the Ancient Egyptians specially Dynasty 2 and 03 could have the knowledge to make jeweled tubular drill, so he insisted on his opinion about the abrasive powder.

Petrie didn't believe that the abrasive powder can be efficient at all.

At the end they did not agree about what was the tool could make such perfect hole into granite, Lucas adopted the idea of using copper tube, this tube will revolve above wet loose abrasive powder from sand. Petrie believed that a tool with fixed points of emery.

In 1995 **Nova team** which consists of Denys Stocks, Roger Hobkins and led by Mark Lehner, this team was trying to prove that the Ancient Egyptians truly used the primitive manual techniques in constructing the pyramids, obelisks and cutting stones especially hard stones.

They brought a long copper saw with teeth to cut a granite block, they first had to make a groove into the surface and then they put sand inside this groove, and they put the saw on top of the sand. They said that this technique will make a cut 04 mm in one hour, in the video the made it shows that after a few days they managed to cut 08-10 cm.

04 mm in one hour!!

We must understand that we are talking about work is being done by humans not machines, so if they will cut 04 mm ion the first hour, they will be tired and cut 02 mm in the second hour and I don't know for how many hours they can keep doing this?

And again, if we look to the result of the cut which was made by a manual tool, it is not the same mark as the cut was made by the Ancient Egyptians.

These holes were made by an advanced tool, a tool like what we have nowadays or even better, a mechanical tool which can provide a continues speed and pressure so it can do the cut in a perfect way.

I want you when you have the chance to see some of these drilled holes to pay attention to the outer shape of these cuts, you will see what we call it key cuts, I think that there was a kind of a metal mechanical design was fitting inside these holes. As an example, the hole on the first granite gate at Hatshepsut temple, it is a part of the door system, it is where they place the door hinge.

The popular theory says that the door has a vertical hinge (top and bottom), the door opens when it revolves, but this movement will lead to the erosion of the hole.

According to many holes with what we call it "key cuts" we understand that the hinge doesn't move (revolve), but it was another piece connects between the door and the hinge (like bearings).

The Obelisks and the challenges of cutting and lifting huge blocks

The Obelisk

The obelisks are very strange designs in Ancient Egypt, there are hundreds of opinions and theories about the functions of all the Ancient Egyptian buildings and structures but not the obelisk, many scholars will tell you, it is a symbolic design, or it points to the sky or to the sun as a holy sign to Ra or Atum.

The ancient Egyptian name for the obelisk is txn (tekhen or techen), and the symbol obelisk is playing as the word mn which means stable (or stability), like in the royal name of king Seti I, mn maat ra which means stable system of Ra, the word mn was replaced by the symbol obelisk to make us understand that obelisk also mean "stable". The plural of the word tekhen (obelisk) is tekhenu (obelisks). The word obelisk was derived from the Greek word obeliskos which means "small spit", the Arabic word for obelisk is mesalah which means big patching needle.

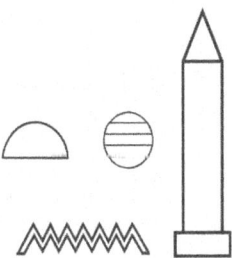

What is the obelisk?

The obelisk is one single piece of stone usually rose granite, it is 4 sided big and long piece of stone, it has a square base and it tapers to the top, the top takes the shape of a small pyramid (pyramidion), this type of obelisks is usually heavy and exceeding 300 tons, like the obelisk attributed to Ramses II at Luxor temple.

According to the mainstream stories, constructing obelisks started by the kings of the Old kingdom, like the small limestone obelisk of king Teti and a similar obelisk for the high priest Idu. But the oldest example of tall rose granite obelisk is one at Al-Matariyyah (north Cairo) which is attributed to king Senusret I (Dynasty 12, Middle kingdom), and then the obelisks of the New kingdom, there are some obelisks were made from different stone rather than rose granite, like the quartzite obelisk of king Seti I.

But we shall not **forget to mention** the giant obelisks which were built at the Sun temples at Abusir and Abu Ghurab and as I mentioned earlier these constructions were attributed to Dynasty 5. According to the image was carved by the Ancient Egyptians and the size of one of the bases of this this construction which still exist at Abu Ghurab, the size of the obelisk on top of this bas will be enormous, I think it will be more than 1000 tones.

Idu Obelisk

We can see the standing obelisks at Karnak temple and Luxor temple, there were many obelisks inside Karnak temple but most of it were destroyed because they were trying to take it out of the temple, because they were using the primitive technique which they claimed it was the technique was used by the Ancient Egyptians to erect the obelisk, the broken obelisk near the lake inside Karnak temple is a great example for this great failure to use the technique which they invented, and by the way, till now this is the mainstream believe, they didn't get the fact that this primitive technique is completely wrong.

I will describe the technique they think it the was used by the Ancient Egyptians to erect the obelisk. They say that the builders will decide where they are going to place the obelisk and they put the base on the spot the chose, they will bring tons of sand and put around that spot, or surrounding the base, as if they design high ground or small hill surrounding the base, and then they will drag the obelisk above this artificial hill to reach the top, they will slide down the obelisk slowly until it droops nicely above the base. I will not put may comment about this fantasy theory, but again I will tell you that, this was the exact same technique the early adventurer and treasure hunters used to take many of our obelisks to Europe, but the broke many of our rose granite obelisk before they figure out that this technique is a great failure, and they started to use another way to take the obelisk, and they had to use tones of wooden bars and steel.

The biggest obelisk in Egypt and in the world is not finished, I don't this was bad luck for the workers who were cutting the obelisk from the granite quarry or it is good luck for us, so we can the methods of cutting in Ancient Egypt.

Although we have an unfinished obelisk still lays down at the granite quarry in Aswan, we couldn't agree about the technique which was used to cut such obelisk, and we became 2 major groups, each group does believe that the obelisk was cut in a specific way and no other.

The first group believes that the obelisk was being cut with dolerite bounders! some round balls a little pit bigger than the hand size were found in the granite quarry at Aswan, these balls are dolerite bounders, and this is the evidence was used by the mainstream academics.

The second group (I'm part of it) believes that the obelisk was being cut with an advance technology, and it wasn't the same tool which cut the other blocks, there were at least 2 tools, the first one cuts straight smoothed edges, we can this edge when we go inside the quarry to the area at the ground level which has water and some green reeds.

The second tool creates rough cuts, and it is a continues cut starts from outside the border line of the obelisk and goes down to the base level and continue up to the obelisk surface, the tool creates similar patterns all the way till the end of the cut. I realized that there is a line of red color on each edge of these long patterns (vertical lines) and sometimes there are some horizontal lines go across the vertical lines, the red color is not a red ocher color or painting, it is something different and it looks like a natural color or vine on the surface. But we won't see these lines on that smoothed wall on the other side.

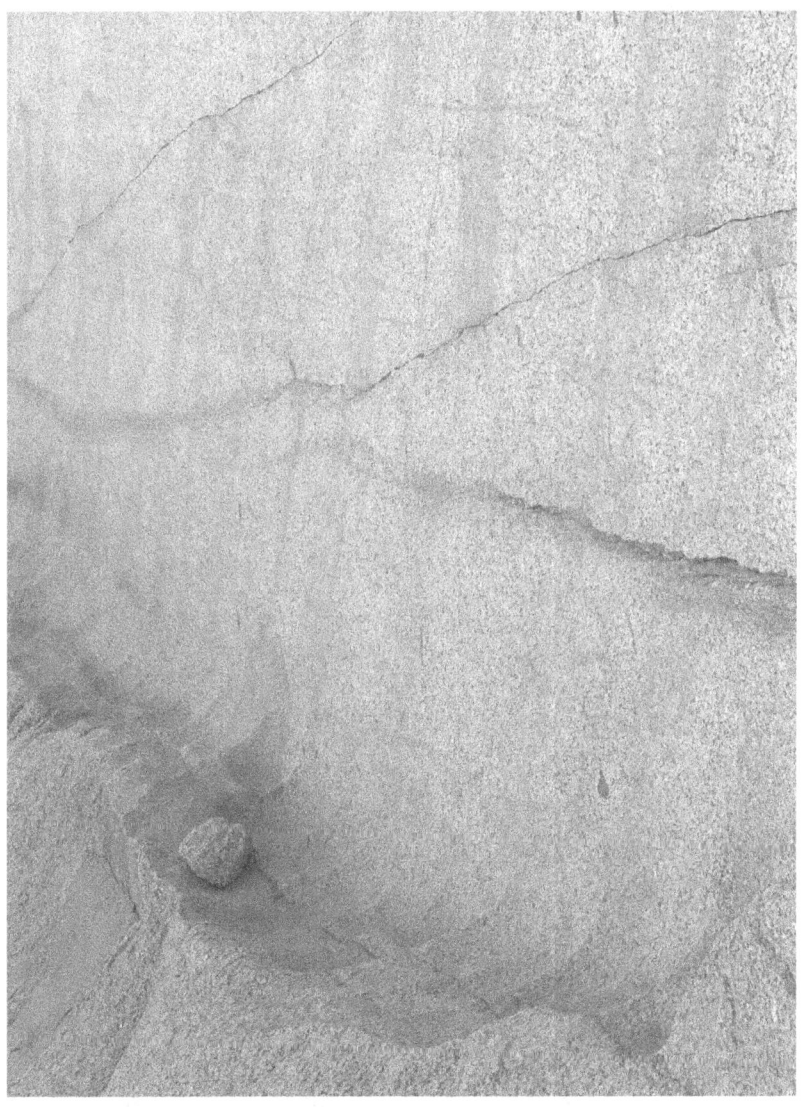

The unfinished obelisk is about 42 m (138 ft), the estimate weight is around 1200 tons, and the trench surrounding the obelisk is almost 70 cm. If you are staying at the top of the obelisk, will see that edge of the quarry from that side is very limited, and the space from the other side is not huge too, so if we talk about a big number of workers it wouldn't fit in these limited spaces.

The workers had left the work at this obelisk after the almost finished 75% of the job because of unknown reason, the famous story says that while they were working the obelisk was cracked from the top part.

I never believed that story and which doesn't make any sense, the ancient workers made what we called test pits to understand if there is a natural crack in there way or no, the surface of the obelisk was cut and shaped in a good way so there was no crack at that point. Cracks happened into the stone because of natural reasons and expand when the block is cut and being moved or vibrated, I believe that the crack occurred into the unfinished obelisk happened after the obelisk was cut and after the workers abundant the location for an unknown reason, as if the workers went for lunch and never come back.

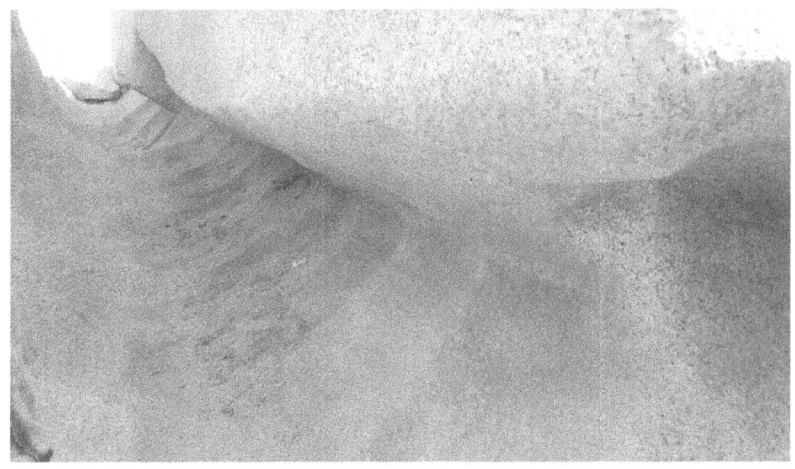

When we check the tool marks in this granite quarry, we will see many different marks, we can clearly see the difference between these so-called "scooping marks" and the other tool mark, which was found in many sections of this quarry, these tool marks were made by iron chisels and hummers (from iron or something else).

This technique was always used to cut a slice of the stone by separating it from a sideway or from the top level.

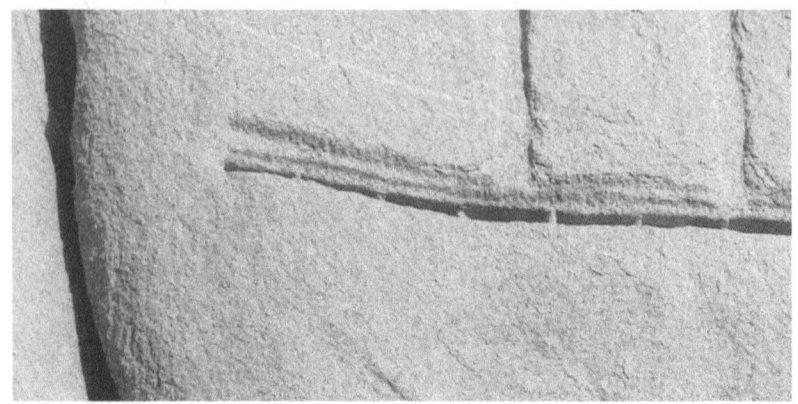

But these strange tool marks "scooping marks" are not a result of any known tool or blade we know.

My friend Timothy Hogan suggested that the Ancient Egyptians poured hydrofluoric acid above the stone, and it milted the stone fabric then they scooped these milted sections.

Egypt Before the Written History

According to the famous story, the word Technology means science of craft, it consists of 2 Greek words τέχνη (techne) and λογία (logia). I say that the source of the word Technology is the Ancient Egyptian word Techen (obelisk) and the Greeks add Logia to it, so it became the Technology (the science of Obelisks).

I believe that the obelisk was used in Ancient Egypt in many ways:

- As an antenna, sending and receiving signals from place to another (from temple to another), the quartz inside the rose granite is the reason for this ability, so we can say it was used for communications.
- As tuning forks, creating certain resonance to affect the visitors of the temple before they enter the place and while they proceed getting inside, that's why they are always in pairs.
- As acupunctures, it was used to absorb negative energies from the bodies of the visitors and recharge their bodies with positive energies, we can see this clear on the seated statue in front of Luxor temple, the one to the right side (it is attributed to king Ramses II).

You will find that in many cemeteries all over the world, especially some Christian cemeteries in Egypt, the tomb stone was made as an obelisk, why?

The answer is, the dynastic Egyptians and the later Egyptians were trying to bring the healing abilities of the obelisks to their dead relatives or maybe communication abilities!

The challenges of cutting and lifting huge stone blocks

When we talk about megalithic blocks of stones either limestone or granite, we must ask ourselves this important question, how they cut this huge piece of stone?

I'm not talking about the cutting tool yet; I'm talking about the ability to identify a location which can allow them to find such long piece without cracks. I understand that if you want to cut a small block of stone (1 m X 1m) it will easy to cut it from many spots at the quarry, but when you want to cut bigger blocks the chances are going to be less and less so you have to go to the deep levels of the quarry and the bigger block you want the deeper level you must go.

I visited a **church** in Cairo in an area called Al Mokattam Mountain or Hills, Al Mokattam was formed during the Eocene era and it has a good quality of limestone. The church was built around 1974-1976 and it is called Saint Simon Church. When I went inside the church I saw a huge cave goes deep more than 200 m with an angle almost 45°, this is what they called the big church and it can house more than 15,000 persons together in the same time, there is another church is called the winter church, it is smaller but it has the same design, it is also a cave but not huge like the main cave, when I saw the 2 churches I immediately understand that these 2 caves were 2 quarries from the Ancient Egyptian times, but not any quarries, quarries for the huge blocks.

EGYPT BEFORE THE WRITTEN HISTORY

And I shall mention again that the huge area near Abu Rawash pyramid is a very good quarry of pure limestone, and there are many huge "caves" under the ground level, so I believe that these were the locations where they cut the big blocks.

Cutting big blocks from deep levels under the ground is adding another challenge to the workers who are going to take this piece out its location and then out of the quarry itself.

I believe that the rose granite quarry at Aswan was much bigger and higher than it is nowadays, but because the Ancient Egyptians cut tens of thousands of huge blocks from there it became smaller and smaller.

After they cut the obelisk and take it outside the quarry, the famous story explains that the Ancient Egyptian prepared a small harbor near the granite quarry and they put the obelisk on top of a large ship, this ship will sail during the flood time (July-September) to the Nile and then to its destination either Luxor, Cairo or another destination.

This story is not correct and the lower level of the quarry in front of the main entrance was not a small harbor because of a simple reason, if go up at the quarry and look towards the west side you will not be able to see the Nile, Why? Because there a high hill between the Nile and the quarry, so how the chips are going to sail above the hill, and no way to claim that the Nile annual flood can reach that height.

Yes I know that there is a scene on the walls of the temple of Hatshepsut showing a boat is carrying 2 obelisks, and most of the guessing are saying that these are Hatshepsut's 2 obelisks at Karnak temple, but again in my opinion this is not true, the size of each obelisk is huge and it will be too much to load one obelisk above such boat, what about 2 obelisks.

The same question will be repeated when you stand in front of the Valley temple at Giza Plateau from east side, how they left these huge blokes??

The limestone blocks which were used to build this temple are weighing more than 50 tones, there are bigger blocks at the 2nd level and at the 3rd level. Every step in moving and constructing these blocks is a great challenge.

The giant statue at the Ramesseum temple in the west bank at Luxor is one of the big questions about the capabilities of the Ancient Egyptians.

This seated statue which is attributed to Ramses II is made from the Aswanian rose granite, the estimate weight for this statute is 1000 tones and the estimate wait for the pedestal is 500 tones. When we talk about this statue we always mention this heavy weight but we don't pay attention to the original weight when it was just a block, the size and weight of the block was bigger than the current statue because they had to hack the space between the head and the thighs, the height of the statute is 19 meters (62 feet), I'm talking about a huge piece of stone was removed from the main block, I think the weight of this piece was 250 tons or more, so in my opinion the original weight of the block was 1250 tones or even more.

There is another huge statute is attributed to King Ramses II, the fragments of these statue are in Tanis, Tanis or San El Hagar I believe it is the modern name for the Ancient Egyptian city Pr Ramses (the house of Ramses), or maybe it was Avaris, the former Hyksos capital. There are hundreds of huge granite and quartzite blocks scattered in a vast area, these huge broken pieces include a huge granite foot, it was one day part of a giant statue, and according to the size of this foot we understand that it was bigger than the statue at Ramesseum, I think it was around 1200 tones, and the original block was around 1500 tones.

When I talk about huge statues, most of the people will expect me to talk about granite statues only, but there are huge statues made from other materials maybe not hard like granite, but we still ask the same question, how they cut these huge blocks?

At West Bank of Luxor there are 2 huge statues from quartzite stone, this stone is not from Aswan this time, it is from Cairo, yes from east Cairo, the quarry is called El-Gabal el-Ahmar, the 2 statues are called the colossi of Memnon, the story behind this name is interesting.

It says that the 2 statues were doing a sound like whistling every day during or after the dawn time, so they connected between the Ethiopian King Memnon who was killed by Achilles and these 2 statues, it was said the Memnon was the son of Eos, the goddess of dawn. Around 200 A.D during the time of the roman emperor Septimus Severus, an attempt to restore the colossi was made, since then the colossi are not whistling anymore. The 2 statues are attributed to king Amenhotep III.

The estimate weight of each statue is 700 tones, but as we understand when we talk about seated statues, we expect that the weight of the original was bigger, so maybe the original weight was 1000 tones.

Another 2 statues which are also attributed to king Amenhotep III, these 2 statues are standing statues and were made from another hard material, made from Conglomerate stone. Conglomerate is originally sandstone, but it contains it can contain clasts of many rock material such as quartz, gravel and chemical cement, so I can say it is like natural concrete, this composition makes Conglomerate is a hard material to cut or carve with primitive tools. These 2 standing statues are in the west bank of Luxor near the Ramesseum temple, the estimate weight for each statue is 400 tones.

When you visit Luxor temple you will see 4 megalithic granite seated statues, 2 statues are in front of the first pylon (tower or gate) and the other 2 statues are in front of the 2nd pylon. These 4 statues are attributed to King Ramses II because his name is written above them, and other scholars believe that these statues are originally made by King Amenhotep III and were usurped by Ramses II.

Each statue is made of one single piece of granite, the estimate weight of each statue is 700 tons, and I think the original weight of the block was 1000 tones. When you are facing the first pylon of Luxor temple you will realize that the statue to the right side (west side) has a hollow rectangular space in the lower level, we think it was made to support the block from being totally cracked by adding hard material inside this hollow space to keep the 2 sides of the block together, also I want to explain that I believe that this crack happened after the statue was put in front of the temple.

- There are so many examples for huge statues from Ancient Egypt, such as:
- The statue of Queen Meritamun at Tell Basta (Bubastis).
- The statue of Queen Meritamun at Akhmim, Sohag.
- The limestone colossal statue of King Amenhotep and his wife queen Tiye at the Egyptian museum in Cairo.
- The limestone statue of King Ramses II at Memphis Museum.

And I can add to this list hundreds of broken pieces of statues, and from the size of these pieces we understand that the statue was huge.

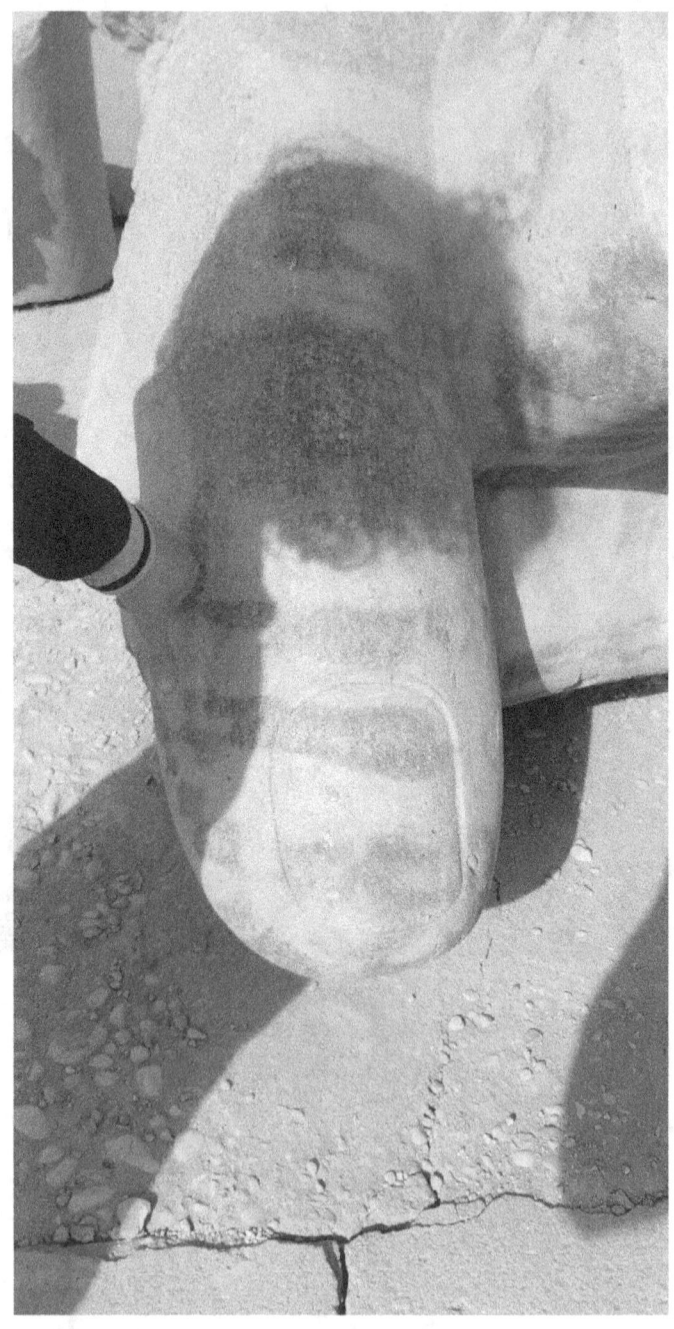

EGYPT BEFORE THE WRITTEN HISTORY

Statue broken kneecap VS Mohamed's kneecap

The Serapeum

The meaning and discovery of the Serapeum

The Searpeum means the place of Serapis, it is the burial site for the sacred Apis Bull, the Apis bull it relates to the Ancient Egyptian "deity" Ptah.

It was found by the French Egyptologist Auguste Mariette, in 1850 he first found a head of a Sphinx sticking out from the sand of Sakkara at the northwest side of Djoser Step Pyramid, after clearing the sand from around the statue he found other sphinx statues creating a sphinx avenue leads to the entrance of the Serapeum (around 600 Sphinxes). Some stories mentioned that she was a lady riding a horse who found the head of the buried sphinx, she was visiting Sakkara and decided to take a horse ride in this area around the Serapeum, the hoof of the horse hit the top part of the head of a Sphinx statue and that was the reason of this great discovery.

The meaning of Serapis

Σέραπις (Serapis) is a Greek name for the Ancient Egyptian sacred bull Ausir-Hap, the Apis Bull was considered as a son to Hathor and it was connected to Ptah first and then Osiris

(Ausir), the cult center of Ptah is the ancient capital of Egypt, Memphis, the name of Serapis is derived from the Ancient Egyptian name for the Apis Bull (Osiris + Hap) Ausir-Ap which became Auserapis and finally Serapis.

During my many visits inside the Egyptian museum in Cairo, especially after they allowed photos, I found a drawing of bull carrying a coffin to the grave, I found this drawing on many coffins, the coffin of the dead person was normally carried by a donkey or by people.

So, I believe that the Ancient Egyptians were connecting between the bull and the afterlife journey.

The reputation of Serapis was in a great level during the Hellenistic period, Serapis for the Ancient Egyptian was the sacred Apis Bull, Serapis for the Greeks was a man with heavy beard (similar to Zeus) with a Modius above the head (modius is a type of flat-topped cylindrical headdress or crown found)

Locations of the Serapeum

There 3 famous locations in Egypt bear the name Serapeum;

1. Serapeum of Ismailia

In Ismailia (Egyptian governorate) we have a town called Serapeum, we are not sure if there is an underground structure or no, no diggings were made to prove it or deny it.

2. Serapeum of Alexandria

The surrounding area of the huge pillar in Alexandria (Pompey's Pillar or Sawary Pillar), there are remains of a huge temple this temple was dedicated to Serapis, it was built during the time of Ptolemy III Euergetes, so the triad of Alexandria was Serapis, Isis and Harpocrates. There is a tunnel system under the bedrock, this area was playing as a substitute to the famous Library of Alexandria.

3. Serapeum of Sakkara

In Sakkara at the northwest side of the Step Pyramid there is a huge tunnel under the ground called the Serapeum, there is no upper structure found for this Serapeum.

Serapeum of Sakkara

When you visit Sakkara and reach the cross roads, if you turn left you will reach the Step Pyramid, if you turn right you will reach Teti's pyramid and some of the Noble's tombs, but if you drive straight you will reach the location of the Serapeum, to visit the Serapeum you must purchase an extra ticket.

The Serapeum is a tunnel under the bedrock, it runs from East to West for more than 500 meters, the height is 3-5 meters and the width of the tunnel is about 3 meters.

There are 24 boxes "sarcophagi" in the Serapeum, all the boxes are made from Granite and Granodiorite, except one box is made of Limestone.

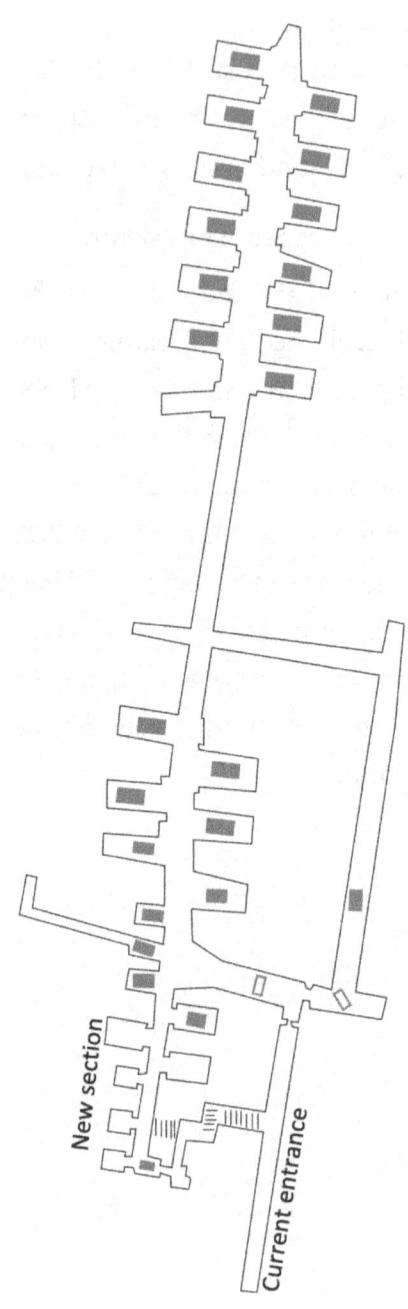

The estimate weight of each box is 55 - 70 tons and the lid of the box is 20 - 30 tons, so each box in total is 75 - 100 tons.

The box itself was made from one single piece of stone, the sides, edges, and corners were cut in a perfect precision. Perfect precision as if it was done by our modern technologies, but the truth is, our technologies will not be able to do this job easily, to be clear in this part I must say that our modern machines can do the job but in a long time and it will cost too much money, so in my opinion we will not find a company or a factory which will agree to do a job like this.

Each box is about 3.5 x 2.5 meters and the height is almost 2.5 meters, so fare there are no analyses done on this magnificent structure, all what we have are some individual work from the interested experts in engineering like Christopher Dunn. When we talk about the Serapeum we cannot ignore the efforts of Chris to show us the great work was done by the Ancient Egyptians who built the Serapeum, but first I must explain to you how we date this magnificent structure.

They attribute the Serapeum to the Eighteens Dynasty, time of Amenhotep III because of some artifacts were found and bear the name of Amenhotep III, prince Khaemweset son of king Ramses II from Dynasty 19 did some work at the Serapeum, some other rulers from different periods like king Psametik I from Dynasty 26 and an unknown ruler called Khababash from the end of the Egyptian civilization. But of course, they also relate the Serapeum to Greek era in Egypt specially Ptolemy III – Ptolemy XII. A big question well come to the scene, did the technologies during these time periods can produce the boxes inside the Serapeum? or can technologies these build the Serapeum underground galleries?

The answer is No, there are so many boxes from the New Kingdom time and the Late Period, but it doesn't match the same quality of the boxes at the Serapeum or even close.

When Chris had the permission to some measurements at the Serapeum he went inside the only box was found closed "intact" and he use his professional tools to check the flat surfaces of the box, he put the straight edge and he pointed his flashlight from the other side, the light didn't go through, which means that the surface is super flat and smoothed which allowed the straight edge to be place above it perfectly.

During my many visits to the Serapeum I discovered things are not mentioned in any book;

- At least one lid has a design from underneath (an edge or lip), so when they close the box the lid will not be slide, to open the lid, it must be lifted.
- Who made these boxes used a kind of a liquid to polish the external surfaces, remans of this liquid were found (leaking) on the bottom edge of one the lids.

Also, during my many visits to the Serapeum I hear many wrong information and stories but there 2 information are completely wrong;

1. The only box available for visit, they say it is made from Basalt stone, this information is absolutely wrong, it was made from Granodiorite, some guides who are not expert in Geology, say black granite which is ok, but it is not basalt.

Basalt stone doesn't have quarts in the molecular structure, granite does, and granodiorite does, and when visit this box you will see clearly the surfaces of box is full of quarts.

2. In our way out, there is an unfinished box in the middle of the second tunnel and after 4 meters we can see the lid, this box is made from granodiorite and it is not finished 100% yet. Guards will tell you a story to explain why this box is not inside its room, they say, king Farouk (1920 – 1965) wanted to take this box outside, I don't know why king Farouk would send his workers to take an unfinished box!! Why he didn't try to take one of the good boxes inside the Serapeum? the truth is that this box was not being taking out, it was on its way inside the Serapeum, but something happened and stopped the workers from finishing the job. As if they went for lunch and never come back.

As I mentioned this box is unfinished, why king Farouk would interested with an unfinished box? But it makes sense when we have an unfinished box in the middle of the tunnel heading to its room, from another unfished box in the main tunnel we understand that the builders did the final work inside the Serapeum.

After they cut, shape, transfer the box to the Serapeum and put the box in its room they smoothed the surfaces and made it in perfect straight edges, and the angles are perfectly done (90 degrees), and finally the add this liquid to make the surface polished and shiny, BUT we have a big question again!!!

One of the rooms which is housing an unfinished box is very small and the box is occupying the whole room, only few centimeters from each side between the walls and the box's surfaces, so how they did that final work, and with which tools, what is the size of these tools to fit in this very tiny space??

When I answer this question people get surprised, because I say that the Ancient Egyptian engineer was using nano tools, yes nano tools and I'm not talking about small or tiny chisels because it is impossible to use chisels even from iron and produce these smoothed straight sides of the boxes of the Serapeum, I'm talking about nano advanced tools.

Also there is an important fact about boxes like these, boxes with great quality, the lid is part from the same block of the main box, and it was cut from the back side of the box, my evidence is the unfinished box in the Egyptian museum in Cairo, you will see that the box is almost done and it is in a great shape, but when you look behind the box you will see the attempt to cut the lid, it was failure job, because half of the lid is broken and the other half is still attached to the box. I understand why the must cut the lid from the same stone block, because the number of quarts in the molecular structure is going to be similar in the box and the lid, this will create harmony between both of them when the box resonates.

An important thing you will realize while walking inside the Serapeum and looking to the boxes, the housing rooms on the right side and the ones on the left side are not facing each other, they are not on the same line, you will find a room on the left side facing a wall on the right side, and a room on the right side facing a wall on the left side.

Also, when you look to the boxes you will realize that they are not identical, or to be precise, the lids are not identical, the lids take the gem or somehow diamond shape, and if there is some angles are not symmetrical to each other they didn't care,

I think they didn't want to lose extra material, in my opinion, the volume of the stone was more important than the good-looking shape.

Another important thing you will realize when you visit the Serapeum and have a good look to the boxes, you will see some scooping marks, mostly on the lids and few on the boxes. There many opinions about what are these marks, one of these opinions was adopted by many visitors to the Serapeum and many people who are interested in the Serapeum, they say, these marks happened because the box and the lid was milted during the activation and became solid again, so these marks happened as a side effect to this change, I disagree with this 100%.

These scooping marks are truly scooping marks, how?

The Advanced Ancient Egyptian realized some small or tiny cracks on the surface of the lid or the box, these cracks will expand when the box resonates and it will turn into big crack later and the box will be destroyed, so they had to scope out these tiny cracks to avoid this future problem. This step must happen before the final step, which is the polishing step, that's why we see all the scooping marks are also polished like the rest of surface of the lid or the box.

Finally, digging the tunnel itself is a challenge to our modern machines, it can be done in modern days, but it will take lots of time and money, so if they claim that the dynastic Egyptians made it, then how and with which tools, there are many questions about the ability to dig in limestone without light and without ventilations. If we think that the Ancient Egyptians had used hammers and chisels to dig the Serapeum then we must know that because of this manual technique those workers are going to die before completing the job because when the workers smash the limestone bedrock, a powder will produced and fill the air, this powder is similar to white cement, which means that the workers who will inhale this powder will have problems with their lungs and maybe die because of that.

There is another problem which is light!!

To depend on the primitive ways to produce light in the ancient world we need fire or flame, inside the Serapeum if they did that and use a kind of candles or oil flames it means that they are going to lose the oxygen inside the tunnel which will create a big problem for their breathing.

If you didn't visit the Serapeum yet, I tell you must visit Egypt and must go and visit the Serapeum.

The Unfinished Box at the Egyptian museum in Cairo

The Egyptian museum in Cairo is one of the very interesting museums all over the world, because of course it contains the biggest collection for the Ancient Egyptian history, it contains around 120,000 items, the size of these items is varying, from 05 centimeters to 12 meters high.

In the Egyptian museum in Cairo you will see statues, shrines, boxes, jars, pillars, coffins, masks, stone scarabs, stelas, discs, shrines, mummies and more.

When you step inside the building, turn left towards the Old Kingdom section, on the far-left side next to the wall you will see a granite box, this box is laying on its side and the backside faces the wall, it is registered under the number JE54938

The dimensions of this box are:

Height: 108 cm, 94 cm, 84 cm (the bottom is not flat)

Width: 126 cm

Length: 245 cm

Thickness: 18 cm

This box was found in the cemetery G 7000 at the eastern side of the Great Pyramid, it was found inside the tomb of Hordjedef (Hor-Djed-Ef), tomb number G 7210 – G 7220.

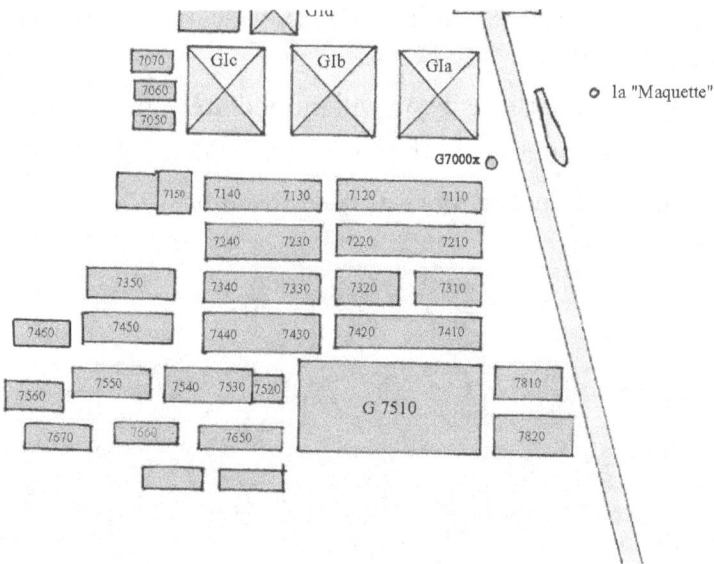

Hordjedef was one of the sons of the famous king of Dynasty 4, king khufu. Hordjedef was a half-brother of two great kings of Dynasty 4, king Djedefre and king Khafre.

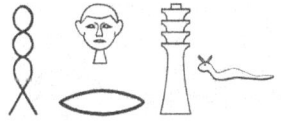

If you stay in front of this box you will realize that it is a good quality box, the edges of the box are done and the space inside the box is already hollowed, but it is not finished 100%, after seeing the front side you may leave the spot to see something else, but if you go behind the box you are going to see a completely different story.

You will see that there was a process to cut the lead from the backside but it seems that something grant happened and part of the lid is broken, we can still see the other piece of the broken lid is attached to the bottom of the box, we can clearly see the cut mark.

Once you see this cut you will immediately understand that it was cut by an advanced tool, by examining this cut we will know more about the tool was used to cut it.

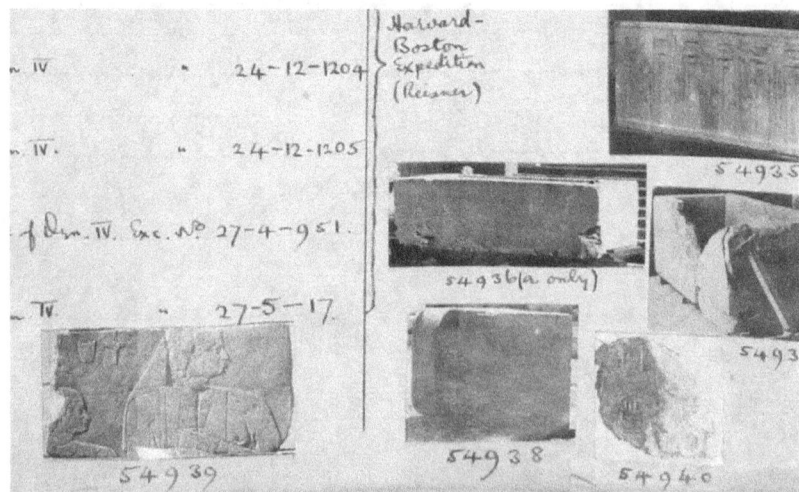

When we look carefully to the cut, we will see that it goes deep into the center and shallow from the top and bottom, also there are striations in the shape of a small crescent, so we understand that the tool was a disc saw. Yes, disc saw like what we have nowadays or even better. But when we look to the cut again we find that it doesn't go all the way through, and there is a similar cut from the lower level, so we now understand that there was another disc saw, this "saw table was prepared with 2 disc saws above each other. There was a third saw, this saw was straight saw, when we check the striations on the right side we will find that it is straight vertical striations so it is clear that there was a straight saw was working behind the 2 disc saws to cut the space will be still attached because of the space between the 2 disc saws.

I used to think that this box was neglected by the Ancient Egyptians, and I had a wrong information that it was found under the sand in Meidum site, near Meidum pyramid, I found that this box was used as a "normal" box by one of the sons of king Khufu, prince Hordjedef.

After I know these facts, I had many questions;

- Why they used a broken box?
- Did they put a lid above the box or no? because there are no stories about a lid was found in that tomb.
- Why didn't they continue cutting the broken lid and make a new lid to the box?
- Academics attribute great constructions to Dynasty 4, so why such box was used by "prince" Hordjedef

who wasn't one of the commoners, his position would grantee great tomb with great qualities.

The only answer for these questions, this box was re-used by prince Hordjedef, he used it with its condition and didn't want to change anything because his workers may have been destroyed it.

There is another important question about this unfinished box, why the one who was making this box didn't cut this piece of the lid, flatten the bottom, and make a new lid from any other granite piece??

To answer this question we need to understand that granite in general contains quartz (05% - 20%), but rose granite contains more quartz (02% - 60%) that's why rose granite was the popular granite in Ancient Egypt, so the ancient Egyptians understood that each part of the rose granite quarry contains different amount of quartz in it molecular structure. They made sure when they are building a structure or doing an artifact to bring the blocks of granite from the same spot.

So, they needed to cut the lid from the same piece of the box to keep the same percentage of the quartz in the molecular structure, but why from the backside?

It seems that this box and the other boxes were used in an important function, this function required certain system and design, so they made sure to stick with the details even if they waste the whole material.

Most of the sources say that granite is not a magnetic rock, but we must understand that granite contains some minerals which can be magnetic (amphibole minerals), it seems that the quartz in the granite fabric deals with the earth magnetism somehow, so my guessing that by cutting the led from the bottom of the box and but that lid on top of the box, it creates 2 fields against each other and I think this filed is a diamagnetic filed.

Microwaves in Ancient Egypt

When you visit the Bent pyramid at Dahshur and stand in front of the northern side and look up to casing stone you will see many eroded spots scattered in many locations on the casing stones, and you will realize that the upper part of the pyramid from the 4 sides had lost its casing stone and had this rough surface.

But if you look carefully you will find out that these erosions are very strange, under every eroded spot there is something looks like water stain, or as if there was a water leak from that spot, I used to think that this happened because of rain or daily morning humid weather, but no, these stain are the same all the time, even after rain or very humid morning, in March 2020 we had an rare phenomenon, a hurricane was called the Dragon hurricane occurred in Egypt and because of it the sky was raining for more than 12 hours, nonstop rain, I visited the Bent pyramid the following day and the stains were the same and there was no other stain because of that rain.

Unfortunately all the pyramids of Egypt lost the casing stone except very few, like the 02nd pyramid at Giza Plateau "Khafra Pyramid", this pyramid still keep the casing stones on the top part of the pyramid, I started to pay attention to the surface of this casing stone and I found the same effect happened to the limestones blocks of the casing stone.

I had to buy a good camera with a good zoom lens so I can have some good photos to these stains above the casing stone of Khafra pyramid.

It seems that the reason which affected the limestone casing stone also affected granite block.

When you visit the valley temple you will find that there are some sever erosions on many of the granite blocks inside the Valley temple, the granite surface in some blocks is peeling off, and as I understand granite doesn't do this in normal circumstances.

Not only the granite of the Valley temple at Giza Plateau but also some granite blocks at Karnak temple in Luxor.

When you visit Karnak temple and reach the so-called holy of holies (Philp Arihadus room), to the left of this room there are 2 rooms attributed to king Tuthmoses III, our target is the 02nd room.

The entrance of this room was made of granodiorite (sometimes it is called grey granite), when look to the granodiorite blocks you will see that the stone is in a very bad condition and there are hundreds of small cracks went through the stone fabric, these blocks still standing in the same location, it didn't fall off, it seems that something hit it badly. When you get inside the room itself, you will see scatted chunks of granodiorite, the strange thing I realized about these pieces of granodiorite that the surfaces are in better condition than the inner parts, some pieces were broken into 2 pieces so we can see the core of each piece, the core is very fragile but the surface is still in better condition.

EGYPT BEFORE THE WRITTEN HISTORY

Right behind the same holy of holies there are 3 granite blocks were arranged one after the other towards the east side (to the backside of the temple), my first time to see these blocks from a distance I thought these are made from mud, because of the very bade condition, but when I got closer I immediately knew it is rose granite block, we all know that rose granite is tough stone and weather conditions can't do these erosion easily to rose granite, there is a missing factor in the 3 stories.

I spent around 8 years trying to figure out how happened these erosions at the Bent pyramid, and the same erosion at the 02nd pyramid at Giza Plateau "Khafra pyramid", and what happened to the granodiorite blocks and the rose granite blocks at Karnak temple.

My first observation, there are remains (stains) of of leaking water, so we must think of water erosion, but is it water from outside? Rain or humidity? I don't think it is rain water or humidity because these stains didn't cover the whole body of the pyramid, and I don't think rain or humidity can do that.

My second obsevation, this erosion happened from inside out. When you climb the wodden steps to go to the entrance of the pyramid you will be very close to the casingstones in that part, so I had the chance to examine some of these erosions closly and I realized that the erosions go deep into the fabric of the block.

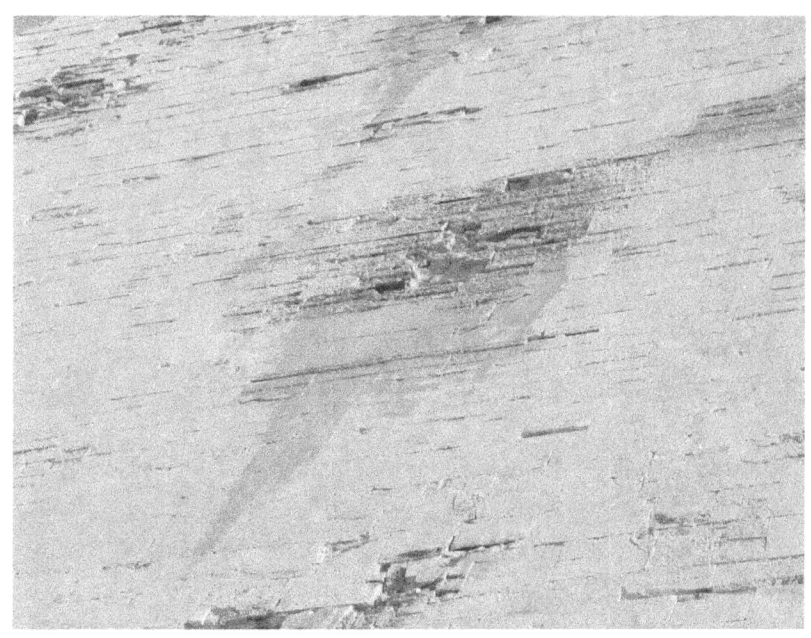

My third observation is that these stains are slightly red in color, so we are talknig about a red liquid, the idea that the surface of the pyramid was painted in red is not supported by evidence. If the limestone blocks were cut from the same quarry as the limestone blocks of the Red Pyramids, we would expect to see red color in the molecular structure of the stone due to the presence of Iron Oxide, this is the reason of that red color of the stains.

I believe the reason for these 3 cases is microwaves. As I understand that our microwave ovens in our kitchens are being used to cook the food or to heat the food, because microwaves are targeting the water or moisture molecules inside the food, microwaves cause these molecules to vibrate and this cause heat.

So I think that the Ancient Egyptian sites or some parts of it were producing microwaves for some reasons, maybe communications and other functions, when these sites were distroyed after a global disaster and the power or the level of microwaves was not under control, or some parts of these sites were exposed to non stop microwaves, the water molecules were overheated and evaporated to very hot steam, that steam needed to get out of the stone, the steam found its way through the weakest parts in the stone fabric, ccausing these erosions and stains on the limestone. It is the same case with granite but because granite is a plutonic rock, it doesn't have much water content or we can sat it has very little, that's why we didn't see the same effect of the microwaves on these granite blocks but we found another effect which matches the conditons and the molecular structure of granite, specially rose granit of Aswan. The inner sections of the granite blocks were overheated and that "toasted" the core of the block, leaving the external parts in better conditon.

Based on the information and evidences I presented in this book, and there are many more observations in my future books, we need to understand that there were so many Ancient Egypt, not only Ancient Egypt but also ancient other civilizations.

The Ancient Egypt we know and study in schools is the last phase of these ancient cycles of civilizations, and it wasn't the most advanced one, acutally the earlier civilizations were more advanced.

The oldest human remains were found in Egypt is the Tramsa child, dating back to 55,000 BC, and the oldest tools discovered in Egypt and around the world are nearly 2.3 million years old. These are flint tools and other flint tools are 1.5 millions years old and we can track the flint indudstry till 5000 BC or even 3000 BC and maybe after this, so the question is:

Did humans spent almost 2,290,000 years in the cycle of flint primitive tools and did not devolop even for once??

If the answer is no, as I believe, it would be unfair for humanty and for the heritage of our ancestors.

The right answer is yes. Our ancestors must have created hundreds of civilizations and they must have reached advanced knowledge, and maybe they were more advanced than us.

The Ancient Egyptians believed in the 5 cycles of the sun, and I call it the 5 cycles of civilizations, 2012 was the end the 5th cycle, the cycle of darkness, we are living now in a new cycle, cycle number one, The Dwan Cycle.

These cycles are not happening for one round only, these cycles are repeated in bigger cycles. The Ancient Egyptian belived that death is not the end of the journey, no, we live in endles actions and reactions.

About the author

Mohamed Ibrahim was born and raised in Badrashien town in Giza, Badrashien is the hometown of many ancient sites like Memphis (the very old capital of Ancient Egypt, Sakkara, Daahsur, Abusir and more.

Mohamed didn't only study Ancient Egypt, he studied Greco-Roman Egypt, Coptic Egypt, Islamic Egypt, and Modern Egypt. He studied history, monuments, art, religion, and Ancient Egyptian Language. He graduated with a bachelor's degree from Helwan University in Cairo in 2000.

Because of Mohamed's great passion about Egypt, he decided to take his research about Ancient Egypt to deep levels of History, and he was lucky to meet and work with so many experts in different fields, all of them were passionate about Ancient Egypt, so he started to gain great knowledge about Ancient Egypt from many aspects. Mohamed is teaching about the Ancient Egyptian Advanced Lost Technologies and the Pre-Diluvian Civilizations of Egypt. Beside this he is teaching about Healing in Ancient Egypt and lately he is talking about new subjects like the Star Gates of Ancient Egypt.

Because of Mohamed's intensive knowledge about Ancient Egypt, he is being invited as a guest speaker in many conferences inside and outside Egypt.

Mohamed is a professional tour Guide for more than 20 years and he is the owner of Saba Tours.

www.ingramcontent.com/pod-product-compliance
Lightning Source LLC
Chambersburg PA
CBHW060938230426
43665CB00015B/1982